Cockpit Resource Management

Other books in the PRACTICAL FLYING SERIES

Cockpit Resource Management

The Private Pilot's Guide

Second Edition

Thomas P. Turner

McGraw-Hill

New York   San Francisco   Washington, D.C.   Auckland   Bogotá
Caracas   Lisbon   London   Madrid   Mexico City   Milan
Montreal   New Delhi   San Juan   Singapore
Sydney   Tokyo   Toronto

Library of Congress Cataloging-in-Publication Data

Turner, Thomas P.
   Cockpit resource management : the private pilot's guide / Thomas
P. Turner.—2nd ed.
     p. cm.
  Includes index.
  ISBN 0-07-065606-1 (hardcover).—ISBN 0-07-065605-3 (pbk.)
  1. Airplanes—Piloting—Human factors. 2. Private flying.
I. Title.
TL553.6.T87   1998
629.132'5217—dc21   97-52225
                                                 CIP

McGraw-Hill

*A Division of The **McGraw·Hill** Companies*

1 2 3 4 5 6 7 8 9 0 DOC/DOC 9 0 3 2 1 0 9 8

ISBN 0-07-065606-1 HC   0-07-065605-3 PBK

*The sponsoring editor for this book was Shelley Carr, the editing supervisor was
Ruth W. Mannino, and the production supervisor was Tina Cameron. It was set in
Times Roman by Kim Sheran of McGraw-Hill's Professional Group Composition
Unit, in Hightstown, NJ.*

Printed and bound by R. R. Donnelly & Sons Company.

McGraw-Hill books are available at special quantity discounts to use as
premiums and sales promotions, or for use in corporate training programs. For
more information, please write to the Director of Special Sales, McGraw-Hill,
11 West 19th Street, New York, NY 10011. Or contact your local bookstore.

This book is printed on recycled, acid-free paper containing a
minimum of 50 percent recycled, de-inked fiber.

Contents

Acknowledgments

I'd like to thank everyone who has helped me in putting together this second edition of *CRM*. Again, if I leave anyone out, it's merely an oversight on my part because I depend upon the expertise of those who help turn my manuscript into a legible and presentable book.

To all those who helped so much in the research and production of the first edition, thanks again. To all those whose work precedes me, and especially those whom I've had the honor of citing in this edition, thank you as well. Special thanks to my editor, Shelley Carr, for prompting me to update this work, to Ruth Mannino for her patience with my revisions, and to all those who participated from manuscript submission to the time the book arrived in stores.

And, of course, once more I thank my wife Peggy and our son Alan for their patience and support on this and my other projects.

Introduction

Human factors, traditionally called "pilot error," cause nearly 80 percent of all general aviation accidents. It's been demonstrated conclusively by the airline and corporate flight communities that teaching the control of adverse human factors is possible with excellent results in the improvement of overall accident statistics. No segment of aviation is safer, for instance, than professionally flown corporate flight.

To date, however, the skills and techniques taught to increase safety in airplanes requiring more than one pilot have not been translated into information readily usable to the single-pilot operator. This sort of information and technique almost never makes it to the biggest segment of aviation, the privately flown light airplane. Although most of the language of crew resource management (CRM) reflects the notion that there is more than one person "up front" to help with the work and to make decisions, the bigger part of the CRM philosophy can be readily applied to help a pilot flying alone handle the risks of VFR, IFR, and night flight. That's the goal of this book: to bring the safety-enhancing concepts of CRM to the cockpits of even the smallest airplanes with the hope that such techniques and information will help make private pilots safer.

I'll make recommendations and point out additions that you might wish to make to your airplane's checklists. Remember that no one can be an expert in all types of airplanes. The pilot's operating handbook for the airplane you're flying is your ultimate guide to safely flying the type. If you have questions regarding the specifics of flying a particular type of aircraft, consult that plane's pilot's operating handbook and seek the counsel of an instructor who specializes in the make and model that you fly.

We'll also be citing a number of accident reports plus near mishaps as a means of illustrating key points. **Please bear in mind that these citations are in no way meant to be a condemnation of pilots, maintainers, controllers, manufacturers, or any other parties, nor are they designed to point fingers or assess negligence** or blame. Instead, the sole reason we'll review actual accident and incident case studies is to point out the lessons all pilots can learn in the hopes that accident history will not be repeated. Where you see actual statistics, the determination of probable cause was made by the National Transportation Safety Board or other related investigators.

The FAA's practical test standard guides for all certificates and ratings call for the evaluation of CRM skills, but the guides do not fully define what the applicant should do to meet the task objective or how the examiner should evaluate cockpit management skills in administering a flight test. Certified flight instructors can use this book as a guide for teaching cockpit resource management to their students. The final chapter shows how CFIs can present cockpit management topics at all levels of pilot training, even in the first few flying lessons.

Recently, cockpit resource management has been criticized for promoting a "feel good" attitude in the cockpit, and one major U.S. airline has removed CRM training from its syllabus after the crash of a Boeing 757 linked to lack of decisive action by that airliner's captain. The opponents of CRM training speculate that an old-style, autocratic captain would not have flown his craft into the side of a mountain. In reality, however, it appears lack of crew communication led to the crew's loss of orientation. This is exactly the situation CRM training hopes to avoid. Whether in an airliner or a light airplane, there must be a clear decision-maker to use the information available.

Remember that you, the pilot, are solely and ultimately responsible for the safe outcome of a flight. Techniques and philosophies have been developed that demonstrably increase the level of flight safety. Here's your chance to truly "fly like the pros" and apply the CRM concepts of airline and corporate aviation to your own flying. I'll say it again in this book: There's no reason you can't be as safe as professional pilots just because you're not being paid to fly.

1
Why cockpit management?

THIS IS NOT A BOOK ABOUT ORGANIZING PENCILS. COCKPIT RESOURCE MANAGEMENT is often broadly referred to but is rarely specifically defined in the aviation training industry. This is especially true in the world of light aircraft (fewer than 12,500 pounds).

Where you do see discussions of CRM in the aviation press, the author is usually addressing the issue of cockpit layout. He or she will provide hints about the number of pencils to carry, the type and size of flashlight to keep in your flight case, and a technique for writing down instrument clearances so as to have the information readily available in flight. That is vital information, to be sure, but it fails to address the basis for the modern study of cockpit resource management. Although this book will certainly include such elements of cockpit organization, I hope to be able to provide information that is even more basic yet more crucial to consistently conducting safe, efficient flights.

This book is about decision making. Historically, about 80 percent of all general aviation accidents have been the result of what is popularly known as "pilot error"— the action or inaction of the pilot that leads to a mishap.[1] The term "pilot error" carries a stigma about it; there is a popularly held sense that when the National Transportation Safety Board investigates aircraft accidents, pilot error is identified as the root cause if no other factors can be found. Such an investigation would be categorized instead as an "unknown" or "other" cause of the accident. Pilot error is the determination only when the NTSB positively finds that pilot action or inaction was the primary cause of the crash (Fig. 1-1).

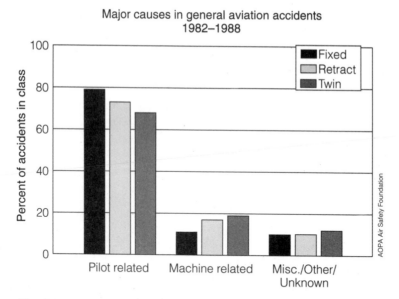

Fig. 1-1. *A comparison of accident causes.*

Pilot-error accidents—I prefer to think of them as "human-factors-related"—are often the result of faulty pilot technique, but in the majority of cases, you can trace the cause back even further to an error in decision making. Had the VFR pilot who penetrated instrument meteorological conditions merely called flight service for a weather briefing, for instance, he or she would have found conditions dire enough to rethink the takeoff decision.

In another instance, after attempting an instrument approach three times, a pilot descends below published minimum altitudes on a fourth attempt to land at a fog-shrouded field, crashing into obstructions short of the airport. What information did he or she have that an approach could be successfully completed when a "missed" was required on three previous attempts? Or an overloaded airplane fails to clear a line of trees on takeoff. What compelled this pilot to violate aircraft limitations and the laws of physics?

These are the sorts of human-factors-related situations that cause the vast majority of accidents. If the pilot in each case had employed the decision-making principles of cockpit resource management, the accidents quite likely would have been avoided.

The FAA's practical test standard manuals for airman certificates and ratings require examiners to evaluate an applicant's cockpit management performance but are not very clear about what examiners are looking for. The *Private Pilot Practical Test Standards* help clarify the matter within "Area of Operation II: Ground Operations, Task B: Cockpit Management." The objective of that portion of the test seeks to determine that the applicant:

- Exhibits knowledge of cockpit management by explaining related safety and efficiency factors.

- Organizes and arranges the material and equipment in an efficient manner.
- Ensures that the safety belts and shoulder harnesses are fastened.
- Adjusts and locks the rudder pedals and pilot's seat to a safe position and ensures full control movement.
- Briefs occupants on the use of safety belts and emergency procedures.
- Exhibits adequate crew coordination.

Most of these objectives are the traditional general aviation approach to cockpit resource management: making sure that maps and pencils are laid out and that seats and safety belts are adjusted. The first and last objectives call for an examination of more subjective CRM tasks: "related safety and efficiency factors" and "crew coordination."

Crew coordination is typically not applicable in a general aviation flight test because the airplane usually has one required crewmember. I suppose that if an applicant makes an effort to brief the examiner that he or she (the applicant) is pilot-in-command for the flight test, the examiner should speak up if he or she (the examiner) notices any safety-related item (other air traffic, for instance); the applicant would have exhibited good "crew" coordination.

"Related safety and efficiency factors" could mean just about anything. What other guidance does an examiner have to tell him or her what to look for when evaluating the CRM techniques of an applicant? The introduction of the practical test standards offers this: "Examiners will place special emphasis upon areas of aircraft operations which are most critical to flight safety. Among these are positive aircraft control and sound decision making. Although these areas may not be shown under each task, they are essential to flight safety and will receive careful evaluation throughout the practical test . . .. Numerous studies indicate that many accidents have occurred when the pilot's attention has been distracted during various phases of flight . . . where safe flight was possible (if the pilot had) . . . divided attention properly . . .. To strengthen this area of pilot training and evaluation, the examiner will provide realistic distractions . . . to evaluate the applicant's ability to divide attention while maintaining safe flight."[2] The practical test standards then go on to list examples of the distractions that an examiner might use.

Translation: An applicant for a pilot certificate or rating might fly perfectly well, technically to the letter of the practical test standards, and still fail the flight test if he or she does not appear to exercise good judgment. It's entirely up to the examiner to decide how to evaluate cockpit management and decision making. One statement says it all when defining what is acceptable performance on an practical test checkride; this statement is also very useful when pilots critique themselves after any flight: The pilot must show "mastery of the aircraft within the standards outlined in the test standards book with the successful outcome of a (maneuver) never seriously in doubt."

This book, to reiterate, is about decision making for pilots. We'll look at the decision-making process and define how a pilot can use standard techniques to determine goals, options, and strategies for safely completing a flight. Along the way we'll discuss some inhibitors to the decision-making process, factors that tend to cloud our judgment and reduce the amount of information available for making a good choice; we'll investigate techniques for overcoming these inhibitors. We'll examine actual accident case histories, not to condemn pilots, mechanics, air traffic controllers, or manufacturers, but instead to learn how a better decision might have been made with a safer and less spectacular outcome.

THE ORIGIN OF CRM

In the early days of aviation, faulty engines and substandard airframe construction led to the majority of accidents. For example, the OX5 series of engines, which powered almost every military and civil aircraft design in the 1920s, had a time-between-overhaul of about 50 hours. It seemed that power-off landings were more common than the opposite and led to a large percentage of all aircraft mishaps.

As aviation progressed, maintenance and construction of airplanes became more reliable, and today the prospect of an engine failure is quite remote. Meanwhile, the environment in which we fly has become much more demanding. All-weather operations are the norm, adding instrument piloting skills and procedures to the tasks that a well-traveled pilot needs to master. Airplanes are much faster and aerodynamically much cleaner, meaning events happen much more quickly; unplanned contact with the ground or an obstacle happens at a faster speed with deadly impact force. Mechanical factors as the primary causes of accidents have been overshadowed by human factors. We would be foolish to say that mechanical systems can stand little improvement, but we would be wise to say that in order to make substantial reductions in the number of accidents, we need to improve on the human factor.

We need to be able to make better decisions.

We can credit the airline industry with making the first inroads toward improving the human factors safety record. Noting the number of decision-making-related accidents, the industry began to look for ways of increasing the level of information in the cockpit because more information generally results in a better decision. Because airline equipment is flown by at least two and sometimes as many as four cockpit crewmembers, the airlines found better decisions could be made if only the crew were more efficient in its communications.

The notion of the gray-templed autocratic captain barking orders at a youthful copilot who struggled to please his master was soon replaced with the model of a skilled leader in the left seat who was open to suggestions from his or her crewmembers yet still retaining the authority to make the final decision once all input was received. The advent of widespread simulator training for airline crews made even more apparent the human infallibility of a single mind and the benefits of synergy or "greater-than-the-sum-of-the-parts" superiority of working as a crew.

Techniques were devised to improve communications and the decision-making process on the flight deck; the techniques were taught under the mantle of *cockpit resource management*. CRM is now generally referred to in the industry as *crew* resource management, belying its airline roots; crews overwhelmingly perform better in simulator training when practicing these techniques, and the overall accident rate is decreasing.[3]

"What good does this do me, the pilot of a single-engine or light-twin airplane?" you might ask yourself. "If the airline safety record improvement is the result of better aircrew communication, what benefit can I derive sitting alone in the cockpit?" To be sure, the principles of cockpit resource management are based upon two-pilot operation, but with a little translation the principles promise a host of workload-reducing and safety-enhancing techniques for the solo operation of a lightplane, whether on instruments or in clear air. That's why cockpit resource management is valid for the private pilot. Practicing the tenets of CRM that have been modified for the lightplane world can serve to improve pilot decision making, thereby reducing risk and making for consistently safer flight (Fig. 1-2).

Fig. 1-2. *Regardless the airplane that you fly, the concepts of CRM will make you a safer pilot.*

THE ACCIDENT RECORD

Lest you have doubts about the validity of cockpit resource management as an aviation safety tool, take a look at the general aviation accident record. In 1991, the AOPA Air Safety Foundation published the *General Aviation Accident Analysis Book*, which was the first compilation of general-aviation-specific accident statistics. Based upon NTSB findings, the book notes that 16,220 general aviation accidents were reported in the United States during the years 1982 through 1988, inclusive; of these:

- 18.7 percent were fatal
- 28.5 percent caused the total destruction of the airplane

- 69.2 percent substantially damaged the aircraft
- 76.9 percent were the result of human factors (action or inaction on the part of the pilot-in-command that is normally referred to as "pilot error")

Human factors were also attributed to the following:

- 79.3 percent of all single-engine, fixed gear accidents
- 73.0 percent of all single-engine, retractable gear mishaps
- 68.7 percent of all crashes in twin-engine airplanes were attributed to human factors[4]

Obviously, eliminating even just a few of the typical human factors mistakes made in general aviation will greatly reduce the number of airplane accidents. As the developers of cockpit resource management discovered, the sorts of errors made on the airline flight deck, which of course are documented to a much higher degree than errors made in light airplanes, are the types of mistakes that would bring down any aircraft, whether it be a Piper Cub or a Boeing 747 (Fig. 1-3).

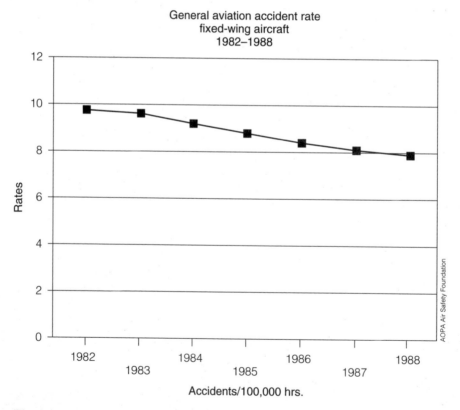

Fig. 1-3. *A comparison of accident rates.*

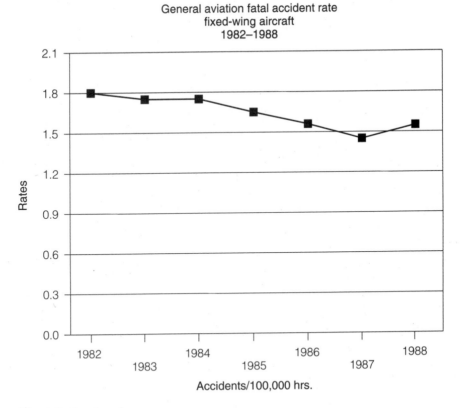

General aviation fatal accident rate
fixed-wing aircraft
1982–1988

Fig. 1-3. *Continued*

In years since this original study, general aviation accident trends have reversed. Possibly because of a change in the way the federal government estimates the total number of general aviation hours flown annually, the accident rate per 100,000 flight hours has shown signs of increase (Fig. 1-4). This suggests that we need to resume emphasis on avoiding the most common cause of aviation accident—pilot error.

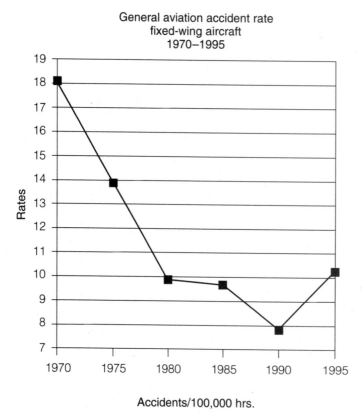

Fig. 1-4. *Accident trends through 1995.*

2
Goals of the flight

T O IMPROVE THE CHANCES OF SAFELY COMPLETING A FLIGHT, CONCEN-
TRATE on ways to improve your decision-making skills. You can quickly and
efficiently make good decisions by knowing what you want to do—knowing the goals
of your trip. This will help you determine options and what information is truly important when faced with making a decision.

Say for instance that you are a VFR-rated pilot and are planning a holiday flight in
the family Skyhawk from your home in Columbus, Ohio, to a vacation in Florida. The
kids are excited about going to Disney World, and you and your spouse just want to escape the dreary cold of a midwestern winter for a week of relaxation in the warm winds
"down south." The plane sits fueled and loaded on the ramp, your family is happily
waiting in the terminal lounge, ready to board, and you're faced with making the final
decision about whether or not to launch southbound. How can you safely make this go-
no-go decision?

Let's take a look at how you can make decisions by establishing your priorities, or
your goals. We'll put it in a context that might be more commonly understood—you're
looking for a new house to buy. If you looked in the newspaper real estate section or
called a real estate agent, you'd be presented with literally thousands of houses, depending on where you were searching, most of which probably wouldn't meet your needs.
You would expend a great amount of wasted time and effort weeding through all those

ads and descriptions; the time it takes to look at all of these houses and decide whether one was right for you might prevent you from attending to other, more crucial tasks.

In order to efficiently go about making a new-home decision, you first have to establish some parameters for the search; the parameters will be the goals that you wish to achieve with your new purchase. You might decide, for instance, that a three-bedroom home is the smallest that is feasible for your family. You might have a growing family, or you might need the extra space for a home office or a hobby room. Smaller houses would be extraordinarily cramped, and you don't want to make this kind of investment and then feel uncomfortable. One of your goals in buying this house, then, is comfort. Provide this information to your Realtor, and you've already done much to narrow down the search and remove extraneous information that will make the decision-making process more difficult and time-consuming.

It would be great if your new house had large rooms, air conditioning for those hot summers, and a backyard swimming pool. More than a place to sleep and eat, your home should also be a fun place to be. Enjoyment, then, is another goal you wish to achieve with your new home purchase.

You might think that you and your family could survive with a single bathroom, but it would be nice to have at least two. You also might really like to have an attached two-car garage. These represent goals of convenience, items that aren't strictly necessary, but have a big impact on the decision you're about to make. Call your agent and mention the desire for a two-bathroom home with attached garage and you've reduced even further the amount of information you'll have to process to decide on a new home.

Cost certainly will be a factor. You examine your budget and decide, for example, that $750 per month is the highest mortgage payment you can afford. You call the experts and find out this means a maximum purchase price of $75,000, so you tell the real estate company to provide information on houses listed at or below that level. This, too, will narrow the search, making your job all the easier.

You want to feel pride in owning your home. In your mind, this means a brick exterior and a tree-lined, fenced yard. Relay these parameters to your agent to avoid extraneous information that might cloud your decision.

And you want to make sure the home provides safety. You want a house with good wiring and plumbing and a sturdy roof. The house should be located in a "good" neighborhood (whatever that means). You need a home that will help you survive the elements. If you're buying a home in Kansas, for instance, you want to be certain you have a basement or at least a storm cellar because you know you'll spend a few hours every year seeking safety when any tornado warnings are posted. If your dream home is along the Atlantic coastline, you might not want a basement at all, but instead look for a house on stilts or sitting on high ground to avoid the floods that accompany storms in the hurricane season. Again, you've added to the framework for your new-home search.

With all this in mind, you call the real estate office and describe the house you wish to purchase: "I want a three-bedroom, two-bath brick home, with a basement, air conditioning and a two-car attached garage. It should have large trees and a fenced-in yard and be in a quiet residential neighborhood. I'd like a swimming pool in the back-yard. The most I can pay for the house is $75,000."

If you give these requirements to your real estate agent, he or she should be able to narrow your search to only those homes that meet all or most of your needs. In many parts of the country, it might even get you laughed out of the office! Anyway, such a list of priorities or goals in finding a house will allow you to quickly reject those that don't satisfy your goals and more easily quantify differences between individual prospects when making your purchasing decision. You won't expend time or effort needlessly; your mind will be free of clutter that might cause you to miss crucial information elsewhere.

Decision making for flight is a lot like buying a new home. Many people approach a new-home purchase without knowing exactly what they want or how much they can afford; many pilots approach flight without clearly evaluating the risks involved, and often the result of such faulty decision making is disastrous.

Back to the vacation flight to Orlando: List the goals. One priority will be family comfort. Given the right weather, the Cessna is a comfortable flying machine, not too hot or too cold and stable enough to provide a smooth ride. It's a comfort also to know that your baggage will be available immediately upon arrival and not at risk of being lost forever in the maze of airline-terminal baggage ramps. This is analogous to deciding on a three-bedroom house; the house or airplane will provide a necessary level of comfort for you to achieve your ultimate goals. Given the alternatives of a crowded airliner or a very long trip by car, going by personal airplane is quite comfortable, so it satisfies this goal.

You want to enjoy this trip. Flying along in the Skyhawk, you'll watch the stark white and brown winter landscape slowly rise to the tree-lined majesty of the Smoky Mountains and then slope gently downward, greening all the way to a white ribbon of sand along the sparkling blue sea. You'd never see these views in memory-inspiring detail from the aisle seat of a DC-9; if you drove, the pace and scope of your view would remove some of its striking impact. Similar to the house's swimming pool and air conditioning, the view from the Cessna will make a long trip more memorable and enjoyable than it otherwise would be.

The Skyhawk is extremely convenient. Scheduled airline travel has become more and more an ordeal with unpredictable schedules and rapid-fire interflight connections at distant terminal airports. In contrast, the luxury of an early-morning takeoff, a refreshing lunch stop along the way, and an afternoon arrival at destination removes all the stress of commercial air travel and still gets you to the waving palm trees around the hotel pool at about the same time the airlines could. You could, of course, load the family into the minivan and drive to Florida, reducing the air carrier stress, but it's a hard two-day drive in each direction, hardly adding to the convenience of the trip. Convenience, which in the purchase of your home mandated that extra bathroom and the garage, dictates again that personal aviation is the way to go.

If you called ABC Airlines and were quoted the total of fares for your family vacation, you'd probably find that taking the Cessna is competitive if not even cheaper. Factor in travel to and from the airline terminal, as well as the expense of parking while you are away, and flying yourself becomes an even more financially attractive option.

Of course, there really isn't a more economical way to travel than personal auto, but if you include the cost of meals and gas and the overnight hotel stays required in each direction, you'd find the price gap between driving and flying to be narrower than you might have originally thought.

You have a big emotional investment in your airplane and your flying skills. You practice takeoffs and landings as often as you can and pride yourself on your ability to pull off a "squeaker" landing most of the time. You spend several minutes at the conclusion of every flight buffing and rubbing your Skyhawk, making it stand out among tens of thousands of homogeneous airplanes with the hopes that it will turn a few heads as you taxi up to the fuel pumps along the way.

Pilots by nature have healthy egos, and yours is no exception; you'll derive a lot of satisfaction in saying "I flew my family down to Florida" when gathering around the coffee machine with your coworkers after the trip. Just as the brick front and tree-shaded yard gives you pride in the house you bought, personal aviation provides a level of satisfaction that builds your self-esteem, and that's one reason you fly. Pride is another goal for your trip to Florida, pride in aviating well in an outstanding airplane.

But most of all, you want to be safe. After all, it's your family strapped into the airplane, and they depend on your judgment and skill to safely reach Florida and return home. You have to be well-rested and fit, and you need to make crucial decisions about routing, time of the flight, fuel reserves, and a host of other considerations that the family regards as "given." Your judgment alone is your family's shelter from the storm, so you consciously consider the safety of your decisions in beginning and continuing a flight.

Here is your list of goals for a trip in a personal airplane:

- Comfort
- Enjoyment
- Convenience
- Cost
- Pride
- Safety

You might even come up with more goals.

How can you use these goals to make better decisions in flight? You can do it by prioritizing your goals and then asking yourself what impact each of your options will have on your primary goals before picking a course of action. Looking at your list of goals, does any single goal stand out as being more important than the rest? It should be obvious that safety is paramount. If your choices are not safe, it's unlikely that your trip will be enjoyable or convenient at best, and the trip can be quite inconvenient and costly at worst.

When you select a course of action, you should do it because it's the safest way to proceed. Taken to the extreme, this means you'd never take off in the first place (or get out of bed, for that matter), so you need to evaluate the risks involved and decide on the safest way to achieve your other goals. Comfort, convenience, cost, enjoyment, and pride are all valid reasons to fly, but all should be subordinate to the primary goal of safety.

Do you make the trip to Florida? Everything points to a "go" decision, but if the weather deteriorates along the way, or the engine runs a bit rough, or if you have a bad headache, or you are tired from a long day at the office, safety might dictate that you decide otherwise. Presented with new conditions that require you to reevaluate your go/no-go decision in order to be safe, you should look at the alternatives and then judge each by whether it improves safety, as well as satisfying your other goals.

I made a trip recently in a Cessna 172, from Louisville, Kentucky, toward my Kansas home. Nestled in the back of the well-equipped, IFR-certified Skyhawk were my wife and our infant son, tired yet relaxed from a week-long tour of relatives' homes in West Virginia and along the East Coast. The weather was warm for January; blotchy cumulus clouds over Kentucky were merging into a broken-to-overcast layer as we fought a strong west wind homeward.

The flight had a late start out of Charleston, West Virginia, after a long deicing effort, and came upon low visibilities and the threat of airframe ice over Louisville, mandating an early landing. When Louisville cleared, we launched west once more, but it was late afternoon by the time we crossed the Mississippi River south of Cairo, Illinois, and the mounting clouds already obscured the afternoon light.

My goal was to make it to Jefferson City, the capital of Missouri, for a fuel-and-feed stop before the final 3-hour leg to Wichita. Headwinds had slowed our progress, however, and I now knew that the final hop would be flown at night. Our groundspeed hovered around 90 knots, much less than I had hoped for, and the easy hop from Kentucky was now becoming a 3½ hour marathon to our fuel stop. I did a quick calculation and found we'd reach Jeff City right around sunset.

I was also a bit concerned about our fuel state. We'd topped the tanks at Louisville, so theoretically we had about 5.0 hours of gas on board, but I was running the engine at 75 percent power and leaning a little richer than "book" to gain maximum speed. I knew from experience that such flying netted about 10.0 gallons per hour fuel burn, and that meant that our "real" fuel endurance was closer to 4.0 hours, not 5.0. I was flying VFR, which meant that we'd have our minimums upon arrival despite high power and headwinds, but it would be close.

It was a good time to reevaluate the goals of my trip and to confirm the wisdom of my decisions. Running down the list, starting with comfort, continuing on to Jefferson City was beginning to wear on my family braving the light turbulence in the back seat of the Cessna. Comfort would be increased by making an earlier fuel stop, although we'd have to find a field with an open pilot's lounge to make stopping short a comfort-increaser. Our route over southeastern Missouri overflew very few airports coded for "services," and I doubted many would be open after 4 p.m. on New Year's Day in any event.

It had been a long day with delays and diversions, and landing early would detract even further from our enjoyment of the trip. We were all getting tired, so the psychological impact of another diversion would cloud our enthusiasm for the trip.

Convenience? Stopping short would be inconvenient. There probably wouldn't be anything to eat except a stale candy bar from a vending machine, and fueling up prior to Jeff City might mandate yet another fuel stop between there and home. It was unlikely I could find another rural airport open for fueling after dark on New Year's Day. An early fuel stop meant we'd have to reroute well out of our way via Springfield or Kansas City to ensure a refueling point on the leg home. That would add even more time to our trip and might translate into arriving at home at midnight or later. Not only would landing short be inconvenient, it would make for a very, very long day.

Cost would be affected minimally. I was renting this airplane "wet," so the typically higher fuel cost near the cities wouldn't impact me directly. A diversion toward an urban area would, however, add to my time aloft and therefore the rental cost, so an early stop would be costly as well.

Pride: My wife has flown enough to realize that diversions are sometimes necessary, so if I told her we were landing at Cuba, Missouri, or some spot other than Jefferson City, it wouldn't make her think less of me for not reaching our goal. I'm lucky in that my wife really likes to travel by personal airplane, but a diversion en route might be a big pride issue for other people.

Yes, all indications were that making an early fuel stop would detract from the trip. It would increase our fatigue, reduce our enjoyment, and make our eventual flight home more costly and inconvenient. Landing early did little to help us meet the goals of our trip.

Yet it was getting dark and cloudy and fuel continued to pour through the carburetor. I had to think in terms of safety. Yes, landing early would detract in every other way, but it would enhance safety just as our options were becoming fewer, and I decided that it was time to pick an alternate. Up ahead about 20 miles was Rolla National Airport, a former military airfield now best known as a DC-3 and Cessna Caravan maintenance base. I tuned the unicom frequency, hoping someone was still on duty, and found the airport manager available to provide gas. On approach to the downwind leg, I saw a motel sign near the airport and decided to talk to my wife after we landed about staying the night here.

Only when I shut down the engine on the darkening ramp did I feel fatigue mounting, and I knew I didn't want to fly another 3.0 hours that night. The airport manager poured 32.0 gallons of fuel into the Skyhawk, meaning that only about 45 minutes of fuel remained in the tanks. If I had continued on toward Jefferson City and encountered even a slight delay for any reason, we would have run out of fuel. My decision to land early and sacrifice my other goals to increase safety was justified.

Luckily, it happened that some very good friends of ours had just purchased a lake home about 30 miles away. After a rest stop and paying for the tank of fuel, we made the quick VFR hop over to Camdenton and had an extremely nice visit with our friends on their first night in their new home.

As if to emphasize the wisdom of choosing "safety" as my primary goal this night, the airplane's attitude indicator failed on the way to Camdenton. A long trip across the sparsely lit plains of western Missouri and eastern Kansas on a dark night beneath a midlevel overcast with a failed attitude indicator after 16 "duty hours" flying from my parents' home that morning might have spelled disaster for my young family.

We've seen the beginnings of how you can set goals for a flight and how you can use those goals, weighted always toward safety as the primary goal, to aid in in-flight decision making. You might think that it goes without saying that safety is your prime consideration and should be the driving force behind all decisions. Unfortunately the accident records are filled with accounts where goals were obviously misprioritized. This is most obvious in the classic case of "continued visual flight into instrument meteorological conditions."

Take a look at the case of a 48-year-old Cherokee 140 pilot on a trip from New Orleans to his home in southern Ohio, as related in the May 1988 issue of *FLYING* magazine. Remember that this book is not assessing blame in looking at examples of aircraft accidents, and the NTSB investigates to find out what probably causes an accident; instead, this book reviews accident histories with the hope of learning valuable lessons. (Speculative comments about any accident or incident are not meant to second-guess any pilot but are meant to foster greater awareness of options that might be applied to similar circumstances.)

The pilot had picked up his son near Fort Worth, Texas, and the two spent an evening in New Orleans. Both were licensed pilots, but the son had little flying experience. The next morning, as the two prepared to fly together to their Ohio home, the weather along their route was deteriorating. A cold front sprawled across their path, filled with the threat of icing, thunderstorms, rain, low ceilings, and fog.

The Cherokee's heading gyro had failed on the trip to Fort Worth, but the pilot didn't get it fixed. An instructor pilot with instrument and multiengine ratings, he elected to continue homeward VFR. The first leg of their journey, to Picayune, Mississippi, was uneventful; they took on fuel and waited two and a half hours for the weather ahead to improve. Less than an hour out of Picayune, they reached Tuscaloosa, Alabama. When flight service briefers pointed out that they had landed while the airport was IFR, the pilot said that he had tried to contact the FSS on 123.6 but had gotten no response.

The pilot obtained a weather briefing for a flight to Chattanooga, Tennessee. The area forecast called for lowered ceilings throughout the afternoon, becoming 1200 to 2500 overcast with 3 to 5 miles visibility in light rain and fog, and mountains obscured after 1300. The briefer told the pilot, as he was required to do, that VFR flight was not recommended.

The pilot then asked for the weather for Meridian, Mississippi, which was VFR. He said he would be returning to Meridian. By now Tuscaloosa was VFR, too; father and son took off, after getting an airport advisory on the flight service frequency at 1313.

Perhaps when they got into the air the weather to the northeast didn't look so bad because they headed not for Meridian but for Chattanooga. The distance from Tuscaloosa to Chattanooga is 157 nautical miles. The route runs parallel to the ridges of the Cumberland Plateau with elevations dropping off to less than 2000 feet to the west and rising above 4000 feet to the east. Interstate 59 runs up to Chattanooga from Birmingham, and they flew alongside that highway as the ceilings grew lower and the visibility worse.

"We were just trying to stay clear of clouds," the son said later from his hospital bed, "but the ceiling just kept coming down . . ... It was raining very hard, there was moderate turbulence and sometimes severe."

At one point during the flight they had descended to 1800 feet or so (MSL—the terrain elevation was between 1000 and 1200 feet) to stay under the clouds. "I remember showing my father an airport on the left side. It was raining real hard and the wind was bouncing us around a good bit. I remember talking about that and then I remember him explaining to me some stuff about the turbulence we were encountering." The airport, the son recalled, was "along a big four-lane highway with a lot of signs that said something about Ruby Falls."

Ruby Falls is a tourist attraction at the southern edge of Chattanooga, but it is heavily promoted on billboards on both sides of the highway both north and south of town. The airport could have been Isabell, some 42 nautical miles south of Chattanooga, or Lowell, in Chattanooga itself.

The pilot-in-command continued. After passing Chattanooga he (apparently) decided to abandon the four-lane highway and track directly to the Hinch Mountain VOR, about 40 nm past Chattanooga. According to the son's account, they were clear of clouds with the ground in sight up to the moment, sometime between 4 and 5 o'clock in the afternoon, when the airplane snagged trees at the 2700-foot level on Hinch Mountain and crashed into rising terrain.

The father was killed and the airplane burned. His son escaped with serious injuries and was found the next morning, walking down the VOR transmitter access road.[1]

This sort of accident is all too common. A sizable percentage of the "continued-visual-flight-into instrument-meteorological-conditions" accidents occurs when instrument-rated pilots blunder into the murk unequipped or unprepared. It's easy to say that pilots should avoid this type of scenario, but in practice it's difficult to foresee the final outcome in many cases because the onset is so gradual, so insidious. Let's look at how goal evaluation might have influenced the outcome of this flight.

This case includes a lot of elements common to airplane accidents, components that tend to cloud judgment and influence goal-related decision making. One such element is that the pilot(s) were headed homeward. This introduces a lot of stress that detracts from making good choices. The accident occurred on a Sunday afternoon. The NTSB should take a good look at the percentage of airplane accidents that happen as a pilot is headed toward home base on a Sunday afternoon. The pressures of completing a trip in time for work Monday are enormous and might influence a pilot to proceed when conditions suggest otherwise. The simple fact that the flight was a return trip at the end of a weekend might have prompted the pilot to rethink his goals.

This represents a "decision point" as a time of the trip when a pilot needs to evaluate her or his options from the standpoint of stating and meeting the goals of the flight. If nothing else, the return trip and the day of the week should trigger flags that the pilot might have his or her decision-making skills clouded by external pressures. Unfortunately, it appears that convenience (the timely completion of the homebound leg) in this case was considered more crucial than safety despite the very obvious weather threats.

The pilot-in-command had his son, also a pilot, aboard. Obviously the pilot had a great deal more experience flying than did his son; there might have been a need, conscious or not, to impress the younger pilot with Dad's piloting skill. Pride as an experienced pilot and pride as a father might have taken precedence over other goals. The elder pilot might have thought it quite important to show his son what Dad could do. This is another decision point, highlighted by a potential increase in risk. Unfortunately for both, the goal of pride seems also to have been given precedence over safety in the pilot's decision making.

The flight began with a known aircraft defect; we'll see this as a causal factor in airplane accidents again. A primary instrument, the heading indicator, was inoperative. The failure occurred on the southbound trip, but the pilot was perhaps worried about time (convenience again) or cost (especially considering shop rates on a weekend) and elected to defer the maintenance and proceed homeward under visual flight rules. Actually, faced with the weather hazards predicted on the morning of their departure from New Orleans, the airplane occupants would have been safer flying in visual conditions than penetrating the clouds IFR; in a roundabout way, this failure contributed to a good decision, staying in clear air. At this decision point and again unfortunately for both onboard, the convenience or cost advantages of waiting to fix the broken indicator might have overshadowed the goal of safety when the pilot decided to take off.

The first leg to Picayune was uneventful. Apparently the pilot checked the weather ahead or the sky to the northeast looked threatening because he and his son waited more than two hours before proceeding toward Tuscaloosa. I've been in situations like this myself and know that each tick of the clock while waiting out weather adds to the temptation to go "give it a look." This might be why the pilot arrived VFR at the FSS-equipped Tuscaloosa airport in instrument conditions. The Class D airspace (at the time, a control zone) was monitored by flight service, and the briefers provided nonbinding airport advisories to arriving and departing traffic. Apparently there was no radio contact between the pilot and flight service upon his arrival; he was told the airport was below visual minimums only when he entered the FSS for a briefing for his continuation northbound. Time pressures and the need to prove to his son that he was capable of getting them home might have begun to actively affect the pilot at this decision point.

Next stop: Chattanooga. Weather farther north was deteriorating; although the ceiling was still expected to be 1200 to 2500 overcast, the visibility was dropping in rain and fog, and the terrain along the route would occasionally penetrate the cloud base. Advised by flight service that VFR flight into the area wasn't recommended, the pilot asked for information toward Meridian. This was a 180° turn back in the direction from whence he came; it might have been an attempt to skirt around the weather pattern, or there might have been some other reason he would rather wait it out in Mississippi, but in either case, it was a good decision. Conditions had improved to VFR at Tuscaloosa, so father and son took off once more with safety a primary goal.

When airborne, the pilot apparently headed straight toward Chattanooga. Whatever was going through the pilot's head at this decision point, he turned northeast, following the freeway toward Chattanooga and into ever-worsening ceilings and visibility.

Soon they were in turbulence and rain, flying lower and lower to maintain visual contact with the ground. Yet the pilot decided at this point to continue even when presented with an airport off the left wing. At this point in the flight, the repetitive delays and late hour of the day might have completely eclipsed notions of safety in the pilot's mind because he ignored the obvious safety choice of a 180° turn into hopefully clearer air and pressed on VFR in an airplane no longer equipped for instrument conditions.

Again, the examples are not meant to condemn the actions of individuals or groups but with the hope that we'll avoid repeating accident history. In this case, issues of convenience, cost, and pride consistently overshadowed safety in a pilot's decision-making process. At each decision point, the pilot was presented a clear choice that would not have sacrificed flight safety in the furtherance of a subordinate goal. For whatever reason, the pilot chose not to exercise that safety valve until events went beyond his or the airplane's capabilities.

Let's look at another case where lesser goals were pursued at the expense of flight safety. As you read this description, as printed in the September 1988 issue of *FLYING* magazine, look for the decision points, think about which goal was being pursued at each point, and ask yourself whether there was an obvious choice available that would reduce risk and heighten the pilot's level of safety.

It was a gray dawn at the north end of Tampa Bay, Florida. Tampa International Information Papa told the story: "Indefinite ceiling zero, sky obscured, visibility one-sixteenth of a mile with fog, temperature and dew point seven-one."

Arriving aircraft were using the Runway 36L ILS approach—except that no aircraft were arriving. The Runway Visual Range (RVR) was shrinking all the time. At about 6:30 a.m., 15 minutes before sunrise, a DC-9 started an approach with an RVR of 1400 feet, and descended to 100 feet above the runway with the approach lights in sight before losing sight of everything, taking the missed approach and diverting to nearby Sarasota. A Cessna 172 three minutes behind the DC-9 was given the minimum RVR report for the approach: 1200 feet. He was in solid fog at 200 feet and went to his alternate, St. Petersburg, just a few miles across the bay, where the weather was 200 and one.

Just after the Cessna started his missed approach, an Apache called from seven miles out. The tower gave him an RVR of 600 feet at the touchdown end of the runway and cleared him to continue his approach.

Seven minutes later, after flying a precise ILS approach to minimums, the Apache pilot called a missed approach. "I'd like to go back and try it again," he said. As the Apache circled toward the outer marker, Tampa Approach gave him new RVR readings: 600 feet at the touchdown end, 800 at the roll-out end, and 3000 in between. The controller thought the improvement in midfield visibility was probably due to the turbulence created by a DC-9 that had just departed, but he didn't say so. "That 3000 sounds better, I hope," the Apache pilot said.

"Yes, it does," the controller agreed.

Two minutes before seven, when he cleared the Apache for a second approach, the controller reported the midfield RVR as 1000 feet. Five minutes later, when the Apache was two miles from the touchdown point, the controller gave another update: 600 feet at touchdown, 800 at midfield, and 800 at roll-out. The Apache pilot acknowledged.

At the same time, a Pan Am 727 was rolling cautiously toward Runway 36L. As the captain peered into the fog, a shape materialized and moved rapidly toward him. It was the Apache, flaring, its wheels feeling for the taxiway. It touched down 200 feet from the jetliner. There was time to swerve the Boeing hard to the right before the small twin, which had pitched up and become airborne again, struck the airliner's nose. The Apache's left engine caught beneath the radome and was wrenched from the wing; the rest of the airplane, its ruptured tanks spewing burning fuel, hurtled under the left wing of the 727 and skidded to a stop 100 feet away, where it lay burning on the taxiway.

The Pan Am first officer called a Mayday to the tower: "Clipper's been hit by a light airplane on the taxiway, I don't think there's any injuries but there may be some damage."

Evidently he wasn't thinking about the pilot of the demolished light airplane, who was dead.

When the news media first reported this accident, it caused many people to say, "Another crazy private pilot. They shouldn't let those guys near airports." But as the details emerged an irony appeared: The pilot of the Apache was a highly experienced Eastern Airlines captain, a 20,000-hour pilot who had been with Eastern for more than 20 years.

He lived at Pine Shadows Airpark near Fort Myers, 120 miles to the south, and was trying to get to work. He had a Newark-bound flight at 8:05 a.m., and was supposed to report at 7:20 a.m. He had called flight service the night before and gotten a forecast for Tampa; the worst it predicted was a 300-foot ceiling and half-a-mile visibility. He decided to fly to Tampa in the morning rather than drive.

During the night the forecast changed for the worse; when the pilot called flight service after getting airborne a little after 6 a.m., he heard about the zero ceiling and the one-sixteenth-mile visibility for the first time.

At this point, he could no longer drive to Tampa and expect to get to work on time. He could, however, land at St. Petersburg, take a taxi across the bridge, and be only a little late. If he were slightly late, his flight would be held for him. He elected, however, to try the approach. Eastern had been acquired by Texas Air earlier in the year, and there had been a lot of emphasis on avoiding crew delays. In addition, it was a company policy to "discourage" private flying within 12 hours of a scheduled flight.

The pilot was late once before. Yet more than three years had passed and, under Eastern policies, that previous incident could not be held against him in determining how another instance of tardiness would be dealt with. But he might have not been aware of the three-year limit. The pressure to land at Tampa, concludes the National Transportation Safety Board in its analysis of the accident, "probably was largely self-generated on the part of the Apache pilot."[2]

The NTSB comment says it all. Conditions were well below instrument minimums the entire time the Apache pilot was in contact with flight service or air traffic control, for more than an hour from first contact to the time of the crash. During that time, every airplane that attempted the approach into Tampa was required to miss, although nearby St. Petersburg seemed to be available as an option. If the pilot had contacted flight service prior to departure and learned of the conditions at Tampa or had simply elected to give himself an extra few minutes for a possible diversion by departing 15 minutes earlier, much of the pilot-induced pressure to land at Tampa might have been removed.

Lastly, the highly experienced airline captain should have maintained the level of discipline that kept him safe on the first approach attempt at Tampa and resisted the urge to diverge from the approach path and "bust minimums" by aiming for the first lights he saw; speculation was that first lights seen by the pilot were the taxiing Pan Am airliner. It's impossible to know what was going through the Apache pilot's mind in the final seconds before the crash, but it was more likely concern over being late and the possible consequences of such an action. He was probably less conscious of the immediate goal of safely completing the flight. The irony is that his scheduled Eastern flight experienced a much longer crew delay than his diversion to St. Petersburg would have created.

As with any other type of decision in life, safely flying an airplane requires you to identify your goals, prioritize them, and then consider the possible impact of options when applied to the goals. Just as when buying a house, you might have to sacrifice some of the subordinate goals (comfort, enjoyment, convenience, pride, cost, and others) in order to minimize risks. Flying a light plane is challenging; your job is to make informed decisions to avert unexpected hazards that arise.

3
The decision-making process

L ET'S DELVE A LITTLE DEEPER INTO HOW YOU CAN MAKE GOOD PREFLIGHT and in-flight decisions. Knowing the goals of your flight with a clear choice of safety as your primary concern does not by itself allow you to make the best, most-informed decision. You need to recognize how a good decision is made in order to make consistently good decisions yourself. Knowing your goals helps you to evaluate the available options.

We can take a hint from the world of business. Developed in business academia and most commonly taught in business management courses is the "DECIDE" model of making a good decision; aviation instructors have adapted this model slightly for aviation purposes.[1] We are going to apply business decision-making principles to making good choices in flight, thereby recognizing the goals of the flight to help make what is hopefully the best possible choice in a given situation.

The DECIDE model, as I've further modified the technique, breaks decision making into six distinct steps:

1. **D**etect that a decision needs to be made.
2. **E**valuate the options available.

3. Choose an option that best meets your goals.

4. Implement that choice.

5. Detect any changes that come about as a result of that implementation.

6. Evaluate those outcomes to determine whether your decision was a good one or if you need to begin the process anew.

This example of an in-flight situation will illustrate how to use the DECIDE model.

You're flying a Piper Archer on a springtime cross-country trip from Oklahoma City to St. Louis, Missouri. When you called flight service on the morning of your trip, you learned that your entire route was under the influence of a cold front extending roughly from southern Michigan through extreme western Tennessee, then bending southwesterly into the Dallas-Fort Worth area. Conditions behind the cold front along your proposed route were 2000–3000 feet overcast with good visibilities beneath the clouds. There was a SIGMET for light to moderate mixed icing in the clouds but no PIREPs confirmed the forecast; cloud tops had been reported in the 6000–7000-foot range over the first third of your route. Isolated light rain showers peppered the radar summary plots.

You decide to give it a go, planning on a rapid climb to 9000 feet through the cloud base to the hopefully clear skies above. On climbout, you encounter only the faintest wisps of ice as you top the cloud layer; you settle in for an uneventful cruise at your planned altitude enjoying a slight tailwind component from the northwesterly breeze aloft.

Over southern Missouri, which is closer to the cold frontal boundary, cloud tops begin to slowly rise to meet you. Time after time you brush through the tops of a small cumulus bulbs rising from the stratus murk; each time a little frost coats the Archer's windscreen only to be melted off again as soon as you return to sunlit air between the buildups. Ahead, the cloud tops appear to rise well above your 9000-foot perch. You've reached a decision point. Let's look at how you can make a good in-flight go/no-go decision.

First, you'll "Detect" that a decision needs to be made; you've already done that, but let's define the situation that exists. You are flying an airplane that is not certified for flight in known-icing conditions. Ice is obviously in the clouds. It appears that if you continue as planned, you'll penetrate the cloud layer for an extended period of time; therefore, continuing as planned exposes you to the risk of accumulating ice on an unprotected airframe with all the attendant hazards of increased stall speed, increased weight, and loss of aerodynamic control. You've certainly detected that a decision needs to be made.

Second, you'll "Evaluate" the options at hand. This is the step where you look at the goals of your flight and evaluate the options on the basis of what effect each will have on achieving your goals. One is to simply do nothing, continuing as planned and hoping that nothing will get beyond your ability to control the airplane. The problem is that continuing toward St. Louis at 9000 feet will almost certainly mean picking up a load of ice, and by the time the situation becomes critical, you might not have any other options within your reach. Option one, continuing on faith, doesn't look so good to you. What else might you do?

You could climb or descend along your proposed flight path hoping to reach clear air once more or at least reach an altitude where ice is less likely. To do this effectively, you need two pieces of information:

- Altitudes that are in clear air
- Altitude of the freezing level

If you didn't already have the answers, the obvious place to find out is flight service. Ask air traffic control for a frequency change to talk to flight watch. Ask the weather briefer if she has any reports of cloud tops or bases along your route of flight, and also request for the reported freezing level along your route of flight. She relates that cloud tops over central Missouri have been reported at 13,000 feet, and the area forecast calls for an overcast ceiling of 3000 feet. Surface observations at Vichy, Missouri, about a hundred miles short of your destination, confirm the area forecast. The observed freezing level over southern and central portions of Missouri was last reported to be at 5400 feet.

How can you use this information? Attempting to climb above the cloud tops would put you at oxygen-breathing altitudes, and you don't have any oxygen aboard; you'll still need to descend through a thick altitude range of suspected ice upon reaching your destination. You could go ahead and descend through the clouds now, where a thinner altitude band of ice exists, and hope that any accumulated ice melts off when you reach clear air beneath the clouds. The minimum en route altitude along your route is 3000 feet and the cloud bases are 3000 feet above ground level; you should have close to a thousand feet between you and the icy bases in which to maneuver. With the information now available, it looks like a descent to 3000 feet is the safest bet if you wish to continue along your filed route of flight. But do you have any other choices?

You could land at nearby Springfield, Missouri, which is served by several airports with instrument approaches. Most likely destination would be Springfield Regional with its precision approaches and big FBO. Landing at Springfield is inconvenient and costly because it would take several hours driving a rental car to reach St. Louis and you'd have to drive all the way back to fetch your airplane. Your passengers might be upset that you couldn't get them to the destination; they might even be frightened out of ever wanting to fly with you again. Nonetheless, an early arrival, even at Springfield, might be the safest bet.

You might divert off course, hoping to circumnavigate the icy clouds. Turning right toward the southeast is out because that's the direction of the cold front and would only expose you to more cloudiness. You should have decided against turning toward the front before you took off unless you positively knew conditions improved in that direction. Turning north or northwest toward Kansas City or Columbia, Missouri, might put you far enough behind the front that the clouds would thin out or hold less ice because it was a farther distance from the source of moisture.

Chapter three

Flight watch tells you that the cloud tops in the Kansas City region have been reported at 7000 feet, with numerous reports of rime ice; there are no reports of cloud tops in the Columbia area. Things are not significantly improved to the north. You think you've just about explored every option available when you decide turning back is always an out. Cloud tops are lower to the southwest, and ice was almost nonexistent in the clouds on climbout. Nonetheless, there was "known ice" (you made it known) back toward Oklahoma City, and you'd like to get as close to St. Louis as possible, so you "Choose" the best compromise decision possible (the third step): Sacrifice a little convenience and economy and put down at Springfield for a rental car or until conditions improve.

Fourth, you need to "Implement" your decision. You call Kansas City Center and ask for a revised clearance to Springfield Regional. You soon have an amendment and turn northwest on vectors descending through the clouds. Pitot heat is on, and the defroster is keeping the windscreen clean; you aren't encountering any ice at all on the descent. Only as you fly through the freezing level do you see a little rime ice form, but it disappears almost as quickly as you pop out of the cloud base at 4000 feet. You've "Detected" the change that occurred (the fifth step). You are no longer exposed to the hazard of airframe ice. Your decision was a good one.

Visibility is at least 20 miles beneath the cloud layer; you're in the clear even above the MEA, and all reports say that you could get all the way to St. Louis at 3000 feet and stay in the clear. It's time to "Evaluate" the decision you've made (step 6). You can land at Springfield and satisfy the goal of safety at the expense of other goals, or you can ask to resume toward St. Louis, flying at the 3000-foot minimum en route altitude to meet all of your goals, safety still being paramount.

You've detected that it's time to make another decision, so start gathering information with which to evaluate your options. You have systematically made a good decision, modifying it for changing conditions as necessary. Using the DECIDE model not only gives you a framework for making a good decision, it also forces you to pace yourself, which is a guard against snap judgments that might not be the best choice you could make in a given situation. Take a look at another decision-making scenario.

You've stopped at Wichita Mid-Continent Airport to pick up a friend in your B55 Baron, after flying up from your home base near Dallas. You had planned to fill the fuel tanks at Wichita even though the hop to Kansas City will take less than an hour, but the fuel truck at the FBO you chose is broken down, and you figure it would take too much time to arrange for another fueler to take care of your needs. Slightly more than two hours of fuel are in the tanks with more than enough fuel for a reserve; habitually, you pop open the left fuel cap, chuckling to yourself when you realize you'll only see the bottom of the fuel bladder this far out on the wing with so little fuel (Fig. 3-1).

It's still early, and a thick fog has begun to lift into a low cloud deck at about 300 feet overcast with 4 or 5 miles visibility. You know you'll be in clear air above the clouds shortly after liftoff, and conditions are expected to improve rapidly, so arriving at Kansas City Downtown Airport should be a breeze. You greet your friend, load up, and taxi to the departure end of Runway 1R at Wichita.

24

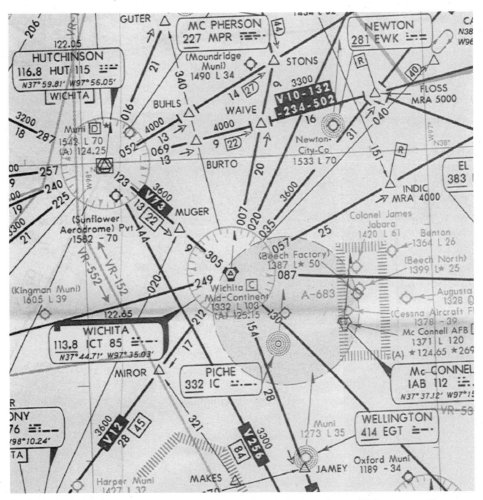

Fig. 3-1. *A portion of a low-altitude en route chart showing Wichita and the surrounding area.*

"Tower, Baron 12345 ready to go, one right," you call, and you're granted permission to go. You accelerate down the runway, reaching liftoff speed quickly with your reduced weight, and fold up the gear as you punch into the fog a couple hundred feet above the pavement.

Only after you reduce propeller speed and settle into climb do you notice an intermittent tapping, a rough banging from the left wing. It's the fuel cap hanging on its chain and slapping against the top of the left wing; you were distracted by something when you checked the fuel level and didn't get the cap completely resecured. When the wing began to generate a lot of lift, the low-pressure area that formed on top of the wing sucked the cap off its mount. Not only that, the low-pressure area was now pulling fuel through the filler port in a thin liquid stream trailing behind the port wing. You're running out of fuel on the left side.

By now you're in clear air above the fog, talking to Wichita Departure, and you've certainly detected the need to make a decision. You engage the autopilot and begin to look at your options. You really have two decisions to make in this scenario: first, what do you do about the fuel problem, and second, where do you go? You have to prioritize these decisions as well. Which is more crucial? Yes, you do have a pressing fuel problem, but you don't want to waste precious time and fuel going away from a safe haven, so you need to decide the "where" first and the "what" afterward.

Where will you go? Wichita is close to instrument minimums. Sure, you've landed there earlier this morning, but whenever you have to fly an approach there is always the chance you might have to fly the missed approach procedure, and you probably don't have the fuel to miss an approach and go elsewhere. Ask yourself a question: "If I did have to miss the approach at Wichita, where would I go?" To answer that, you need some information. Ask Wichita Approach for the nearest VFR or marginal VFR airport. That's what you would probably do if you had to miss Wichita's approach; why not avoid wasting time and precious gas and simply aim for that airport to begin with?

It so happens that Hutchinson, Kansas, only around 30 miles to the west, is marginal VFR in lifting fog; this might be your best bet even if it's not the most convenient for your passengers. You've quickly evaluated your options with a little help from ATC, and you choose to fly toward Hutchinson. You could have made this decision before you ever left the ground: "If a problem presents itself shortly after takeoff, I'll fly to Hutchinson." (The workload-reducing technique of picking a "departure alternate" is discussed elsewhere in this book.)

A vector from ATC helps you implement your decision to divert, and now you're en route to Hutchinson, Kansas. You engage the autopilot and start gathering information for the approach. You know that the next step in the decision-making process is to detect the changes that result from your decision, and that reminds you of the reason you diverted in the first place: the rapidly dwindling supply of fuel in the left wing. You've detected that it's time to make another decision: What do you do about the fuel state?

One option is to do nothing, to let the fuel blow out until the left engine quits. There is an attraction to this decision, and that is that both engines remain operative for the greatest amount of time. It's possible that the engine failure won't occur until after you're on the ground at Hutchinson. You know that two engines are better than one, especially during an approach. The problem is that you doubt that the fuel will last long enough for you to reach your new destination, and the engine failure is likely to occur at an inopportune time, such as just as you've begun your approach. It's tempting to hope that nothing will go wrong, but wishful thinking is not a guarantee you'll satisfy your goals. Doing nothing is rarely a good choice and certainly not so in this instance.

You might go ahead and shut down the left engine now, at altitude, on the way to Hutchinson. You'll take longer to reach the airport (but not much), but at least the engine failure will occur on your terms—when and where you choose. File this option for a moment and think whether there's anything else you can do.

You could crossfeed and burn fuel from the right-wing tank in both engines. A simple flip of the switch ensures that both engines remain running for as long as there's fuel in the right wing. The problem is that there wasn't a lot of gas in either wing to start with. Oh, you had plenty to safely get to Kansas City if nothing went wrong, but you might not have enough to fly the short distance to Hutchinson and land if you effectively double the fuel-flow rate from the right wing by running both engines from that side.

Remember, you can't count on any fuel being available later from the left wing because it's siphoning out at an unpredictable rate. Crossfeeding is an initially attractive option that might actually make things worse, and you've pretty much decided that would be contrary to your mandate of flight safety.

Is there anything else you haven't considered? You decide there isn't and your evaluation of your fuel-related options helps you choose what seems to be the best overall, which is shutting down the left engine now while well above the ground and not distracted with the minutia of flying an approach. It's time to implement your decision.

Here's where people sometimes get themselves into trouble. You're on the autopilot in clear and smooth air above an undercast that is parting to reveal patches of ground, and you've got plenty of time. You know you need to secure an engine, and the only time you might have ever practiced the procedure is in the heat of a simulated engine failure close to the ground, but you don't have to start snatching and yanking handles.

It would be too easy in this already stressful situation to secure the wrong engine or at least in some way upset the power development on the "good" side of the airplane if you blindly start tugging on controls without thinking about what you're doing. Somewhere in the airplane (very close by, if you're doing your job) you've got a pilot's operating handbook or other approved checklist for a precautionary engine shutdown.

Don't do anything until you've read the procedure through completely, and then methodically work your way through the checklist, being ready for the swing in pitch, yaw, and roll that accompanies the failure of an engine. One of the purposes of a checklist is to pace you through a difficult or repetitive procedure, to help prevent an improper action that you might otherwise have done in your haste to complete what's not really a time-critical procedure. Use the checklist, and shut down the left engine.

After you've got the airplane retrimmed and back on the autopilot, try to detect the changes that have come about by making this decision. Evaluate the impact. Recalculate your time en route to Hutchinson, and compare it to your new fuel burn on one engine. If the margin of fuel remaining on landing is small, think about reducing power and slowing down. You'll probably find that you can increase endurance dramatically with even a small reduction of power, especially propeller speed; it will take the least amount of power to remain airborne at your "blue-line," or best-single-engine-rate-of-climb speed because this velocity has the least total amount of drag. If a power reduction makes it difficult to hold altitude, try trimming for this least-drag speed to see if you can increase performance.

Have you noticed a pattern? Every time you make a decision, you alter the conditions of the flight, and quite often those altered conditions require you to make yet another decision to safely meet your goals. Flying is, after all, a constant string of making decisions, so it's not difficult to see why one poor decision can snowball into an accident. (This phenomenon, called the judgment chain, is subsequently investigated in this book.) Let's look at a real-life example of the decision-making process.

The pressurized single-engine airplane was climbing to 15,000 feet when its pilot noticed a low oil-pressure light. Asking ATC for a vector to the nearest airport, he was told that Jimmy Stewart Field was at about his 11:30 position and 15 miles away. After the pilot asked "Is that a tower field," the controller replied that he didn't know. Instead, ATC offered Westmoreland Field, a controlled airport, and provided a vector and altitude for the airport, which was also about 15 miles from the Malibu. Westmoreland's tower had already closed for the evening, however, and the controller advised the pilot as much.

The pilot, still uncertain about where to divert, next asked about Pittsburgh Airport, about 35 miles away. The pilot turned toward Pittsburgh before reporting zero oil pressure and a low-fuel light. He declared an emergency and was cleared to nearby Allegheny County Airport. The aircraft crashed soon afterward, the victim of a loose turbocharger oil-feed line and poor decision making on the part of the pilot.[2]

The pilot of this aircraft met with tragedy by making a poor decision—not landing as soon as possible. It's quite likely that he could have made it to Westmoreland or another area airport, but he apparently fixated on the perceived need for a controlled airport when in such a case any airport should suffice. After detecting the need for a decision, by noting the oil-pressure indications, the pilot began to evaluate his admittedly limited options. He could attempt to make it to Pittsburgh, a certainly more convenient place for an emergency landing, or he could put it down at nearby Westmoreland.

Regardless of how he might have arrived at his decision (through experience, insight, or divine intervention), the pilot forgot that he needed to evaluate options based upon the goals of his flight. Safety was represented by a "sure thing," an airport nearly beneath the airplane's wings. The safety of the nearest airport should have won out as the ultimate priority, displacing the very tempting goals of convenience and comfort that might have prompted him to try to land at a controlled airport. When his goals were clearly in sight, his choice of an option should have been easy, and he might have made an uneventful landing at the nearby airstrip.

Beginning to implement that decision, he might have detected the need to make another decision. He could keep the engine running, maintaining power for as long as possible, or he could have shut it down when the airplane was within gliding distance of the airport, perhaps preventing further destruction of the engine. A second "decision wheel" began to turn, and again the pilot needed to consider his options based upon the impact each would have on attaining his goals. There was absolutely nothing to be gained by shutting the engine down prior to arrival except the possibility of saving some money on a rebuild. He reasoned that a botched approach without engine power, which might be unrecoverable, would be more expensive and certainly less safe than a go-around under power.

When he realized that economy was the only goal he could attain by shutting down the engine in flight, and that such economy would be at the expense of flying safety, he wisely chose to keep the engine running as long as it would.

Can you think of another decision the pilot could have made to improve flying safety and avoid the possibility of a crash? Obviously he was observant of engine indications because he noted the oil abnormality shortly into the flight. A loose oil line in the Malibu's turbocharger might have resulted in slightly less than normal manifold pressure at full throttle on takeoff, however, so he might have been able to detect a problem earlier. He might also have found evidence of an oil leak on a thorough pre-flight inspection. It would be pointless to speculate further on what he might have done before flight because there's no way to tell exactly what he saw. If the pilot had taken the time to give the airplane a meticulous examination before takeoff or noted a lower-than-normal power setting on takeoff, tragedy might have been averted.

I faced a similar circumstance a few years ago when I was the lead instructor for the factory-authorized pilot training program for the Beechcraft Bonanza, out of Wi-chita. After a week of intensive classroom and simulator training, I was ready to con-duct a day's worth of flight training with my client in his A36 Bonanza. His airplane, which had originally been equipped with a 285-horsepower IO-520 engine, had re-cently been modified with the more powerful IO-550. I'm not certain exactly how much time the owner had put on the new engine, but I do know that it was probably fewer than 50 hours.

Our flight training started with an extended preflight inspection that was designed to translate a week's worth of academics covering airplane systems and techniques into information that the pilot could use on a daily basis. Opening the cowling, we looked at the engine and its systems. Across the top of the fuel-injected Continentals, there is a squarish mounting bracket over which run the individual fuel injector lines on the way to the cylinders. At the point where the fuel injector lines cross the mounting bracket, the lines are held in place by a metal clip. To keep the lines in place, they're held by rubber wraps, or grommets, as they pass through the clips.

At this point, I thought that the purpose of the grommets was to keep the fuel lines from rubbing against the bracket. In fact, there was a rental Bonanza nearby that I'd of-ten flown, and I'd noticed once that the fuel injector lines were getting a flat spot where they rubbed against the bracket. So I made a point of this in class and again during pre-flight inspections.

On this particular morning, my client and I noticed that one of the rubber grom-mets on the center cylinder on the right side of the engine was cracking badly. Think-ing that preventing friction was the only function of the grommet, I looked closely at the underside of the fuel line and detected no evidence of wear. Without thinking any more of it, except to make a written note on my "debriefing pad" that the owner should have a grommet installed at his earliest convenience, we completed our walk-around and climbed aboard.

It was a good day for instrument training. We had a midlevel overcast and smooth air that was warm enough that we didn't have to worry about ice. After a couple of hours of maneuvering, we landed for lunch at a nearby controlled airport. After a little more briefing, we took off for some instrument approach practice. After a time or two around the airfield, the owner and I started to notice the very faint smell of fuel in the cockpit. The Teledyne Continental IO-550 employs an automatic mixture control sys-tem, so IO-550 pilots don't normally need to manually adjust mixture settings on takeoff. I had noticed in this case, however, that the fuel flow during takeoff was several gallons per hour higher that the pilot's operating handbook would suggest.

Although we manually adjusted the fuel flow to "book" specifications on each takeoff run, I dismissed the fuel smell to excessive fuel flowing through the engine at the first moments of each practice missed approach, before we had a chance to fiddle with the mixture control. My client allowed that this was a reasonable explanation, but after about the third time around the approach course, the scent was strong enough that we decided to land and check things out.

Taxiing up to the FBO, we lifted the cowl and began to look. At this point I was locked into a mind-set that we'd find evidence of fuel staining around the seal drains (overflow ports where excessive fuel vents overboard). Neither the owner or I even considered the fuel injector line we'd found without padding earlier, even though in retrospect I remember voicing that the cracked grommet was now missing entirely. A mechanic came out and volunteered a look, finding no more than did we. Convinced now that our fuel smell was the result of a malfunctioning automatic mixture control, which we could easily overcome manually, we took off once more toward our starting point on the east side of Wichita.

Above the clouds, we practiced a few more procedures on the 40-mile flight to Colonel James Jabara Airport; ready to end our session, I contacted Wichita Approach to resume our IFR clearance for the VOR approach into Jabara. This procedure called for a vector well to the east of Jabara and then a turn back nearly westward for the final approach course. Passing somewhere north of the city of Wichita, I commonly kept the Newton, Kansas, NDB tuned during vectors into Jabara; at around 25 miles nearly due north of Jabara, Newton was a good indicator of my position on the eastbound vector (Fig. 3-1).

We were at 4000 feet, in the clouds, when a sudden vibration commanded our attention. The noise level seemed to increase tenfold as I scanned the gauges. All seemed well, including the EGT on the Bonanza's single-cylinder unit, except that the fuel flow was well above the redline, reading around 35 gallons per hour. In the interest of safety, I took the controls and began the engine emergency procedure: change fuel tanks (since the fuel selector is on the far left in a Bonanza, I instructed the owner to do that for me), turn the auxiliary fuel pump on, and check the mixture. I found it curious that the fuel flow didn't change at all as I leaned in an attempt to eliminate what I figured was an overly-rich mixture; I left the mixture control about three-quarters of the way forward and asked the owner to check the individual magnetos for me. Nothing seemed to work.

At the same instant that I had taken the controls and we began the emergency procedure, I put the Bonanza in a standard-rate right turn, changing heading roughly 180° in the direction of the Newton NDB. That was the only direction I could determine that would take me straight toward an airport. I keyed the microphone and in what was probably a rather high-pitched tone told Wichita Approach that I had a partial power loss and was turning toward Newton. The controller didn't ask and at this point I didn't request anything about declaring an emergency; instead, the controller, perhaps sensing my workload, issued me a clearance via vectors direct to Newton, and told me that I needn't reply immediately.

Exhausting our emergency checklist actions, the owner and I became very aware of a *strong* fuel odor in the cockpit. Again I leaned the mixture, but to no avail. I did find that full throttle was giving us just enough power to maintain our 4000-foot altitude, as long as our airspeed hovered around 110 knots. Without planning it, I found a new use for best-glide airspeed; it is the speed where the airplane has the least total amount of drag and therefore will get the best performance on minimal power. I discovered that if I tried to go even a little faster or slower than the best-glide airspeed, I couldn't maintain 4000 feet.

I'd certainly detected the need to make a decision because I had a partial power loss. The emergency procedure demanded quick action; it was one of the few cases where time wasn't available to complete the entire DECIDE model methodically. In fact, decisions in emergencies can be said to follow a shortened version of the DECIDE model, with the unfortunate mnemonic DIE:

1. **D**etect the need for an action or decision.
2. **I**mplement the preprogrammed response as dictated in the emergency procedures checklists.
3. **E**valuate the changes that occur as a result.

This is why regular practice and review of emergency procedures is crucial. In an actual emergency, you might not have the time to remember what to do. Instead, you might need to react instinctively, at least long enough to get the crucial actions under way. In my Bonanza example, I detected a problem, implemented the emergency procedure, and evaluated the outcome—nothing had changed. I also detected a need to aim for the nearest airport, implemented a heading change toward the nearest strip of pavement served by an instrument approach, and began to evaluate where my emergency procedure was taking us. Now I had time to shift gears, to slow down and begin the entire decision-making process.

To make an informed decision, I needed to gather facts. We had minimal power. At best-glide speed, we could maintain 4000 feet. The scent of fuel was strong. We were headed toward Newton, and ATC knew of our plight.

Newton, however, is a solid 45-minute drive from Wichita. I wasn't certain there would be anyone on the ground that could fix the airplane. I would have to call my wife, who had just driven from her job, 10 minutes south of Newton back home to Wichita, and have her drive all the way back up to Newton to get us. I was sorely tempted to get to Jabara Airport if possible, to avoid the logistical mess landing at Newton would create.

But I managed to think in terms of my flight's primary goal, safety. If the engine were to soon fail, I'd like to be as close to an airport as possible. Although I have nothing in principle against IFR flight in single-engine airplanes, I wished at this point that I were flying a Baron instead, and I could simply shut down the offending powerplant and limp home on the other. No such luck this day, however.

It would be really nice to go to Jabara, though, I remember thinking, so I finally called Wichita Approach and asked a question: "What is my distance from the Newton airport?" The answer was 7 nautical miles. Then I asked my distance from the Jabara airport, and the reply was 8 nautical miles. I'd flown my 1946 Cessna 120 low and slow around the northeast side of Wichita for years and knew that there was nothing but flat, unobstructed fields beneath the undercast from my present position all the way to Jabara. Newton and Jabara were about equal in terms of distance; the north wind aloft would make the time en route about identical, if not actually favor Jabara.

It might have been rationalization, but I told the controller I wanted a vector directly to Jabara. I was immediately granted an amended clearance direct to Jabara via a radar vector and instructed to descend to 2000 feet. I exercised my rights as pilot-in-command and said "No" because I wanted to stay at 4000 feet until I was within gliding distance of Jabara, just in case the engine quit. The Bonanza handbook promises 1.7 nautical miles forward gliding distance for each 1000 feet of altitude lost. Figuring a pessimistic 1.5 nautical miles per thousand feet, I reasoned that I needed to stay at 4000 feet until I was within 3 nautical miles of my destination, and I told the controller as much. My request was immediately granted. When ATC advised that I was 3 miles out, I began a gentle descent, broke out of the clouds at around 1000 feet above ground, and made an uneventful landing. I thanked the controller and canceled the IFR clearance.

Lots of decisions. I tried to make each successive choice based upon the impact it had on landing safely. You may debate the wisdom of each of my decisions; I often wonder whether I should have gone ahead and landed at Newton anyhow or if I should have shut down the engine when the emergency occurred and landed in a field northeast of Wichita. There was probably no absolutely correct answer; however, I did make what I thought were the best-informed decisions I could at the time.

What caused the engine's power loss? As you might have suspected, I learned that day that the rubber grommets on the fuel injector lines have a second important function. They dampen out vibrations caused by engine operation. The grommet that broke loose in flight allowed the fuel injector line to vibrate. The vibration worked the line loose at the injector nozzle, and raw fuel began to spew into the engine compartment. I guess that so much air was flowing through the cowling that the fuel couldn't burn, or you'd be reading about this in an accident report and not by my own account.

Apparently the fuel leak started off slowly, which gave us merely the faint smell of fuel in the cockpit; when the injector line broke free, the fuel smell increased as the air around the cowling ducted fuel through the wing-root vent on the right side of the airplane. The fuel-flow indication became so high and seemed unresponsive to movements of the mixture control handle because there was no longer any back pressure in the line. Fuel gushed overboard, wildly spinning the waterwheellike transducer that provides the fuel-flow indication.

What's my point with all this? Faced with an emergency en route, my training and experience with emergency procedures allowed me to quickly detect the problem, implement both the power-loss procedure and a turn toward the nearest airport, and evaluate the fact that my checklist efforts were fruitless, all without having to think much about what I needed to do. That done, the next objective was to shift gears, to slow down and make a good follow-on decision about where to go and what to do using the DECIDE model and evaluating options based on their impact on meeting the goals of my flight. There were numerous decisions to be made and no "right" answers, but I made decisions methodically, using the best information available at the time.

How could I have made the flight even safer? The whole incident, which could have potentially ended in an off-airport landing or even a fire in flight, could have been avoided if I had bothered to have the cracking fuel-line grommet replaced before take-off. Since that day I've emphasized that grommet with my students; it makes me wonder what other little "gotchas" await unsuspecting pilots. The answer is simply to ask questions and check over any discrepancies found on a preflight inspection. An inexpensive fuel-line wrap could have prevented a possible accident.

Do you have a decision to make? Consider the DECIDE model:

- **D**etect the need to make a decision.
- **E**valuate your options, considering the goals of your flight.
- **C**hoose the option that best meets your goals.
- **I**mplement that choice.
- **D**etect the changes that result from your decision.
- **E**valuate the result and your need to make further decisions.

Whether related to flying or in any pursuit in your life, having discipline when making choices, having a firm grasp of your goals and their priorities, and utilizing as much information as you can gather will enable you to make good, informed decisions.

4
Factors affecting decision making

IT'S EASY TO READ A BOOK AND PRACTICE THE DECIDE MODEL DESCRIBED IN chapter 3, but real life has factors that tend to impair our ability to use the process objectively. Let's take a look at some factors that impact your ability to make good decisions.

FATIGUE

Fatigue's role in accident statistics is just beginning to be measured. Occasional articles in the local newspapers note the dangers of all-night over-the-road trucks on the highway and the number of accidents that occur after drivers have apparently fallen asleep. I know I've driven at times when I could barely stay awake, and to be honest, I'm lucky to still be alive. Fatigue is also becoming an issue in extremely long airline travel; transoceanic flight crews have fallen asleep short of destination, and the FAA is considering not only allowing but actually mandating rotating nap periods among crew members to refresh them for landing.

How does fatigue affect a pilot? Fatigue's effects are similar to those of alcohol impairment: reduced perception, lessened motor skills, and the inability to control one's actions. That's a worst-case scenario, just before you're ready to fall into deep sleep.

What's really dangerous is how fatigue can begin to sneak up on you before it becomes an obvious factor. Let's look at one pilot's experience with fatigue and how the weariness led to tragedy.

The pilot obtained a preflight weather briefing for his flight. The forecast was for midlevel clouds, turbulence, and good visibilities. Flight precautions were noted for coastal mountain obscurations due to low clouds. Rain and low ceiling were forecast to move in several hours after the planned estimated time of arrival.

The pilot did not file a flight plan and either did not heed or failed to receive notice that conditions were deteriorating as expected, but much sooner than forecast. The airplane was seen flying about 500 feet AGL through a valley along a highway. Just before reaching an oil refinery smokestack, the airplane turned sharply to the right and impacted fatally with a mountain ridge. It was shortly after midnight local time.[1]

We don't know how long the pilot in this instance had been awake before making the ill-advised flight, but it's likely that fatigue was an important factor in his decision making. The physical skills required for low-level flight underneath an overcast in mountainous conditions should also be factored in. Additionally, the forecast was a player because it warned of worsening conditions, but not until after the proposed conclusion of the flight.

Fatigue is a very difficult thing to measure. Some folks are "night people," and are at their best in the evening. An early morning flight for them might be an extremely hazardous undertaking. On the other hand, some folks are "morning people," and they are at their best in before noon. I'm a morning person; I get up at 5 a.m. every day and write for 2 hours before going to work. Most of the time my typing skills are as good as they're going to get; however, if I try to write at night after my son goes to bed, the number of "typos" my computer has to correct for me increases dramatically.

Because I know something about my fatigue-related limitations, I've come up with a rule about flying in the late afternoon or evening that helps me overcome them. If I'm going to fly anytime after 4 p.m., I want to have the chance to sit down in a quiet room for about half an hour before the trip. Whether or not I nap, this helps refresh me for the trip ahead. If any part of my flight will take place after 6 p.m., I make sure I've been able to sleep at least half an hour that afternoon. If the weather is marginal VFR or worse, and any part of my flight will take place after dark, I don't go; I'd be much better off to rent a hotel room after a long day's work and wake up around 3 a.m. for a departure in time to make it home for the next day's work.

Think about your personal sleep patterns and the level of difficulty you have concentrating or performing motor tasks at different times of the day, and see if you can't come up with a rule or rules about fatigue that will help you avoid its effects.

STRESS

Stress, too, has unpredictable yet measurable effects on human performance. There are all sorts of stress, and they are not all bad. Without some sort of deadline, for instance, most people would have a great deal of difficulty motivating themselves to get things done. There comes a point, however, when stress begins to have negative effects (Fig. 4-1).

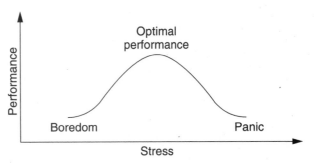

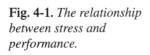

Fig. 4-1. *The relationship between stress and performance.*

The destructive types of stress are those that cause the conscious mind to focus (fixate) on a problem to the point that other mental functions are suppressed. At this point, the "stressed-out" person relies on rote or subconscious memory and repetition to accomplish mental and physical tasks. A stressed person can fix breakfast or brush his or her teeth or even drive a car while under this mind-numbing stress because those sorts of functions are practiced so often that the subconscious mind has experience in dealing with most of the variables likely to be encountered. Unfortunately, that's not usually the case with flying.

Let's say that you have a morning flight to make a business presentation in another city and just before liftoff you call the office for a final status check. Suddenly you learn that your multimillion dollar client is likely to do business with your competitor unless you can really convince your client's CEO that your firm is better. You get so locked into the pending presentation and the consequences if it isn't successful that you start to miss checklist items that you usually verify without thinking about. This might not be as crucial if your flight is short and easy in a low-horsepower runabout, but if you're launching into hard IFR or in a high-performance single or twin, it might be fatal.

Family pressures are also hard to overcome. Let's say you are flying to a family re-union and weather or mechanical problems have kept you on the ground at home until the day of the event. When you wake up for the flight, you find that the weather is marginal VFR with patches of IFR in fog along your route of flight. You never quite got around to taking your instrument checkride, but you've got more than 40 hours of in-strument dual instruction logged, and your family airplane is equipped and signed off for instrument flight. Weather at your destination is marginal VFR in fog and haze, but you've flown into the "old homestead" airport dozens of times, so you know all you have to do is to pick out the river or the highway and it will take you directly to the air-port. Can you see the potential for disaster?

You might normally decline to make the trip, postponing it until later in the day when conditions are forecast to improve, but you have an external stress: the family re-union. Your parents made a big deal of the fact that you are a pilot and would be flying to the event, and relatives you haven't seen in years are waiting to visit. You might just decide to try it; probably your flight will be uneventful, but then again . . ..

Perhaps it's a job schedule or a friend along for the ride that adds additional pressure to make you rush a trip. Here's an example.

A noninstrument rated pilot and his three passengers planned a pleasure flight to Mexico in a high-performance single-engine airplane. Despite weather below VFR minimums, the pilot elected to make the flight. Several minutes after departure, the airplane was observed to enter an area of snow showers. The cloud base was estimated to be 200 feet above ground level, and the visibility varied from 50 feet to one mile. A witness observed an aircraft flying below the clouds in a steep left bank; the aircraft suddenly pitched upward and rolled right and flew into the clouds. Another witness, in a house about 150 feet from the accident site, heard what could be described as an aircraft engine in a power dive, then a loud thud. The witness looked outside to find the aircraft in an apple orchard. There were no indications of mechanical failure prior to impact, and there were no survivors.[2]

Perhaps driven by the presence of his friends to attempt the flight regardless of conditions, or maybe lulled into a sense of urgency by the warm breezes and sunny skies that awaited to the south, this pilot and his passengers fell victim to the external stresses placed upon the pilot to complete the trip regardless of the risk. An experienced instrument pilot should think twice about flight in conditions as adverse as this VFR-limited pilot undertook.

These scenarios all are the result of external pressures driving pilots to make poor go-no-go decisions or failing to adequately prepare themselves for a flight undertaken under the pressure of stress.

MEDICATION AND HEALTH

Depending on the type of flying you do, you need to demonstrate your body's fitness for flight from every 3 years to as often as every 6 months. Regardless of the interval between issuances of your medical certificate, however, the flight physical is a measure of your fitness at that point in time. When you've established your body's basic "airworthiness," it's up to you to make the determination before each flight that you're still capable of piloting.

Even seemingly innocuous illnesses might become serious cockpit distractions. I served in the Air Force with a fellow officer who "washed out" of pilot training because of a toothache. It seems that at some point early in his life he had some rather extensive dental work done. Whoever performed the oral surgery had failed to completely eliminate pockets of air beneath the jaw line; whenever this prospective pilot flew above about 5000 feet, the expansion of this pocket of air gave him a toothache excruciating enough to just about disable him. Eventually, I believe, he had the surgery corrected, but not in time to allow him to continue a military flying career.

Consider what a "slight" head cold or sinus infection might do. As you climb in altitude, the gases trapped in your nasal and ear passages blow up like a balloon. Without some way to escape, these trapped pockets of air swell, creating a sinus headache or an earache that will at least distract you from critical cockpit chores and at most could rob your attention until you're incapable of safe flight.

Think of the difficulty you'd have flying an approach and landing with a gastric disorder or a flare-up of arthritis.

Approach flight with a medical condition with extreme caution. Be especially careful about flying after dental work or any medical procedure because pockets of air might have been trapped that will cause pain at altitude.

If you don't feel completely well, don't attempt IFR or night flight; if you feel downright sick, to the point where you take extra medication to ease the symptoms, simply don't fly at all.

ALCOHOL

The effects of alcohol consumed the night before a flight might carry over until morning, affecting pilot performance and decision making well after the party is over. Use the 8-hour "bottle-to-throttle" rule merely as guidance. You might find that you need more time than that to recover from the effects of alcohol, especially as you age.

Thankfully, the incidence of alcohol-related aviation accidents is quite low. Statistically, however, drunken flying leads almost inevitably to fatalities. The whole premise of cockpit resource management is that safe flying requires proper planning, good decision making, and good judgment. Alcohol inhibits your ability to do any of these things well.

PERSONALITY

A pilot's own personality traits can aid or hinder his or her decision-making skills and aptitude as a pilot. Pilot mind-sets can be distilled into five categories:

- Macho
- Impulsive
- Invulnerable
- Antiauthority
- Resigned[3]

Looking at the list, you might think that one or more of these traits are actually good. I doubt very much that a person could fly an airplane without a balanced measure of each of these characteristics. You probably would never have learned to fly without an antiauthority streak; most people probably thought you were a little crazy to be "going up in one of those little airplanes" in the first place. A pilot could never launch on a long cross-country or IFR flight without a good dose of machismo, or confidence, to cite another example. The situation can become dangerous when one or more of these personality traits become dominant to the point that your thinking is clouded and your sight is blinded regarding the true goals of a flight.

Let's look at how you can recognize when a personality trait begins to destroy your decision-making and piloting abilities.

Self-assessment
of hazardous attitudes

This assessment will help you learn about the five hazardous attitudes affecting pilot judgment and how to understand these attitudes as they apply to your flying. In subsequent chapters, you will learn ways to limit your own hazardous attitudes and to reduce the effects of high stress.

As a first step, you are now to take a self-assessment inventory to give you a personal insight for the following discussions and training. This information is only for your own use. It is not intended to be shared with your flight instructor or anyone else, unless you choose to do so.

This assessment asks you to decide why you, as a pilot, might have made certain decisions. Ten situations will be presented, each involving a flight decision. After each situation, you will find a list of five possible reasons for a decision. No "correct" answer is provided for any of the 10 situations. You may indeed be correct in believing that a safe pilot would not choose any of the five alternatives. Be assured that most people know better than to act as described in the situations. Just recognize that the inventory presents extreme cases of incorrect pilot decision making to help introduce you to the five special types of hazardous attitudes described later.

Instructions: Attitude Inventory

1. Use the answer sheet provided.

2. Read over each situation and the five choices. Decide which choice is *the most likely reason* why you might make the choice that is described. Place a numeral 5 in the space provided on the answer sheet.

3. Continue by placing a numeral 4 by the next most probable reason, and so on, until you have filled in all five blanks with ratings of 5, 4, 3, 2, and 1.

4. Do all 10 situations and *fill in each blank*, even though you might disagree with the choices listed. Remember, there are no correct answers.

Example:

a. __1__ (your least likely response)

b. __3__

c. __5__ (your most likely response)

d. __2__

e. __4__

ATTITUDE INVENTORY

Answer sheet

Situation 1

a. _____

b. _____

c. _____

d. _____

e. _____

Situation 2

a. _____

b. _____

c. _____

d. _____

e. _____

Situation 3

a. _____

b. _____

c. _____

d. _____

e. _____

Situation 4

a. _____

b. _____

c. _____

d. _____

e. _____

Situation 5

a. _____

b. _____

c. _____

d. _____

e. _____

Situation 6

a. _____

b. _____

c. _____

d. _____

e. _____

Situation 7

a. _____

b. _____

c. _____

d. _____

e. _____

Situation 8

a. _____

b. _____

c. _____

d. _____

e. _____

Situation 9

a. _____

b. _____

c. _____

d. _____

e. _____

Situation 10

a. _____

b. _____

c. _____

d. _____

e. _____

ATTITUDE INVENTORY

Situation 1

You are on a flight to an unfamiliar, rural airport. Flight service states that VFR flight is not recommended since heavy coastal fog is forecast to move into the destination airport area about the time you expect to land. You first consider returning to your home base where visibility is still good, but decide instead to continue as planned and land safely after some problems. Why did you reach this decision?

a. You hate to admit that you cannot complete your original flight plan.

b. You resent the suggestion by flight service that you should change your mind.

c. You feel sure that things will turn out safely, that there is no real danger.

d. You reason that since your actions would make no real difference, you might as well continue.

e. You feel the need to decide quickly so you take the simplest alternative.

Situation 2

While taxiing for takeoff, you notice that your right brake pedal is softer than the left. Once airborne, you are sufficiently concerned about the problem to radio for information. Since strong winds are reported at your destination, an experienced pilot who is a passenger recommends that you abandon the flight and return to your departure airport. You choose to continue the flight and experience no further difficulties. Why did you continue?

a. You feel that suggestions made in this type of situation are usually overly cautious.

b. Your brakes have never failed before, so you doubt that they will this time.

c. You feel that you can leave the decision to the tower at your destination.

d. You immediately decide that you want to continue.

e. You are sure that if anyone could handle the landing, you can.

Situation 3

Your regular airplane has been grounded because of an airframe problem. You are scheduled in another airplane and discover it is a model you are not familiar with. After your preflight you decide to take off on your business trip as planned. What was your reasoning?

a. You feel that a difficult situation will not arise so there is no reason not to go.

b. You tell yourself that if there were any danger, you would not have been offered the plane.

c. You are in a hurry and do not want to take the time to think of alternative choices.

d. You do not want to admit that you may have trouble flying an unfamiliar airplane.

e. You are convinced that your flight instructor was much too conservative and pessimistic when he cautioned you to be thoroughly checked out in an unfamiliar aircraft.

Situation 4

You were briefed about possible icing conditions, but did not think there would be any problem since your departure airport temperature was 60°F (15°C). As you near your destination, you encounter freezing precipitation, which clings to your aircraft, and your passenger, who is a more experienced pilot, begins to panic. You consider turning back to the departure airport, but continue instead. Why did you not return?

a. You feel that having come this far, things are out of your hands.

b. The panic of the passenger makes you "commit yourself" without thinking the situation over.

c. You do not want the passenger to think you are afraid.

d. You are determined not to let the passenger think he can influence what you do.

e. You do not believe that the icing could cause your plane to crash in these circumstances.

Situation 5

You do not bother to check weather conditions at your destination. En route, you encounter headwinds. Your fuel supply is adequate to reach your destination, but there is almost no reserve for emergencies. You continue the flight and land with a nearly dry tank. What most influenced you to do this?

a. Being unhappy with the pressure of having to choose what to do, you make a snap decision.

b. You do not want your friends to hear that you had to turn back.

c. You feel that flight manuals always understate the safety margin in fuel tank capacity.

d. You believe that all things usually turn out well, and this will be no exception.

e. You reason that the situation has already been determined because the destination is closer than any other airport.

Situation 6

You are forty minutes late for a trip in a small airplane, and since the aircraft handled well on the previous day's flight, you decide to skip most of the preflight check. What leads you to this decision?

a. You simply take the first approach to making up time that comes to mind.

b. You feel that your reputation for being on time demands that you cut corners when necessary.

c. You believe that some of the preflight inspection is just a waste of time.

d. You see no reason to think that something unfortunate will happen during this flight.

e. If any problems develop, the responsibility would not be yours. It is the maintenance of the airplane that really makes the difference.

Situation 7

You are to fly an aircraft which you know is old and has been poorly maintained. A higher than normal RPM drop on the magneto check is indicated, and you suspect the spark plugs. Your friends, who are traveling as passengers, do not want to be delayed. After five minutes of debate, you agree to make the trip. Why did you permit yourself to be persuaded?

a. You feel that you must always prove your ability as a pilot, even under less than ideal circumstances.

b. You believe that regulations overstress safety in this kind of situation.

c. You think that the spark plugs will certainly last for just one more flight.

d. You feel that your opinion may be wrong since all the passengers are willing to take the risk.

e. The thought of changing arrangements is too annoying, so you jump at the suggestion of the passengers.

Situation 8

You are on final approach when you notice a large unidentified object on the far end of the runway. You consider going around, but your friend suggests landing anyway since the runway is "plenty long enough." You land, stopping 200 feet short of the obstacles. Why did you agree to land?

a. You have never had an accident, so you feel that nothing will happen this time.

b. You are pleased to have someone else help with the decision and decide your friend is right.

c. You do not have much time, so you just go ahead and act on your friend's suggestion.

d. You want to show your friend that you can stop the plane as quickly as needed.

e. You feel that the regulations making the pilot responsible for the safe operation of the aircraft do not apply here since it is the airport's responsibility to maintain the runway.

Situation 9

You have just completed your base leg for a landing on runway 14 at an uncontrolled airport. As you turn to final, you see that the wind has changed, blowing from about 90°. You make two sharp turns and land on runway 11. What was your reasoning?

a. You believe you are a really good pilot who can safely make sudden maneuvers.

b. You believe your flight instructor was overly cautious when insisting that a pilot must go around rather than make sudden course changes while on final approach.

c. You know there would be no danger in making the sudden turns because you do things like this all the time.

d. You know landing into the wind is best, so you act as soon as you can to avoid a crosswind landing.

e. The unexpected wind change is a bad break, but figure if the wind can change, so can you.

Situation 10

You have flown to your destination airfield only in daylight and believe that you know it well. You learn that your airplane needs a minor repair which will delay your arrival until well after dark. Although a good portion of the flight is after dark, you feel that you should be able to recognize some of the lighted landmarks. Why did you decide to make the flight?

a. You believe that when your time comes you cannot escape, and until that time there is no need to worry.

b. You do not want to wait to study other operations, so you carry out your first plan.

c. You feel that if anyone can handle this problem, you can do it.

d. You believe that the repair is not necessary. You decide you will not let recommended but minor maintenance stop you from getting to your destination.

e. You simply do not believe that you could get off course despite your unfamiliarity with ground references at night.

SCORING INSTRUCTIONS FOR ATTITUDE INVENTORY

Now that you have completed taking the inventory, the next step is to score it to determine your hazardous attitude profile. You will need to use your answer sheet, the scoring keys that follow these instructions, and the profile graph that follows the scoring keys.

1. Place the left side of the answer sheet on top of the first scoring key (Anti-Authority) so that it is lined up with the scoring key blanks for situations 1 through 5. Add the numbers written on your answer sheet which appears next to the "x" letters on the scoring key. Keep these totals on a separate piece of paper.

2. When you have done this for situations 1 through 5, move the answer sheet so that its right edge now lines up with the blanks for situations 6 through 10. Add the numbers next to the "x" letters for situations 6 through 10 to the first total which you recorded on a separate piece of paper.

3. Write this sum on the top of the profile graph at the end.

4. Repeat this procedure for all five scoring keys.

See the example below for the use of the scoring key.

EXAMPLE OF SCORING KEY USE

Scoring key for Anti-Authority   Answer sheet

Situation 1   **Situation 1**

a. _____   a. __4__

b. __x__   b. __3__

c. _____   c. __1__

d. _____   d. __5__

e. _____   e. __2__

Situation 2   **Situation 2**

a. _____   a. __3__

b. _____   b. __2__

c. _____   c. __5__

d. __x__   d. __1__

e. _____   e. __4__

    3 (number next to "x" on scoring key at 1-b)
  +1 (number next to "x" on scoring key at 2-d)
  =4   subtotal for situations 1 and 2
+ . . . (numbers next to "x's" for situations 3 through 10)
    Grand total of all 10 numbers next to x's.

Transfer this total to the "Anti-Authority" blank at the top of the profile graph.

SCORING KEY FOR ANTI-AUTHORITY

Situation 1

a. _____

b. __x__

c. _____

d. _____

e. _____

Situation 2

a. __x__

b. _____

c. _____

d. _____

e. _____

Situation 3

a. _____

b. _____

c. _____

d. _____

e. __x__

Situation 4

a. _____

b. _____

c. _____

d. __x__

e. _____

Situation 5

a. _____

b. _____

c. __x__

d. _____

e. _____

Situation 6

a. _____

b. _____

c. __x__

d. _____

e. _____

Situation 7

a. _____

b. __x__

c. _____

d. _____

e. _____

Situation 8

a. _____

b. _____

c. _____

d. _____

e. __x__

Situation 9

a. _____

b. __x__

c. _____

d. _____

e. _____

Situation 10

a. _____

b. _____

c. _____

d. __x__

e. _____

SCORING KEY FOR IMPULSIVITY

Situation 1

a. _____

b. _____

c. _____

d. _____

e. __X__

Situation 2

a. _____

b. _____

c. _____

d. __X__

e. _____

Situation 3

a. _____

b. _____

c. __X__

d. _____

e. _____

Situation 4

a. _____

b. __X__

c. _____

d. _____

e. _____

Situation 5

a. __X__

b. _____

c. _____

d. _____

e. _____

Situation 6

a. __X__

b. _____

c. _____

d. _____

e. _____

Situation 7

a. _____

b. _____

c. _____

d. _____

e. __X__

Situation 8

a. _____

b. _____

c. __X__

d. _____

e. _____

Situation 9

a. _____

b. _____

c. _____

d. __X__

e. _____

Situation 10

a. _____

b. __X__

c. _____

d. _____

e. _____

SCORING KEY FOR INVULNERABILITY

Situation 1	**Situation 5**	**Situation 8**
a. _____	a. _____	a. __X__
b. _____	b. _____	b. _____
c. __X__	c. _____	c. _____
d. _____	d. __X__	d. _____
e. _____	e. _____	e. _____

Situation 2	**Situation 6**	**Situation 9**
a. _____	a. _____	a. _____
b. __X__	b. _____	b. _____
c. _____	c. _____	c. __X__
d. _____	d. __X__	d. _____
e. _____	e. _____	e. _____

Situation 3	**Situation 7**	**Situation 10**
a. __X__	a. _____	a. _____
b. _____	b. _____	b. _____
c. _____	c. __X__	c. _____
d. _____	d. _____	d. _____
e. _____	e. _____	e. __X__

Situation 4

a. _____
b. _____
c. _____
d. _____
e. __X__

SCORING KEY FOR MACHO

Situation 1	Situation 5	Situation 8
a. __X__	a. _____	a. _____
b. _____	b. __X__	b. _____
c. _____	c. _____	c. _____
d. _____	d. _____	d. __X__
e. _____	e. _____	e. _____

Situation 2	Situation 6	Situation 9
a. _____	a. _____	a. __X__
b. _____	b. __X__	b. _____
c. _____	c. _____	c. _____
d. _____	d. _____	d. _____
e. __X__	e. _____	e. _____

Situation 3	Situation 7	Situation 10
a. _____	a. __X__	a. _____
b. _____	b. _____	b. _____
c. _____	c. _____	c. __X__
d. __X__	d. _____	d. _____
e. _____	e. _____	e. _____

Situation 4
a. _____
b. _____
c. __X__
d. _____
e. _____

SCORING KEY FOR RESIGNATION

Situation 1	**Situation 5**	**Situation 8**
a. _____	a. _____	a. _____
b. _____	b. _____	b. __x__
c. _____	c. _____	c. _____
d. __x__	d. _____	d. _____
e. _____	e. __x__	e. _____

Situation 2	**Situation 6**	**Situation 9**
a. _____	a. _____	a. _____
b. _____	b. _____	b. _____
c. __x__	c. _____	c. _____
d. _____	d. _____	d. _____
e. _____	e. __x__	e. __x__

Situation 3	**Situation 7**	**Situation 10**
a. _____	a. _____	a. __x__
b. __x__	b. _____	b. _____
c. _____	c. _____	c. _____
d. _____	d. __x__	d. _____
e. _____	e. _____	e. _____

Situation 4

a. __x__

b. _____

c. _____

d. _____

e. _____

PROFILE GAME

1. Enter the raw scores obtained from each scoring key in the correct blank space below. The sum of the five scores should equal 150; if not, go back and check your work.

Anti-Authority   _____

Impulsivity   _____

Invulnerability _____

Macho   _____

Resignation   _____

TOTAL 150

2. Now look at the hazardous attitude profile form on the next page. Notice that there are five columns, one for each of the raw scores. Place a mark on each line at the height that matches your score. Now draw lines connecting the five marks.

HAZARDOUS ATTITUDE PROFILE

Anti-Authority	Impulsivity	Invulnerability	Macho	Resignation
_____50	_____50	_____50	_____50	_____50
_____	_____	_____	_____	_____
_____	_____	_____	_____	_____
_____	_____	_____	_____	_____
_____	_____	_____	_____	_____
_____	_____	_____	_____	_____
_____	_____	_____	_____	_____
_____	_____	_____	_____	_____
_____40	_____40	_____40	_____40	_____40
_____	_____	_____	_____	_____
_____	_____	_____	_____	_____
_____	_____	_____	_____	_____
_____	_____	_____	_____	_____
_____	_____	_____	_____	_____
_____	_____	_____	_____	_____
_____30	_____30	_____30	_____30	_____30
_____	_____	_____	_____	_____
_____	_____	_____	_____	_____
_____	_____	_____	_____	_____
_____	_____	_____	_____	_____
_____	_____	_____	_____	_____
_____20	_____20	_____20	_____20	_____20
_____	_____	_____	_____	_____
_____	_____	_____	_____	_____
_____	_____	_____	_____	_____
_____	_____	_____	_____	_____
_____	_____	_____	_____	_____
_____	_____	_____	_____	_____
_____10	_____10	_____10	_____10	_____10

PROFILE EXPLANATION

You now have a profile graph which indicates the comparative strength of each of the five hazardous attitudes for you. (Remember, your scores are confidential and need not be divulged to anyone!) The higher the relative number, the greater the likelihood that you will respond with that hazardous attitude. Keep your results in mind as you read further. Let us begin the explanation of your profile by describing an all-too-common flight situation.

A pilot of a single-engine airplane checks the weather and notes that there is a possibility of a thunderstorm at his destination airport. He has never operated an aircraft in bad weather, and he knows that his flight instructor would advise him not to fly. Despite this, he takes off, crashes in poor weather, and seriously injures himself.

Why does this occur so often? Because many accidents involve pilots who allow themselves to be influenced by one or more of the five hazardous attitudes. These attitudes get pilots into trouble by causing them to take chances that invite accidents. (The five hazardous attitudes are the ones recorded on the assessment inventory which you just completed.)

SUMMARY

If you have not already done so, look back at your profile to see which hazardous attitudes most often matched your own thinking when you answered the questions. This shows which patterns you tend to use when your judgment becomes influenced by hazardous thinking. The inventory does not show that you are bound to act in the manner of one or more of the hazardous thoughts. Having thoughts similar to the ones described as hazardous is common and normal. But as you progress in your flight training, you will find yourself thinking fewer and fewer hazardous thoughts as you become able to identify and counteract them. The important thing to learn is to balance all your thoughts against possible outcomes so that you act only in a safe manner. A critical part of your training, then, is learning to examine your own thinking and control hazardous attitudes. Whether you now engage in one or more of these thought patterns, often or only rarely, learning to control them will be worthwhile; you will become a safer pilot the less often you act upon a hazardous thought.

THE FIVE HAZARDOUS ATTITUDES

1. Antiauthority:
"Don't tell me!"

This thought is found in people who do not like anyone telling them what to do. They think "Don't tell me!" In a sense, they are saying, "No one can tell me what to do." They may either be resentful of having someone tell him or her what to do or may just regard rules, regulations, and procedures as silly or unnecessary. However, it is always your prerogative to question authority if you feel it is in error.

2. Impulsivity:
"Do something—quickly!"

This is the thought pattern of people who frequently feel the need to do something, anything, immediately. They do not stop to think about what they are about to do; they do not select the best alternative—they do the first thing that comes to mind.

3. Invulnerability:
"It won't happen to me."

Many people feel that accidents happen to others but never to them. They know accidents can happen, and they know that anyone can be affected; but they never really feel or believe that they will be the one involved. Pilots who think this way are more likely to take chances and run unwise risks, thinking all the time, "It won't happen to me!"

4. Macho:
"I can do it."

People who are always trying to prove that they are better than anyone else think, "I can do it!" They "prove" themselves by taking risks and by trying to impress others. While this pattern is thought to be a male characteristic, women are equally susceptible.

5. Resignation:
"What's the use?"

People who think, "What's the use?" do not see themselves as making a great deal of difference in what happens to them. When things go well, they think, "That's good luck." When things go badly, they attribute it to bad luck or feel that someone is "out to get them." They leave the action to others—for better or worse. Sometimes, such individuals will even go along with unreasonable requests just to be a "nice guy."

The macho pilot

Flying involves a certain measure of confidence. As your flying skills improve with practice, you'll feel more capable of making a trip when conditions get more difficult. Be careful that this feeling of increased ability is measured with a realistic review of your true capability. Weather is a good example of how machismo can impair pilot decision making. A VFR pilot might cancel or delay a number of flights on the basis of the flight service comment "VFR flight not recommended" only to learn that conditions were better than forecast and the trip could have been flown.

As she builds flying time, she might decide that she can go "take a look" when such warnings are given; she'll probably complete a flight or two without incident, serving to "disprove" the judgment of the forecasters. At this point, she can choose one of two paths for the rest of her flying career:

- She can learn how to supplement her weather briefings with her own knowledge of meteorology and take off with a set of options in mind in case the weather turns out to be bad after all.

- She can decide that calling flight service is a waste of time and press on even when dire warnings are available through proper channels.

Unfortunately, many pilots choose the latter course, trusting in their own abilities to get them through unaided. Why might this be? Flying itself is a "macho" thing to do, a me-against-the-elements sort of thing, a satisfaction for the need to be in control. Self-reliant people learn to fly in the first place, so pilots on the whole are susceptible to the "macho mind-set" and its pitfalls.

Back to the example: She now regularly takes off cross-country into some of the worst weather, knowing that she'll get around it or through it simply because she has made it alive up to that point. In extreme cases, she'll become the type who flies IFR without a rating or a clearance, groping her way through the clouds with little thought of the danger she's created for herself, her passengers, and others outside of the airplane.

Or she might regularly bust minimums once instrument rated or fly in ice in a non-certified airplane. She might exceed maximum loading in her airplane because deep down she "knows" she has a special ability to handle these situations. Polls indicate that something like 87 percent of all pilots feel that they are "above average" in their flying ability. That's good to a point, I suppose, because pilots need that level of confidence to fly, but it also reflects a trait of machismo that is likely responsible for a good number of accidents.

How can you use this knowledge to make safer flying decisions? If you find yourself deciding on a course of action because you feel you're better than most pilots or you can make it when others can't, it's time to step back for a moment and evaluate whether that's really the case or if instead you're using one of the traits that caused you to become a pilot in the first place to justify an otherwise unjustifiable decision.

The impulsive pilot

Pilots should be able to make quick decisions and take action in a crisis without taking the time to think. Much time is spent during pilot training to develop a pilot's quick-reaction skills by drilling on engine failures, fires, and other types of procedures; however, this snap-decision situation is rarely required in the cockpit. Usually it's the little things that add up to an accident, and the pilot has a great deal of time to evaluate a decision and choose a course of action.

Because pilot-type personalities tend to be decisive to begin with and the quick-reaction response is so ingrained in pilot training, persons for which this trait is particularly dominant might actually create emergencies where none exist or make a small problem a much greater one. Here's an example.

A student of mine, who already had a great deal of time flying his Beech Baron, was preparing for a commercial checkride with another instructor when he came to me for "factory-approved" training. He had done quite well in the Baron simulator, and we were in his airplane practicing V_{MC} demonstrations. For readers not familiar with the term, a "V_{MC} demo" is an illustration of the fact that when one engine on a multiengine airplane is shut down, it takes progressively more and more control deflection to fly straight ahead as airspeed is reduced. Eventually the pilot reaches "minimum controllable airspeed," which is that speed where full control deflection is reached, and any further airspeed loss causes the airplane to roll, pitch, and yaw in the direction of the "dead" engine.

The purpose of the demo is to drill the pilot in proper airspeed control during emergencies. The recovery requires reduction of power on the "operating" engine (reducing the imbalance of power on one wing versus the other) and a pitch downward to return airspeed to a value that provides adequate control.

I had already told my client that we would have to be very careful about the possibility of a real engine failure near V_{MC}. We were gradually decelerating for the demonstration at about 5000 feet atop a broken cloud layer in clear and smooth air when the right engine quit; the noise dropped dramatically, and the plane began to yaw, roll, and pitch.

The pilot did an admirable job of maintaining directional control and the pitch attitude necessary to assure proper airspeed. Also to his credit, he masterfully processed the memory items of the engine failure checklist; to this point, his experience in the simulator all week served him well. When he completed the step to turn on the auxiliary boost fuel pump for the failed engine, the engine sprang back to life, and the plane yawed, rolled, and pitched against the asymmetric trim the pilot had set. Again, he did a great job of maintaining control.

With both engines turning, the pilot then reached up and turned off the boost pump that had just restarted the engine. He seemed surprised but still maintained control as the engine's noise again dropped and the airplane again skewed to the right. I reached over and quickly snapped the boost pump back on, and the indications reversed themselves. "In a Baron," I reminded him, "if the auxiliary pump restarts an engine, it's because the primary pump has failed, and the aux pump must stay on for the engine to continue to run."

Our lesson had been cut short, so I negotiated with the controllers for an instrument approach back into Colonel James Jabara Airport on the northeast edge of Wichita. We were just getting established on the inbound course of Jabara's long VOR approach when, without warning, the pilot reached up and turned off the right engine's boost pump. Once again the noise deadened as the right prop blades slowed, and the airplane heaved to the right side; once again the pilot appeared startled even though he did a good job of countering the engine failure's effects. I reached over and turned the switch back on, restarting the engine, and helped the pilot long enough to keep us established on the inbound course of the approach. "The approach checklist calls for boost pumps 'off,'" the pilot explained, then added "I forgot about the failed fuel pump."

We broke out of the bases well above minimum descent altitude, and visibility was around 20 miles, which made finding our destination easy. The VOR approach into Jabara brings you into the runway at a right angle where you can cross over at midfield and break left or right for the appropriate circling pattern. As we turned left for the downwind, the Baron owner once more reached up and turned off the boost pump, which he later explained as "being part of the prelanding checklist." I was ready for him this time and reset the switch before much change in performance occurred. The pilot's landing was excellent, but on rollout he again killed the switch; the right engine sputtered and stopped immediately, making it difficult for our combined efforts to keep us from rolling into the grass.

I hope the Baron pilot realizes that I am merely illustrating how impulsiveness in an airplane (doing things without first assessing the impact of those actions) can sometimes create a more dangerous situation than doing nothing. I'm equally guilty because I spent the week spring-loading the pilot for engine failures; it obviously worked, given his response to five in a single flight, but it also reinforced the faulty notion that quick action is always correct action.

Backed by drilled-in checklist steps to turn off the Baron's auxiliary fuel pumps at various phases of flight, this prevalence for action—so necessary and so common in the successful persons lucky enough to be able to own and operate a light twin— could have turned a minor problem (an engine-driven fuel pump failure at altitude) into an out-and-out catastrophe. The pilot was repeatedly confused by the failure of the engine when he performed a normal-procedures checklist step "correctly."

Put another way, it's the rare situation that requires an immediate rote-memory response in an airplane, and although pilots need to constantly drill for those few emergencies, most accidents are caused by the "little things" that are best countered with the decision-making process, evaluating the outcome of an act before taking action. If you seem to be the sort that finds yourself occasionally running upstairs only to forget why or making a purchase without comparing prices elsewhere or sealing an envelope without first enclosing the contents, you exhibit the trait of impulsiveness. Be careful in your airplane to evaluate the effects of each decision you make and each checklist step you perform.

The invulnerable pilot

I have to watch out for this one in myself. The invulnerable pilot thinks that nothing can happen to him, that he or she has the luck to avoid accidents and the skills it takes to overcome obstacles along the way. It is a close partner to the "macho" characteristic. The "justification" for this attitude is that nothing catastrophic has happened so far, and therefore there's no reason to believe anything bad will happen in the future. Title and position come into play as well.

We assume that the knowledge and confidence exhibited in professional careers will carry over into everything else; however, skills that make us successful in our chosen fields do not necessarily give us credit for the lessons to be learned in aviation. A flight I took a few years ago points out how this attitude could have brought me to grief. My wife refers to the episode as a "stupid airplane trick."

> I was flying and teaching in high-performance airplanes at the time, but still owned the 1946 Cessna 120 that I had used to build most of my time toward my commercial pilot certificate. It was time for the 120's inspection, and after a bad experience with a local mechanic the year before, my wife and I decided to have the job done elsewhere.
>
> I have a good friend who runs a one-man maintenance shop in Sedalia, Missouri, where I had instructed prior to moving to Wichita, and I made arrangements for him to do the annual. It was October, and I rose before the dawn to launch the 200-or-so miles to Sedalia, planning to arrive at about the time the mechanic usually gets to work. Arriving uneventfully, I set about removing the cowling, access panels, seats, and anything else I could get loose prior to the mechanic's scrutiny.
>
> I hoped to be able to get everything done in time to fly home that night, but I had made contingency plans to spend the night with some friends in case something required a little extra time or attention. I had my overnight bag in the hangar alongside the "airplane pieces" through the day as we labored on; I called my local friends around noon, and they were hopeful to be able to see me that evening.
>
> I figured that I needed to get off the ground by around 4:30 to make it home before dark. My Cessna had an electrical system and all the required lights, but it didn't have a radio, so I didn't fly it at night. The lights are always left on at the "home airport" near Wichita, but I just didn't want to fly

over the empty prairies of eastern Kansas at night without a radio, even though the night was to be cloudless.

Around 3:30 it looked as though I'd make my departure time, so I cleaned off my hands long enough to call my local friends once more, thanking them for the offer but advising them I would head home that afternoon. I also left a message on my answering machine at home, telling my wife I'd be on my way.

As the mechanic and I were "buttoning up" a fairing on the left wing, we noticed that the aileron bellcrank was rubbing against metal in the wing. A closer look revealed that I had installed the bellcrank backward when we replaced an aileron crossover cable; I had to remove the bellcrank, reattach the cable, and reinstall the device correctly. It was close to 5 p.m. by the time I was ready to go, which was outside of my previously prescribed "launch window."

Nevertheless, I had already "canceled" my invitation to stay locally, and I had told my wife I would be home that evening, so I packed the logbooks and my overnight bag into the little taildragger and got ready to go. My first warning should have been this rush for departure, despite the fact that I had 2 hours before sundown. It was about a 2-hour flight home to Wichita into the usual westbound headwinds, and the weather promised to be spotless all the way. My second warning should have been when I flipped on the battery master switch and didn't hear the usual "click" of the relay snapping into contact. The battery was dead.

Here's where I began to rationalize. I figured that something I did in the course of the day might have shorted out the electrical system, depleting the battery, and that it would charge back up as soon as I got the engine started. I also began to exhibit the trait of invulnerability. I decided that although I would be pushing it to arrive home before twilight, I was "night current" (albeit in other, tricycle-gear airplanes), and I could easily find the home airport by following the only lighted highway from El Dorado, east of Wichita, to the always-illuminated runway at Benton, Kansas, where I kept the 120. All I had to do was to get my airplane started, and my mechanic obligingly pulled the prop for me, turning it into a blurring disc.

Takeoff into the cool autumn air was smooth, and I cruised westward along an abandoned rail line at 1000 feet above the rusty trees. The visibility was endless and the air without a burble; I saw the occasional fellow traveler high or low as I passed small towns and private grass strips; it was a beautiful evening for a sightseeing flight. The sun began to press the horizon as I crossed the Kansas border and picked up the turnpike to my north, a highway to my south. I knew from experience to stay between them and they would converge at El Dorado, a few miles from home.

The west wind was stronger than forecast, slowing my progress, and the sky began to turn red with the dusk. I quickly figured my new time to destination and learned that it would be about half an hour after sunset. Off my right wing I could see the bright lights of the nuclear reactor near Burlington,

Kansas, and the Coffey County Airport. There would be a place to spend the night at Burlington, I was sure, but I thought I could see one of the oil-field gas fires glowing in the orange ahead that would serve as a beacon taking me directly to my intercept point of El Dorado, and once again my assumed invulnerability prodded me to continue.

El Dorado was definitely in sight, although creeping toward my craft slowly, as the last of twilight began to fade. I had the navigation lights on now, and the single red panel light mounted above my left shoulder didn't do a good job of illuminating the panel. It didn't light up the ammeter at all, and I failed to notice its steady discharge. Perhaps I was lucky, or perhaps I had subconsciously set myself up for this moment, but I had no fewer than three flashlights in the bag beside me; I propped one on the seat, only to see the ammeter hit the peg as the last of my red light extinguished.

Okay, here I was, a thousand feet above the Flint Hills of Kansas, without electrical power. I was aimed for home less than half an hour away, and I could indeed find the airport when I got there, but I had no lights to warn others of my approach and only flashlights to illuminate the instrument panel. I could land at El Dorado if the runway lights were on or even turn and run with the wind to always-illuminated Burlington, but I decided that the chance of a collision was remote, and I could easily find Benton with its runway lights and my car for the trip home. "I'm a top-notch professional instructor," I must have told myself, "and have 300 hours in this Cessna 120. Nothing will go wrong," I was certain.

I didn't see another airplane as I cruised low down the highway to Benton, the lights of El Dorado beneath my dark wings reminding me of the Paris scene at the end of "The Spirit of St. Louis," starring Jimmy Stewart. Ridiculously slowly, Benton finally hovered into view; I could even see the illuminated wind sock, nearly limp but showing a slight breeze from the northwest. I maneuvered for a 45° entry to the downwind leg, just in case anyone else was out there, and ended up in position as I flew along the runway on downwind.

I told myself to be careful for signs of airplanes back-taxiing on the runway or anything else that looked unusual on final approach, and that I could always go around if I needed to. Carb heat on and throttle back, I flew more by feel and the sound in the air vents as I lined up on the narrow runway, my heart racing and sweat rolling down my neck. Everything looked fine until it was time to flare, when I realized that pulling the nose up to the landing position meant I could no longer see the runway lights ahead of me. I put the 120 in a three-point landing attitude and held on (perhaps in retrospect a wheel landing would have been better) until the airplane settled into one of the nicest touchdowns I've ever done. I could taxi between the lines of lights to the blue-lit taxi turnoff, and then the 20 or 30 yards to my tiedown spot.

One of the scariest points in my flying career was when I left the runway at the taxiway lights to find that I could see absolutely nothing along the unlit taxiway. Shining my flashlight out the open door did little good; in near panic, I made one of the best decisions of my entire life when I shut it down on the taxi strip to push it the rest of the way. I'm glad I did. Not 10 yards ahead of me, dark in the night air, sat an unoccupied Cessna 150 in the middle of the taxiway while its pilot and instructor sat in the line shack discussing some night dual. Had I continued to taxi in, I probably would never have seen the 150 before the 120's prop chewed into the 150's rudder.

Physically shaking and after tying my craft in the grass, I called my wife on the pay phone outside the line shack. "Oh, you're home?" she asked, surprised I wasn't calling from an airport along the way. Not yet a pilot, she did nail down my decision making that evening even before I described the flight when she added, "That was stupid."

I learned a lot that evening. Foremost is the fact that I tend to have a feeling that I can handle any situation, and that false security caused me to pass up first a perfectly enjoyable and preplanned evening with friends in Missouri. I even passed up a series of alternate airports that would have been perhaps inconvenient and cost me a little money, but that would have satisfied my goal of safety above all else. I lost sight of my goals and failed to make good decisions because of my personality.

The "antiauthority" pilot

Face it, you have a rebellious streak. You wouldn't defy the masses and fly a "little" airplane if you didn't. By being a bit "antiauthority," what you're really doing is assuming authority yourself, and most of the time that's a good thing when flying an airplane. When your independence starts to let you break the rules—most of the rules were made admittedly by trial and error in the aftermath of airplane accidents—you're letting your personality get in the way of good decision making.

I was flying an instrument-instruction flight one summer afternoon. Aloft at 7000 feet in my flight school's Skyhawk, I watched as my student deviated left and right around some growing cumulus buildups. I'd heard a forecast of thunderstorms for the afternoon, the convective sigmets, and a center weather advisory for a line of storms mounting to the east of my IFR practice route.

The quiet of an underused center sector frequency was broken by a Mooney pilot checking in. The pilot was cruising from the southbound at 9000 feet. It was to our south, in the area of Springfield, Missouri.

When the Mooney checked in on a heading toward Vichy, Missouri, the center controller offered that level 4 and 5 thunderstorms had been reported in that area. The Mooney pilot, perhaps rushing to an appointment in St. Louis, made no reply to the report. When the controller suggested that the Mooney reroute directly north to near Columbia and then due east along the airway to St. Louis, the Mooney pilot barked that he could not take such a wide diversion. "I need to go direct Vichy, direct as filed," was an approximation of his curt reply.

Again the controller provided thunderstorm information, going so far as to read the convective SIGMET and center weather advisory texts, even though it was not the scheduled time. The Mooney pilot remained unimpressed and still requested his filed route.

Taking matters into his own hands, the controller issued a clearance: "Mooney 12345, amend your clearance, fly heading 010, vectors direct Columbia, and expect further clearance shortly." Although unwise, it was entirely within the authority of the Mooney pilot to decline the clearance, but I could scarcely believe my ears when he did. "Negative," returned the pilot, "I want to continue on as filed."

Because weather avoidance is the pilot's responsibility and no other traffic was so inclined to be in the area of reported thunderstorms to provide a spacing conflict, the controller had absolutely no authority to do anything but to grant the request. The Mooney flew into some of the blackest skies I've seen through a cockpit window. It must have been a wild ride. I never heard about a Mooney going down over the Ozark foothills that afternoon, so I guess he made it through alive. How easily that might not have been true.

I've used this as an example of an antiauthority attitude because the Mooney pilot seemed simply not to recognize that anyone besides himself had any influence on the safety of his flight. The controller, to his credit, did everything he possibly could to try to change the Mooney's flight path away from the storms. But the pilot was just too strong-willed for his own good and pressed on into the churning murk. Have you ever known a pilot whom others called an "accident waiting to happen"? It's this sort of strong, antiauthority attitude that can get people—often innocent passengers—killed.

The only pilot I've ever worked with who I've known to die in an airplane crash did a superb job in the VFR aspects of flying his turbocharged Bonanza, but admitted on the first day of his training that he had a habit of setting the autopilot and flying IFR without a clearance and without an instrument rating. He had flown to Wichita at 21,000 feet without contacting anyone and with his transponder turned off to avoid detection and then descended through more than 10,000 feet of solid cloud cover to reach clear air underneath.

Eventually this antiauthority "I-can-do-it-because-I-or-my-autopilot-have-the-skills" attitude caught up with him; he reportedly flew into the side of a mountain in instrument meteorological conditions under autopilot control. Ironically, my pleadings had been at least partially successful; he was scheduled to return to earn his instrument rating two weeks after the fatal crash.

Do you find yourself "bending the rules" a bit or occasionally arguing with the air traffic controllers in the hopes of getting your way? You exhibit a strong antiauthority attitude, so remember that the rules are not meant to be broken.

The resigned pilot

Sometimes the external pressures to make a trip are just too great. Family and friends are anxious to get to a destination on schedule. You need to carry just a little bit more baggage. You have to leave simply to get away from the stresses of home and work.

With external pressures urging you to fly, you sometimes have to assert your authority and intercede in the interest of safety.

Unfortunately such a safety mind-set is difficult to justify to passengers, and it's possible that a pilot might instead delegate (consciously or not) the go/no-go decision to some other party instead of disappointing the family or annoying a passenger. To some extent, pilots need a little sense of subordination (you need to resign yourself to the fact that you will not fly in thunderstorms, for instance), but when you let others make the primary go/no-go decision for you, you've let personal pressures get in the way of sound decision making. Take for example this instructional flight in a Piper Malibu.

Three persons boarded the high-performance pressurized single for the short flight from Santa Maria to Paso Robles, California. It was a cloudless day with at least 10 miles visibility; the pilot was receiving dual flight instruction from an instructor in the right seat. At about 5800 feet above the airport, the instructor shut down the airplane's engine to simulate an engine failure. The pilot being trained was instructed to guide the airplane to a safe landing at the Paso Robles airport.

Several times during the descent the pilot being trained asked his instructor when the landing gear should be extended. Witnesses reported that the pilot lowered the gear at a very low altitude, using the emergency extension procedure. The left main gear did not lock into position and collapsed upon making contact with the runway. No one was hurt.[4]

The pilot of this airplane was in what I call the classic "resigned pilot" dilemma; despite over 11,000 hours logged flight time and 367 hours in the Malibu before the crash, he was resigned to do whatever the instructor asked of him. Too often there is a natural tendency to defer to the experience of an instructor. There are safer and less costly ways to simulate an engine failure. If the pilot truly wanted this training, facilities offer simulator training for the Malibu at much less expense than this local training eventually cost.

Perhaps the underlying cause of this accident was the failure of the pilot to challenge the judgment of his instructor. We are all "students" of flying, and we don't want to second-guess our instructors very often, but we should not be resigned to do whatever is asked, especially under questionable circumstances.

You can be in a similar situation flying for fun or for business when external factors start to make decisions for you. Are you pointed homeward or on a tight schedule to make an important business trip? Did the line service accidentally fill the auxiliary tanks against your wishes, putting you over maximum gross weight for takeoff with the passengers you're carrying? Are you committed to a narrow "launch window" because of the weather? These are examples of situations where a pilot's sense of resignation— he or she has no control over events and therefore will "give it a go" regardless—might emerge as dominant elements of decision making. If you feel that you're being unduly pressured to fly against your better judgment, it's time to step back, define your goals, and reevaluate your choice of "go" or "not to go."

Review the results of your "Attitude Inventory" evaluation. Regardless of the ratings you hold, this exercise will point out which of your decision-making personality traits are dominant, allowing you to anticipate their effects and recognize when you need to recheck your choices to remain safe. It was only after taking this inventory a year and a half after my nighttime trek across eastern Kansas in my Cessna 120 that I clearly understood why I allowed myself to get into such a predicament; I finally learned the true lesson of that flight, that I have a sense of invulnerability that affects my decisions. Since then I have consciously considered the effect of that personality trait numerous times before takeoff and made a few no-go decisions; who knows how many times I saved myself and my passengers from a mishap?

Personality traits such as confidence, independence tempered with the willingness to receive help from others, and a prevalence toward action are brought together to make you a good pilot. When those individual components of your personality rise to dominance, however, they might begin to cloud the judgment your remaining traits normally inspire and you start to make bad decisions that might affect the outcome of your flight. Watch for the signs of decision making based upon individual personality traits. Take the personality assessment test in the appendix of this book *periodically* to see how life's changes are making one or more of your decision-making-related traits emerge (Fig. 4-2).

Hazardous attitude	Antidote
Antiauthority: Don't tell me.	Follow the rules. They are usually right.
Impulsivity: Do something quickly.	Not so fast. Think first.
Invulnerability: It won't happen to me.	It could happen to me.
Macho: I can do it.	Taking chances is foolish.
Resignation: What's the use?	I'm not helpless. I can make a difference.

Fig. 4-2. *Hazardous attitudes and their antidotes.*

5
Phase of flight: Takeoff

YOUR ABILITY TO MAKE WELL-INFORMED, SAFETY-RELATED INFLIGHT decisions depends on several variables. These variables can be lumped into two broad categories that have a direct impact on the wisdom of your decisions:

- Information available with which to make a decision
- Factors that affect your ability to receive and analyze that information

One of the biggest determinants of your ability to receive and analyze information is pilot workload. The rate at which raw data reaches your perception can get to be so great that eventually your mind is no longer able to process it. If the information rate exceeds your capacity to receive, you've reached what the United States Air Force calls *task saturation*; the decision-making processes in your mind actually shut down, leaving you with but instinct and rote learning to continue. This is obviously an extremely dangerous situation in an airplane because safe aviating is the process of continually detecting and managing new, unexpected pieces of knowledge.

Pilot workload varies predictably in different phases of flight. Although circumstances (weather, aircraft emergencies, etc.) might cause localized "spikes" in the workload curve, the level of tasks required of a pilot generally follows the slope depicted in Fig. 5-1. Workload is low during the start-up and taxi phase of operation,

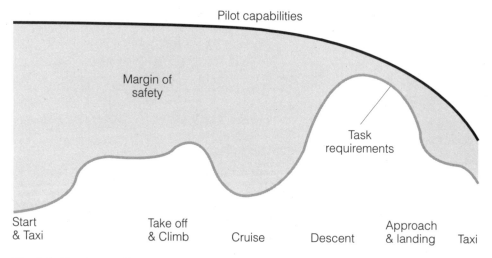

Fig. 5-1. *Varying workload levels during various phases of flight.*

and increases dramatically on takeoff and in climb. Upon reaching cruise altitude, task levels return to a level near that while on the ground; there's not a lot of physical control manipulation required to maintain cruise, at least nothing like that necessary to change a state of flight. Upon descent, your workload begins to increase once more; gearing up for the approach, you'll be required to perform a number of cockpit chores, increasing workload even further. Converging with the ground at slow speed and with flight variables changing rapidly, the landing phase represents the highest workload portion of your trip, followed by the low-stress taxi in to parking and shutdown.

Because the vast majority of general aviation accidents are the result of human factors and pilot decision making, as we have already seen, it's not surprising to also see a correlation between the inflight workload curve and the number of accidents incurred. Let's look at some paraphrased observations from AOPA's Air Safety Foundation.

> A predominance of the accidents (in the study years 1982–1988) occurred during the landing phase of flight (Fig. 5-2); however, the emergency or malfunction that lead to the accident did not necessarily occur during that phase.
>
> The phase in which the emergency occurs identifies where the system malfunctioned or where the accident causal factor occurred (Fig. 5-3).

The intent is to show that although a high percentage of the accidents occurred during the landing phase, many emergencies that led to the accident occurred prior to landing, and if proper actions had been taken prior to or immediately following the emergency, an accident might have been prevented or minimized.[1]

In other words, systems failures rarely cause an aircraft accident. Instead, it's the action or inaction of the pilot that is the ultimate precipitator of most airplane mishaps.

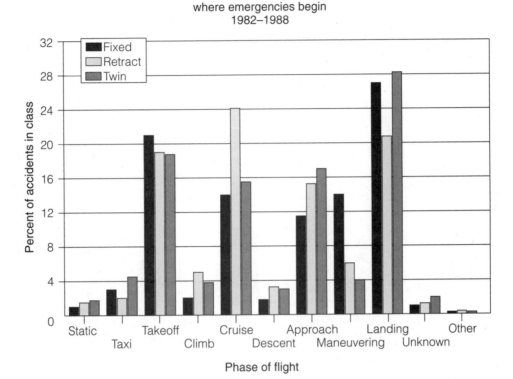

Phase of flight
where emergencies begin
1982–1988

Fig. 5-2. *Phase of flight where emergencies began.* AOPA Air Safety Foundation

Because accidents therefore are the result of human factors, we can compare the work-load curve shown in Fig. 5-1 to the phase of flight where emergencies begin shown in Fig. 5-2 and accidents happen in Fig. 5-3 to illustrate the effect that workload has on pilot decision making.

How can you use this knowledge to become a safer pilot? Realize that a lot of in-flight decisions can easily be made on the ground, prior to takeoff, or in the cruise phase of flight when cockpit demands are low. By preparing beforehand for the indications and decisions required in the high-workload phases of flight, you can skillfully reduce the workload you'll experience when actually conducting those phases. Let's review the various phases of flight and discuss how to approach inflight workload reduction.

START-UP AND TAXI

During the initial start-up and taxi phase of flight, workload is typically very low. There simply isn't a lot of stress while operating on the ground; if the least little prob-lem or a major change in plans arises, dealing with it means simply stopping where you are or at worst shutting down and getting out of the airplane. If you feel rushed or

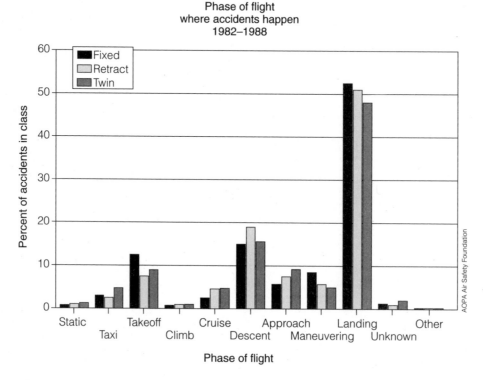

Fig. 5-3. *Phase of flight where accidents happen.*

"stressed out" during the start-up and taxi phase of your flight, it's because you're allowing outside forces such as family or job worries influence your thinking. My friend LeRoy Cook, senior editor of *Private Pilot* magazine, likes to point out the warning sign of a pilot rushing toward an airplane (Fig. 5-4).

Fig. 5-4. *A safe flight begins with thorough and meticulous preflight planning and inspection.*

A good example of stress management before takeoff might be a trip I took with my family one winter's day. The FBO at which we had left our Cessna had promised to put the plane in a heated hangar overnight; when we arrived for an 8 a.m. departure, we found that they had failed to do so. Faced with an all-day flight westbound into mounting headwinds, the knowledge that any delay meant we were more likely to encounter the adverse effects of an approaching cold front added external stress as I assisted in the laborious task of removing a large accumulation of frost and ice on the Cessna. That my wife and our baby boy sat for nearly an hour in freezing temperatures as we tried to start the airplane's engine gave me even more external stress when the powerplant finally roared to life.

When the time came to launch westward, I had to make a conscious decision to simply concentrate on the task of flying and to put behind me the three-hour delay and the impatience of my passengers. I was in a low-workload phase of flight; I didn't need to artificially increase my stress and erode decision making prior to the natural workload increase of takeoff.

Your workload will multiply dramatically during the takeoff and initial climb phase. At this point you're making the transition from one phase to another, and just like any other time when status is changing quickly, a huge amount of information is available, much of which is necessary to safely conduct the flight. Your job is to find and use the information you need and to weed out that which is extraneous. You'll discover that it is much easier to do if you know what indications to expect and make some preliminary decisions in advance.

TAKEOFF

Getting ready for takeoff, you should have a firm grasp of the indications you expect to see so that you'll be able to immediately detect if an abnormality occurs in time to correct the problem before a disaster results. I wrote much of the remainder of this chapter for the November 1994 issue of *Private Pilot* magazine.

"You are cleared for takeoff." Lined up with the runway, anticipating once again the rush of adrenaline that comes with advancing the throttle and pointing your airplane skyward, you increase power as your craft begins to roll. Slowly at first, the tempo of runway light posts quickens in your peripheral vision until you feel the airplane begin to lift. You're airborne, almost subconsciously guiding the plane upward as your thoughts drift to the trip ahead.

But something's wrong. You think you've done everything right, but the airplane isn't climbing like it should. Suddenly your vision locks on the line of trees ahead, and you begin to wonder whether you'll have the altitude to clear it. You push hard on the throttle, although it's already on the forward stop, and start to pull back on the yoke. Airspeed drops and the airplane begins to settle; just before your wings clip the trees, the horizon whirls over, filling the windscreen with a spinning green blur. Later, from your hospital bed, you wonder what you could have done to avoid the crash.

According to the AOPA Air Safety Foundation, 18 percent of all piston-engine, general aviation accidents in the years 1982–1988 occurred during takeoff and the transition to climb. Despite the inherent dangers of relatively slow speed close to the earth, however, many pilots are not taught what to look for in the takeoff process to verify that things are going according to plan. Four years as a Beech Bonanza and Baron simulator and flight instructor revealed that few pilots noticed abnormalities on takeoff in the first days of training until I pointed them out.

Think back to your very first flight training lesson. If you trained in a tricycle gear airplane, it's very likely that the instructor let you make the first takeoff (under close guidance, of course); this might suggest that taking off is a very simple thing to do, when in fact there's a lot to be watched during the takeoff roll and transition to initial climb. It's just as crucial in a low-powered trainer as it is in the fastest "kerosene burner." Lack of emphasis on proper takeoff indications in initial training and the natural expectation of successful flight can conspire to lull pilots into a false security when advancing the throttle and pointing skyward. Nonetheless, pilots all too often do crash while attempting takeoff; clues that "all is not well" can usually be seen in time to avoid tragedy.

You can break the takeoff process down into a list of tasks, and assign goals, or targets, that let you know you've successfully completed each task. If you fail to achieve one of your defined targets, interpret that as a command to abort the takeoff without delay. Likewise, anything confusing or out of the ordinary means you should abort and sort things out. It's like a game of golf; if you don't complete one hole, you don't move on to the next. Does this mean you might one day abort a takeoff needlessly? It's possible, but a properly executed abort erring on the side of caution is certainly preferable to spinning into the trees.

Consider a takeoff to be a string of five successive tasks; review the pilot's operating handbook for the airplane you're flying to identify specific targets for each phase. The five phases of a takeoff are:

1. Pretakeoff
2. Power
3. Acceleration
4. Rotation
5. Initial climb

Here's how you can establish targets for each phase.

The pretakeoff phase

The pretakeoff phase includes all preflight planning, inspection, and ground operations up to the runway hold line. You should know the pressure and density altitudes and the effect that they will have on airplane performance; know also the runway length as compared to your takeoff requirements and the rotation and initial climb speeds recommended in your airplane's manual (Fig. 5-5).

Let's say you're taking off from Jeffco Airport, near Denver, Colorado. You call flight service and find that the outside air temperature is 80°F, and the altimeter setting

Fig. 5-5. *Pilots should know exactly what to expect from their airplanes prior to taking the runway for departure.*

is 29.35. With a field elevation of 5671 feet, this means a pressure altitude of 6241 feet and a density altitude near 9000 feet. The briefer reports that the wind at Jeffco is from 260° at 12 knots; you can expect to use Runway 29L or 29R with a computed head-wind component of 10 knots.

Your F33A Bonanza sits loaded on the ramp. When you board, it will weigh close to 3100 pounds for today's flight. Looking at the pilot's operating handbook, you compute a takeoff roll of roughly 1800 feet; you'll be nearly 3600 feet (more than one half a nautical mile) from the beginning of your takeoff roll when you reach 50 feet above the pavement. You might want to add a 20 percent or so margin to the "book" figures to account for time's effect on the airplane and engine, as well as less-than-perfect pilot technique. The shorter of Jeffco's two northwesterly runways is 7000 feet long, so you have an ample margin regardless of which runway you're assigned.

Remember that takeoff performance is predicated on a specified technique. In the Bonanza, the specified technique is full power before releasing the brakes, rotating (at this weight) upon reaching 68 knots, an obstacle-clearance speed of 74 knots at the 50-foot point, and gear retraction immediately upon achieving a positive rate of climb. Be sure to look at the "associated conditions" for the performance chart in your airplane's manual to determine takeoff technique; if you use any other method, you have no way to predict airplane performance.

You can make a "quick-reference" list of your pretakeoff targets to review just before you call for clearance to go:

- Runway required: 1800 feet
- Runway available: (29L) 7000 feet, (29R) 9000 feet
- Obstacle clearance distance: 3600 feet
- Rotation speed: 68 knots
- Initial climb speed: 74 knots

Write your "quick-reference" notes on your lapboard, or on a "sticky-note" for the instrument panel so you'll be able to see them when you need the figures. Then climb aboard, start the plane up, and run your before-takeoff checklist to ensure you're ready to go. You've completed the pretakeoff phase.

The power phase

When you line up on the runway, try to visualize the expected point of rotation. If runway distance markers aren't available, remember that one runway stripe plus a space is about 100 feet long. Advance the throttle to takeoff power and check the engine readings. If you're flying an airplane with a fixed-pitch propeller, look for the static RPM that's normal for the type. I usually see around 2200–2300 RPM at the beginning of the takeoff roll in a Cessna 172, for instance; if I see less, I know something is calling for my attention. If your craft sports a manifold pressure gauge, like the Bonanza in our Denver example, look for the expected manifold pressure. But how much manifold pressure should you expect?

The manifold pressure gauge indicates the air pressure in the engine's induction manifold, aft of the throttle plate. In other words, it tells you the amount of air available in the engine for combustion. With an airplane engine, you set the amount of power by varying the air in the cylinders. We talk about "opening" the throttle; this opens the throttle plate all the way, admitting the maximum amount of air and supporting maximum power. When you "close" the throttle, you're cutting off air flow and reducing power output. The manifold pressure gauge doesn't directly tell you the power output of the engine, but it does tell you that the potential for power development exists. You do want to be able to anticipate the manifold pressure reading to tell whether you're likely to be achieving maximum power.

So again, how much manifold pressure should you expect? If your engine is normally aspirated (not turbocharged), subtract from 29.92 (30 for an easier calculation) 1 inch of manifold pressure for each 1000 feet of pressure altitude. Reduce that value by another inch for loss of airflow efficiency around the throttle plate (which creates something of a venturi effect). The final result is the manifold pressure that you should see indicated at full throttle in most airplanes.

For your Jeffco Airport takeoff, anticipate about 23.5 inches of manifold pressure when you advance the throttle fully (30 inches at sea level, minus 5.5 inches for Jeffco's roughly 5500-foot elevation, minus another inch for loss of efficiency in the engine). If you see less, you have a problem that is usually related to slipping throttle connections or an obstruction in the intake; see more, and you know you have a manifold pressure gauge calibration error. Whether you're flying a 150- horsepower Super Cub or a 300-horsepower Super Viking, the manifold pressure is the same. Manifold pressure gives the potential for power development; it's up to the compression, the ignition, and the fuel flow to do the rest.

If your engine is turbocharged, the goal is clear: expect the rated takeoff manifold pressure as indicated in the pilot's operating handbook.

Propeller speed, another element of power, should rise smoothly with your throttle application to the takeoff setting. Some propellers, especially fixed-pitch props, run several hundred RPM slow until forward motion begins and the changing air load spins it to takeoff speed. The Skyhawk that I often fly, for example, spins up to around 2550 RPM during the takeoff roll; my experience in Bonanzas, on the other hand, is that they come up to full RPM (2700) immediately upon power application. Know how the airplane you fly will perform, and look for any abnormality.

Fuel flow is directly related to engine power. If your airplane has a fuel-flow gauge, your pilot's operating handbook specifies expected fuel flows based upon pressure altitude; you need the right amount of fuel for the volume of air in the engine. Often you'll need to lean the mixture to obtain best power for takeoff. You can do this at full throttle by leaning to 100° to 125° rich of peak and referencing the exhaust gas temperature or turbine inlet temperature gauge, if your plane is so equipped, or by looking for the maximum propeller RPM in airplanes with fixed-pitch propellers. Many airplanes have an altitude reference mark on the fuel-flow gauge itself to make this leaning easier. Remember that this reference is pressure altitude to match the manifold pressure reading.

Because the takeoff manifold pressure setting of a turbocharged engine is a constant, the fuel flow is also; the pilot's operating handbook will tell you what fuel flow to expect at takeoff power. If your engine has an altitude compensating unit to automatically lean for best power (versions of the Teledyne Continental IO-550, for instance), you'll likewise have a handbook table specifying fuel flows for a given pressure altitude. In either of these cases, you might need to manually lean to achieve best power if the automatic system provides an excessively rich mixture.

Don't get too aggressive with leaning, however, because the engine requires extra fuel for cooling at high power with slow forward airspeed; the "cooling fuel" is accounted for in the handbook figures.

Looking at the airport elevation and the pilot's operating handbook for your F33A at Jeffco, you can come up with some more takeoff targets for your quick-reference checklist:

- Takeoff manifold pressure: 23.5 inches
- Propeller RPM: 2700
- Fuel flow: 19 gallons per hour

Advance the power and look for these indications. Adjust the mixture as necessary. Check the other engine instruments (oil temperature and pressure, cylinder head temperatures, exhaust gas or turbine inlet temperature readings, and electrical gauges, as appropriate) against what experience tells you is normal for your airplane. If you fail to reach a takeoff target, abort now and check things out on the ramp. If all is well, you may try again, watching the indications as before.

The acceleration phase

Having achieved your power targets, release the brakes and begin acceleration. Unfortunately the measure of reaching the acceleration target is subjective; does it "feel right?" With the lack of acceleration charts for most general aviation airplanes and the increase in workload that would result from trying to time the acceleration while operating in single-pilot cockpit if you had such a chart, you must depend on experience to tell whether the airplane is accelerating properly. Indicated airspeed should increase steadily, but remember that acceleration will be sluggish at higher density altitudes.

Scan the engine instruments during the acceleration phase to confirm that your power targets are still being met; take a critical look at the instruments about 10 knots before rotation speed to catch any problems before you run out of time on the ground to abort. Call out airspeeds and their relationship to rotation speed ("Airspeed off the peg." "40 knots looking for 65.") as if this were a multipilot airplane to keep you "in the loop" and not simply along for the ride.

If you haven't reached rotation speed before passing your visualized rotation point, the acceleration target hasn't been met, and it's time to abort and check things over. Remember that driving off the end of a runway at 20 or 30 knots during a takeoff abort is better that ramming into a hill doing 70 or more.

The rotation phase

Reaching your rotation-speed target, bring the nose smoothly up to the recommended initial climb pitch attitude. You want to clear the ground at or near V_X speed to have the greatest amount of altitude as quickly as possible in case an emergency occurs. In the Bonanza, this is about $7°$ above the horizon on the attitude indicator for a high-density-altitude takeoff. Consistent with the airplane type and its pilot's operating handbook, retract the landing gear.

The "associated conditions" of the Bonanza's takeoff performance chart calls for retracting the gear immediately upon achieving a positive rate of climb, not when running out of usable runway, however that might be judged. Do it differently and you won't get the "book" obstacle clearance performance. If you know the pitch attitude that results in V_X speed for your airplane, you won't have to worry about overrotating and a stall on takeoff; if things get bad and you ever doubt you're going to clear an obstacle, you'll instantly be able to achieve the best angle-of-climb performance.

The initial climb phase

Maintain the initial takeoff pitch attitude, which allows the airplane to accelerate through its recommended obstacle-clearance or V_X airspeed. This airspeed might vary depending upon the airplane's takeoff weight; check your pilot's operating handbook. When passing approximately 100 feet AGL or after clearing the last obstacle, lower the pitch to the V_Y attitude, which is usually $2°$ or $3°$ lower than V_X on the attitude indicator.

For your Bonanza takeoff, this is about $5°$ at high-density altitudes. The airplane will accelerate to the best-rate-of-climb speed. Retract any flaps used for takeoff. Maintain this attitude, airspeed, and power setting consistent with any power limitations on your engine or noise abatement procedures until you're a couple of thousand feet above the ground. Only then adjust propeller RPM, throttle, and pitch attitude for the cruise climb.

Using takeoff targets isn't as daunting as it might seem. All you're doing is determining beforehand exactly how you expect your airplane to perform and then comparing anticipated conditions to actual conditions to see whether it's prudent to continue the flight. Reference your pilot's operating handbook for precise techniques to use in the airplane that you are flying. It's actually easier to evaluate takeoff performance by having your targets listed on paper in the cockpit; you'll be able to detect any abnormalities more quickly, in time to safely abort the takeoff before you end up in the trees.

Ninety-nine percent of the time everything will be just fine, but if ever your airplane does have a problem, you'll turn what might have been a disaster into a slightly annoying trip to the mechanic. Regardless of the capability of the airplane you fly, knowing and using your takeoff targets will give you greater safety and control in this crucial phase of flight and should reduce the number of takeoff and initial climb-related accidents.[2]

I'd like to add another indication to watch for during the initial climb phase: climb rate. From your airplane's pilot's operating handbook, you can find a climb figure to anticipate the performance you'll achieve immediately after takeoff and in cruise climb (sometimes called "normal climb"). Back to the Jeffco Bonanza: You determined that the initial climb rate should be 1200 feet per minute and the cruise climb should net 700 fpm. List these figures on your lapboard.

After rotation, targeting the initial climb pitch attitude, a quick glance tells you all is well. Are you not getting the climb rate you expect? One of two things might be wrong: You have too much drag or you're not developing full power. This is the indication that points out if you've forgotten to raise the gear or flaps. Have you ever forgotten to retract the landing gear after rotation? This by itself is not a dangerous situation, but uncorrected it prevent clearing an obstacle that you expected to fly well above, or it might tempt you to raise the nose higher and higher trying to net the expected climb rate, fixating you away from other important data that keeps you from an unintended stall.

Lest you think that predicting and monitoring takeoff targets is the sole province of high-performance airplane drivers, take a look at the following account of the short but memorable flight of a Cessna 152 related to me by an acquaintance and fellow flight instructor.

As most flight instructors know, mistakes are a common occurrence. It is normally the human factor that we must closely monitor; however, airplanes do fail. This is the story of such an instance when I was instructing a student pilot on a maximum performance takeoff.

The incident occurred one late-autumn afternoon at an airport that was undergoing construction to lengthen a runway. On this day, a portion of the runway was closed starting at an intersection with another runway. Approximately 2700 feet of runway remained, which is more than enough for a normal takeoff in a Cessna 152.

It is routine for the student to preflight the airplane while the instructor finishes with the previous student. This was the case this day. The student pilot had recently soloed and was quickly learning self-reliance. Everything began without incident. The aircraft had been flown several times throughout that day and quickly started. The student obtained clearance from ground control and taxied to the makeshift runup area. A routine check was performed using the checklist with no notable difficulty. At this point, I informed the student that I would demonstrate a maximum performance takeoff.

Upon receiving instructions from the tower, I taxied onto the runway at the intersection held for clearance. After clearance was received, I performed the proper procedure of applying full takeoff power while holding the brakes. We began to roll with everything appearing normal. I continued to instruct the student as the airplane accelerated. At 50 knots I rotated and began to climb at the desired 54 knots.

As we crossed the end of the runway, I noticed the aircraft was not climbing as expected. It took a couple of seconds for my mind to verify that my instincts were correct. We were now crossing the road south of the airport, and I began to do the emergency procedure. The student was now sensing that something was wrong because I was no longer verbalizing the instruction. I quickly checked the airspeed indicator for 54 knots, and the vertical speed indicator showed a climb between zero and 50 feet per minute. I further checked the fuel selector, mixture, and carburetor heat and found them to be in the correct position. The throttle did not need to be checked because my hand never moved, and I was now pressing it hard enough to push it through the firewall. The tachometer showed 2000 RPM.

I started considering the options in front of us. It was obvious we were not yet above the treetops at the south end of the golf course that borders the airport to the south, and we were now over the north end. I remember alternately thinking about my option of the trees versus the golf course. We had now been airborne for approximately 10 seconds. It only seemed like eternity.

I decided that we would clear the trees, but I continued to scan the area for a place to land if necessary. We cleared the trees by 10 to 20 feet, which seemed close enough to touch. Once over the trees, my main concern became that we gain sufficient altitude to turn back to the airport. South of the golf course there are few places to safely land. We continued to climb but at a very slow rate. After flying approximately 1 mile from the end of the runway and gaining a meager 200 feet, the tower finally noticed that we were having difficulty and called.

For the first time, I removed my hand from the throttle to pick up the microphone. Tower asked us if we were having difficulties, and I replied affirmatively. I was not however ready for their response. They went on to ask us if we were on fire because we were trailing smoke. Now my mind was really working fast. I have a keen sense of smell that I concentrated like never before. I did not smell anything burning nor did I see any smoke. A quick check of the oil temperature gauge showed normal readings.

By this time we had traveled almost 3 miles south of the airport, and I felt we had sufficient altitude to make a safe turn. The entire time I had kept my airspeed at 54 knots. I performed a gentle turn 180° to downwind. Apparently the controller was no more comfortable with my situation than I was, so he asked me if I wanted to declare an emergency. By now I had a full dose of adrenaline in my system. I quickly decided that we could safely glide back to the runway if necessary and that we probably wouldn't blow up, so I declined; besides, I didn't want to do the paperwork.

I entered downwind and was cleared to land on any runway. As I came abeam the tower, I reached my maximum altitude of 1400 feet MSL, only 800 feet above the ground. I lowered the aircraft nose for the first time to begin the approach for landing, throttled the engine back, dropped flaps, and turned base abeam the displaced threshold. Upon turning final, I was quite high, which was a new feeling for this flight.

I lowered the pitch into a steep dive just in case there was any fire. As my airspeed started to increase to the upper end of the white arc, I eased the aircraft over into a forward slip. The remainder of the landing was without incident. I taxied clear of the runway where I met a member of the airport maintenance crew. We radioed that we could taxi and went directly to the flight school's maintenance ramp.

Upon getting out of the airplane, I realized exactly how much adrenaline I had. It was difficult to stand still and I could have jogged the 4 miles home with ease. I then returned to flight operations where I wrote up a squawk on the aircraft. After retelling the story countless times to all who had been near a radio during the incident, I discussed the situation with the student. When I was able, I went home to try to relax.

I was back at the airport a few hours later for a scheduled night flight. The first thing I did was to talk to the mechanic to find out what went wrong. The venturi on the carburetor had broken, which accounted for the partial loss of power. He went on to say that if I had pulled the throttle out a little I would have gotten more power. I had to laugh. I then explained that it is difficult to experiment with power settings, especially reducing power, when you are not too sure you are going to clear the trees.

We made several mistakes in preparation for this flight. Although it was unlikely that this type of failure could be observed during preflight, it is important to learn at what point the problem became evident. Because similar aircraft are not exactly alike, I did not notice any peculiarity during the runup. Closer attention might have encountered the abnormality before takeoff. During the performance of my emergency procedure, I also failed to check the magneto switch. Although this was not the source of the problem, it could easily have caused a significant loss of performance with similar results. Additionally, I failed to declare an emergency when I should have. By the time I cleared the trees, I should have made the emergency declaration, long before the tower noticed anything was wrong.

Many lessons are learned from an experience this intense. The first is that *experience* is important. On this flight, one pilot had approximately

1000 hours and the other one maybe 20 hours. The student did not notice anything was wrong until I quit talking. It was important that we identify that we had a problem quickly in order to allow ourselves better options for a safe recovery. If the student had been flying the aircraft on this particular day, the results likely would have been quite different.

The limited ability of most students would have delayed both the identification of the problem and the subsequent recovery. Positive airspeed control allowed me to observe the airplane's poor performance earlier than if we had been flying at any other pitch attitude. Because we had little margin for error, this fact is of obvious importance. It is also not uncommon for the instructor's attention to be diverted, slowing the recognition of a problem when the student is controlling the aircraft.

Throughout the training process it is continually stressed that the pilot should always be prepared for an emergency on takeoff. By planning the takeoff properly and reviewing emergency procedures immediately before takeoff, a pilot improves the possibility of success should anything occur. All too often, pilots neglect this phase of preparation in their haste to begin the flight. I once watched a Beech Baron begin flight from the same runway intersection on the field because there were five aircraft awaiting takeoff at the end. As long as the aircraft performance is normal, the pilot will not notice the error of his decision; however, it only takes once. It is equally important that a pilot does each takeoff with precision so that he or she will not get caught short if an emergency occurs.

Finally, the information a pilot receives in an emergency can be severely limited. Here the only visible symptom to the pilot was a lack of performance. Because a Cessna 152 has limited performance capability to begin with, it took a discerning eye to notice that a problem had even occurred. Furthermore, solutions to these emergencies are not always obvious. The simple answer is not always the best answer. I would have never considered that reducing the throttle would have increased power. Of course this solution makes sense when you find out about the malfunction. Cockpit resource management deals with solving situations by using all possible sources of information. Because information is sometimes limited, this is of considerable importance.

A pilot's ability to survive an emergency depends upon experience, proper training, and the ability to properly analyze the situation. Solutions to problems are as varied as the pilot who encounters them. This experience provided valuable knowledge that will help me to prevent future situations from becoming possible tragedies.[3]

The instructor obviously did some things right because he and his student survived the encounter with but an interesting story to tell and an experience to hopefully make their future flying a little safer. How could the pilots have used the concept of takeoff targets to have detected the problem earlier and thereby reduced the chance of a mishap? After all, their safe arrival in this case was in large part a matter of luck; if the tree line were just a few feet higher or located a few yards closer to the end of the runway, we'd have read about this case in an accident study. I don't want to fault the instructor or student in this instance, to be sure; I want to point out how they and others in similar situations can avoid being in that climbing situation to begin with.

In the pretakeoff phase, the instructor and student should have calculated takeoff performance together. That the first takeoff would have been a demonstration of maximum performance short-field technique might not have been "breaking news" to the student just before takeoff; instead, he could have been briefed beforehand, and then two sets of eyes in the cockpit would have been looking for expected performance. The two could have calculated takeoff distance and been able to visualize a rotation point along the runway. They could have determined an anticipated initial climb rate to immediately detect that things were not as planned and begun their emergency procedures earlier.

Where perhaps the two were lacking this day was in detecting indications in the power phase of takeoff. Most obvious probably would have been propeller speed, which likely was not as expected for a Cessna 152 on takeoff. Even a hundred RPM or so less than normal indicates a problem; if they had detected a lack of meeting the power target, their choice of an aborted takeoff would have been automatic, and they'd never have been exposed to the risk of a slow-climbing airplane.

With a loss of power, the acceleration target would not have been met, although it is difficult to subjectively measure this goal, especially in a training situation where the instructor flies a variety of airplanes; however, you can judge the acceleration target indirectly by picking out that anticipated takeoff point along the runway and aborting immediately if you fail to reach rotation speed at that spot, plus or minus a little margin.

To his credit, the instructor knew about the initial climb target. Practicing a V_X climbout, he knew approximately what climb to expect. At least he could tell when he obviously wasn't achieving maximum performance climb when actual performance fell far short, regardless of whether he actually knew in feet per minute what the instruments should indicate. By this time, however, he was committed to at least a short flight; earlier detection of the problem by knowing pretakeoff, power, and acceleration targets would have prevented the scenario from developing into a near-accident.

Once faced with such a meager climb rate, the instructor began the decision-making process. Information slowly trickled in that would help him to make his decision. First, he elected to retain direct control of the flight. He did not transfer control to the student, instead relying on his greater knowledge and experience to increase the margin of safety. He also maintained best-angle-of-climb airspeed because his instruments and the outside world told him he needed to get the best possible climb out of the airplane.

The instructor ran through the engine failure checklist, verifying that the fuel was turned on and that carburetor heat was off. He had the throttle fully forward. He concluded that he forgot to check the magnetos; it turned out in hindsight that this wouldn't have helped, but he noted that a magneto problem could provide the same degradation of performance. How could he have remembered to check the magnetos? If he had referenced the printed engine-failure checklist, the magneto step would have been clearly noted. You might reply that he was too busy at the time to pull out a checklist, and you'd probably be right. He did have a resource in the cockpit, however, that would have helped immensely: his student. He could have asked the student to read, step by step, the emergency checklist to catch any items that had been missed. If the problems had been ignition-related, this could have saved the day. Anytime you have anyone else in the airplane with you, you have an extra set of hands to help in a situation such as this.

There are three components to power development: air, fuel, and ignition. It stands to reason that if a power problem occurs that can be fixed from the cockpit, you'll fix it by manipulating those three systems. In the 152, air flow could not have been increased; the throttle was wide open, or at least the control in the cockpit was fully forward. We've already discussed how the ignition system might have been manipulated to increase power development, if the lack of power was due to a magneto system fault. That leaves fuel as a possible fix for the power loss.

The instructor verified that the fuel was turned on, but didn't mention the mixture control. One shortcoming of many pilot's operating handbooks and other printed checklists is that they are somewhat simplistic. For instance, most will state "Mixture—Full Rich" in the engine failure emergency checklist, leaving pilots to miss what could be a small but lifesaving adjustment to the controls because leaving the mixture control fully forward might prevent a solution to an engine-power emergency. In this example, the power loss was later found to be the result of a reduction in air flow through the engine's induction system. The resulting fuel/air mixture was excessively rich with much more fuel flowing into the cylinders than was air available with which to burn. In other words, the engine was flooding, and that resulted in a dramatic reduction in horsepower.

The instructor stated that his mechanic recommended a throttle reduction to increase power in this case. Reducing the throttle might have altered the internal air pressure in the carburetor, reducing fuel flow, but if it had worked, the resulting throttle setting still might have not netted the power necessary to climb over the trees. Instead, a better solution might have been to manually lean the mixture. This is why I think the situation would have been different if the instructor had been accustomed to flying at high field elevations where the air is thin because pilots are routinely taught that mixture leaning is required to get full power, and it's an everyday practice to reduce the fuel flow on takeoff and during climb. In an emergency, a pilot familiar with high-density-altitude takeoffs would probably lean for more power without giving it a second thought. On the other hand, pilots who typically fly at airports at lower elevations aren't often taught the true dynamics of fuel and air in the development of full power and equate "full-rich" mixture settings to "takeoff power."

If the instructor in the Cessna 152 example had leaned the mixture when faced with the emergency, he likely would have found near-normal performance as the result. Did he know this at the time of his emergency? Of course not. If he knew, however, that power is the result of air, fuel, and ignition and had verified full throttle and checked the magnetos, leaning the mixture would have been his only remaining option. If he had experimented with the mixture, he would have found it worked; he would have sweated less when crossing the line of trees and had better options for returning to the airport or for dealing with a complete power failure if the engine had died completely.

Our instructor had another hint that mixture was the likely culprit, and the hint came from an unlikely source: air traffic control. At one point the controller asked if the airplane was on fire. There are only three things that will burn on the engine side of the firewall (ruling out a catastrophic conflagration that would be immediately obvious): fuel, oil, and electrical equipment. The instructor did look at the oil pressure when asked and found it to be normal. He could have referenced the Cessna's ammeter; a big discharge would have indicated an electrical short, which would have been a possible source of an electrical fire.

The only remaining source would have been fuel. The fuel that was burning could have been the result of a fuel-line break, which would also have reduced engine power. Or the fire could have been due to unburned fuel leaving the cylinders, burning instead in the hot exhaust manifold and leaving a trail of smoke. This is often the indication of an excessively rich mixture.

Cockpit resource management deals with, as the instructor put it, "solving situations by using all possible sources of information." Given a power loss, he could have had his student help with completing the emergency checklist; with ATC's input he might have narrowed the problem down to fuel, and a fuel problem in a Cessna 152 has only three solutions: verify that the fuel is turned on, which he did; adjust the mixture toward rich or lean, which he did not; or land as soon as possible (even on a golf course) if neither previous action works to increase power.

DEPARTURE ALTERNATE

The baggage door of your single-engine airplane pops open just after takeoff. Departing for a business meeting in a high-performance single, you remember that your briefcase is sitting on the FBO counter. Climbing out in a light twin, an engine sputters and dies as the airplane climbs into the low-scudding clouds. What do all these situations have in common? They might require a quick return to the ground.

We've already seen that the takeoff and initial climb are among the high-workload phases of flight, second only to the approach and landing. Trying to turn an airport departure into a safe arrival without some advance planning might exceed your capacity to manage. Before each takeoff, especially at night or into instrument conditions, ask yourself what you would do if some unforeseen event mandated a rapid return to the pavement.

The seemingly simplest plan is to return to the airport from which you departed. This is certainly going to be the first option that pops into your mind if you're faced with an in-flight abort. Returning to the pavement behind you is not without its hazards, however. You need to continue to climb straight ahead to a safe altitude, then turn back into the pattern, much like the instructor that was cited in the Cessna power-loss scenario. If the reason for your return is one of convenience (the forgotten briefcase, for example), this is but a matter of having the discipline to climb and safely turn back at a moderate rate of bank.

If you're aborting the climbout because of a mechanical problem, objects far from the airport grounds might become significant clearance obstacles. Another airport, a golf course, or a deserted stretch of highway might be more or less aligned with your departure path. You might decide before takeoff or perhaps determine immediately after takeoff that an off-airport landing site is safest if you have trouble during the initial climb.

Although not a regulatory requirement for FAR Part 91, it's commonly accepted practice not to depart an airport in instrument conditions if the airport you're departing has weather below the minimums required for a return. In most cases, this is a very good idea. I've had to make a return for a minor mechanical reason in the past, and it's nice to be virtually assured that you'll see the runway before reaching the missed approach point.

Use a little common sense with this rule, however. A good example is the Wichita area, where for four years I routinely departed the Beech factory field and Colonel James Jabara Airport into conditions below the VOR approach minimums. It's very tempting to launch into a 600-foot overcast even if it is below arrival minimums if you know you'll be in clear air by the time you reach 3000 feet, and I did this all of the time; however, I was ready to make a quick turn toward an ILS approach with a 200-foot AGL missed approach point at Wichita Mid-Continent Airport just 7 miles away. That departure alternate was decided beforehand and briefed with my student during the low-workload preflight planning process before takeoff and not in the throes of some emergency in the clouds a few hundred feet off the ground.

Pilots of multiengine airplanes are drilled in the task of handling an engine failure immediately after takeoff. Given enough practice, most get pretty good at it; trained regularly on the procedure, most are perfectly safe if the unexpected occurs. When that prop is feathered, though, what do you do? This is where a lot of engine-failure accidents in light twins take place. If you look at the single-engine climb performance chart for most general aviation twins, you'll find that even on the best days single-engine climb rate is minimal. The Beech Baron is one of the best-performing light twins, but it's not unusual at modest airplane weights and genial density altitude conditions to see no more than a 300-fpm climb rate doing everything correctly with an engine shut down. On paper, that doesn't sound too bad, but take a look at what this really means to the pilot in trouble.

Best single-engine climb rate is based on flying the "blue-line" airspeed, which nets the least total drag and therefore the best performance for a given amount of power. Fly just a few knots faster or slower than "blue line" (adjusted for aircraft weight), and drag increases significantly, resulting in dramatically reduced performance. When I was a Baron simulator instructor, I used to talk clients through a demonstration of this crucial need for airspeed control. Giving the pilot an engine failure shortly after takeoff, after he or she had become proficient in the task, I waited for him or her to set up the approximately 7° nose-up attitude that results in "blue line" in a Baron. When the propeller was feathered and the airplane trimmed, I asked for a vertical speed readout. I usually gave this demonstration on a simulated high-density-altitude day; the climb rate came out to roughly 300 feet per minute.

Next I asked the pilot to raise the nose 2° and trim accordingly. The airplane usually decelerated approximately 5 knots; the resulting vertical speed, affected by the increase in induced drag at this higher angle of attack, dropped to a 50 to 100 feet per minute descent. The temptation students often encountered was to raise the nose even farther, to regain climb rate; students who did raise the nose often got a demonstration of minimum controllable airspeed and a "V_{MC} roll" as well.

Reestablished on "blue line" and 300 fpm climb, I then told the student to lower the nose 2°; the airspeed increased, the parasitic drag built, and the vertical speed again dumped to a 100-fpm descent. I had allowed the pilot to discover the absolute need for pitch and airspeed control if an engine fails.

We weren't done yet, however. The pilot was still just a few hundred feet above simulated ground; the only runway around was the one he or she had departed. After reaching 500 or 600 feet above ground, which seemed to take an eternity, I instructed the pilot to begin a half-standard-rate turn back to the field, being careful to maintain "blue-line" speed. The client quickly found that even a half-standard-rate turn increased the load factor and drag enough to result in that 50- to 100-fpm rate of descent. Many students said that it was very tempting to pull the nose up and increase the bank. I saw many pilots roll into the ground the first time I presented this simulation.

What does this mean to the pilot of a light twin? If you experience the dreaded engine failure just after takeoff, you're committed to flying straight ahead long enough to climb to pattern altitude. Only then can you safely return to the airport. You're going to go a long way to gain that height, which is apparent in this calculated example. The Baron's blue-line airspeed varies from model to model at around 100 knots. Add a little headwind for ease of calculation, and you can expect about a 90-kt groundspeed at blue line, which is approximately a mile and a half per minute. If the best climb you can expect is 300 fpm, it will take a little more than 3 minutes to reach pattern altitude. At 1.5 nm per minute, then, you'll be roughly 5.0 miles from the airport before you can turn back. All the while the temptation will be to do the wrong thing.

Your best bet in this situation might be to continue to an airport that's more or less straight ahead, if one is available. For instance, I used to brief my Baron flight students that if we lost engine power just after takeoff from Jabara Airport southbound, we would make the minor dogleg turn to the left and land straight ahead at nearby Beech Field. Departing out of Beech to the south, McConnell AFB would be our safest option because it is a few miles and a minor heading change to the southwest. Northbound out of Wichita Mid-Continent, Newton, Kansas, might be a good choice, especially if there isn't much headwind (Fig. 5-6).

Regardless of whether you're flying a twin or a single, high performance or low, you need to have a departure abort aim point in mind before takeoff, chosen before events require the decision to be carried out. This reduces your workload dramatically if events require a departure abort.

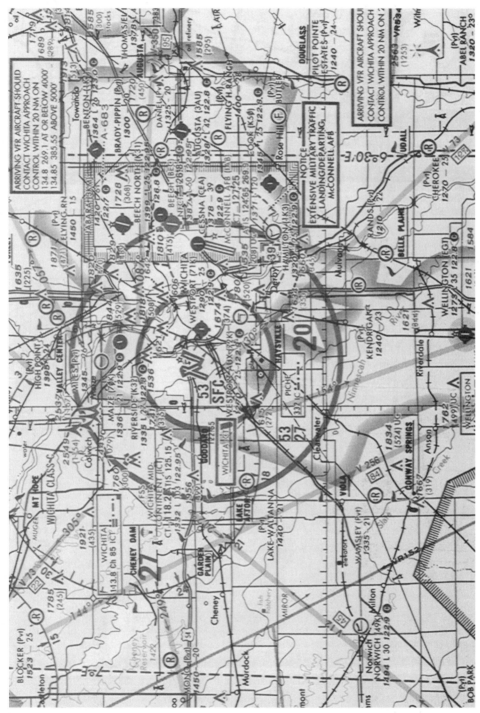

Fig. 5-6. *What's your safest landing spot if you have a problem just after takeoff?*

COCKPIT SETUP

Because events happen fast on takeoff, the less extraneous work you have to do, the more skillfully you can manage the variables that add to or subtract from flight safety. You should identify your takeoff targets, accomplish all steps of predeparture checklists, and choose a departure alternate airport and/or off-airport site before taking the active runway for departure.

Organizing your cockpit is a very personalized task. You'll have to discover through trial and error what works for you. The techniques are based upon how I try to reduce my workload on takeoff; please realize that this is not the only right way to do things and that my techniques are constantly evolving to improve safety and convenience.

Regardless of your method, you'll get the best results if you try to do things the same way every time. This one precept of cockpit management reduces workload phenomenally simply because it means you aren't experimenting with entirely new techniques during high workload phases of flight. If you want to try a new way of doing things, try changing one variable at a time, only one new technique per flight, and don't make big changes in your personal procedure when launching into a 300-foot overcast in gusting winds.

Recall that a lot of takeoff workload reduction is the result of planning before entering the cockpit; obtain the weather briefing, plan the route, and file the flight plan. Based upon weather conditions and the airplane's weight, determine a set of takeoff targets to verify that all is well during the takeoff, and list those targets on a lapboard or sticky-note where they'll be ready for a quick review just before takeoff (Fig. 5-7).

Fig. 5-7. *A quick-reference checklist of takeoff targets.*	Air pressure/OAT	/
	Density altitude	ft
	Runway length	ft
	Runway required	ft
	Manifold pressure	inches
	Propeller speed	rpm
	Fuel flow	gph
	Rotation speed	kts
	Initial climb rate	fpm
	Departure alternate:	

Based also upon the weather conditions and the relative position of obstacles and other airports, pick a departure alternate airport. Tell yourself that if you have a power problem after liftoff, for instance, you will tell ATC what your intentions are based upon preplanned actions; if the emergency landing is to be at a nearby airport, put that approach plate on the top of the stack of charts where you won't need to hunt for it, and prior to departure, take a few minutes to review that approach as if inbound for landing.

I like to fold my en route charts and VFR charts to depict the route with enough margin to get a bigger picture of unfamiliar areas and to reveal frequencies required to get cross-bearings. I paper-clip the charts to hold this new shape and arrange them in a stack in the order I'll use them (the first en route, with a WAC chart underneath, then the next en route, the next WAC chart, etc.). This stack and the departure alternate's approach plate go in the top of my flight bag, where all I have to do is pull them out when I get in the cockpit.

If my trip is long and has stops along the way, I put the charts and plates for the second hop somewhere completely out of the way. I treat each leg as a completely independent flight and don't need the clutter of extraneous charts.

My bag contains the plotter I've come to want in flight more and more, a set of pencils, some sticky-notes, my E6B, a calculator, and the collection of about four flashlights that I've managed to scrounge over the years, each tested before flight to make sure at least one will work if I need it. (I still use the E6B; I tell people my undergraduate degree is in history, which is why I know how to use it.)

I throw in a nut bar and some pieces of hard candy to stave off hunger and thirst, and I put in anything else that I might need to reach along the way. All else is banished to behind the seat; if I won't need it, it shouldn't be in the way. I do like to put the pilot's operating handbook within reach, even if I have a separate checklist, just in case something unusual crops up.

Getting in the airplane, I arrange my flight bag and stack of charts. I use the checklist for all normal starting and check procedures. Setting up the avionics, I like to be as consistent as possible. I remember times early in my flying career when I was confused about whether I was speaking on the #1 or #2 comm radio, or if I were navigating with the #1 or #2 VOR receiver. Now I prefer using the #1 comm and #1 nav, with the #2 units relegated to the role of backups or a reserve for the future. I listen to ATIS, call clearance delivery, and contact ground control all using the #1 comm radio. This is especially important in some airplanes when antenna placement might degrade communications on the ground using the #2 radio.

Your clearance, by the way, should always come in a particular order, whether you pick it up on the ground or in the air. I remember the mnemonic CRAFT:

- **C**learance limit
- **R**oute
- **A**ltitude
- **F**requency (for departure control)
- **T**ransponder code

I actually arrange the letters for CRAFT vertically on my lapboard, leaving space to write in the particulars when I call clearance delivery.

One exception to my rules is that I put the tower frequency in #1 just before calling to go, and the departure frequency is entered in the #2 radio; now a quick flip of the selector switch will put me in touch with departure control when required (Fig. 5-8). When I am settled into cruise climb, I'll dial departure into the #1 and resume operating on that radio (Fig. 5-9).

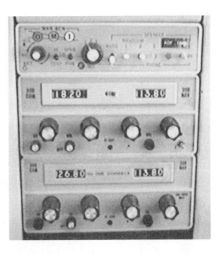

Fig. 5-8. *Before takeoff, the tower frequency is on the number 1 transceiver and the departure frequency is on the number 2 transceiver. When the tower issues a handoff to departure after takeoff, a simple flick of the transmitter selector switch puts you in touch with the next controller.*

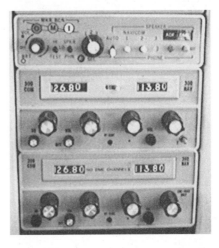

Fig. 5-9. *As time permits, tune the number 1 transceiver to the departure frequency, and set the transmitter selector switch back to number 1.*

After the hand off, I'll see the departure control frequency displayed on both the #1 and #2 comm radios, and the selector will be indicating COMM 1. If the flight is to continue IFR or with VFR flight following, eventually I'll be handed off to another controller. Given a frequency change, I tune the #1 radio to make contact. If the hand-off goes well, all's fine, but if I can't make contact, I still have the previous controller's frequency in the backup radio. I'll switch to #2 briefly to verify the handoff frequency, and retune #1 as necessary for another try. Regardless, I don't need to hunt for the previous frequency if a handoff doesn't go as expected (Fig. 5-10).

Assuming the handoff was okay, I'll tune the new frequency in the #2 radio as time permits, so again both radios display the same. I'm ready for the next handoff, and if something should go wrong with the primary radio, my backup is already tuned to the frequency currently in use (Fig. 5-11).

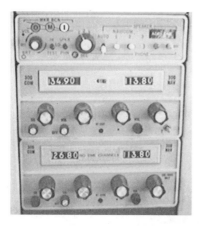

Fig. 5-10. *When the handoff to center occurs, dial the new frequency on the number 1 transceiver and check in. The last assigned frequency is still on the number 2 transceiver in case you can't make contact on the new frequency.*

Fig. 5-11. *After establishing contact on the new frequency and as time permits, retune the number 2 transceiver with the new frequency. Now you're set up for your next handoff.*

If I want to talk to flight watch, or call a unicom or listen to ATIS while still under ATC control, after I receive ATC approval to do so, I'll switch to the #2 radio and monitor the untouched primary frequency on #1. Regardless of the circumstances, I'll always switch to #2 to go off frequency for secondary communications and switch back to #1 to resume primary communications. I should never be confused about which radio I want to speak on, and I should never accidentally lose the primary frequency by tuning the wrong radio.

I play the game the same way even when blessed with "flip-flop" radio designs, where I can store a backup frequency. After a handoff I'll have the last controller's channel in two places: the backup side of the #1 radio and the active side of the #2. When I have time, I'll retune the #2 active side to the new frequency and step my way across the sky using #1 as primary all the way.

That's how I keep the primary frequency and radio in mind and reduce my workload in high-stress situations, such as when a handoff doesn't work in terminal airspace. You might have another procedure that works for you, but as I've heard it said, the most common failing of pilots is not that they have bad procedures, it's that they have no procedures at all. Do it the same way every time, and you'll be amazed at how much more in control you'll feel.

I do the same thing with navigation radios. Setting up for departure, I tune and identify the departure alternate frequency into the #1 nav radio with the first VOR for the trip in #2 with the OBS heading properly set for the first leg. If I'm going via loran or GPS, I load the first waypoint but still set up the nav radios for the departure alternate. If I'm not using the ADF for anything else and an outer marker is available for the departure alternate's approach, I'll tune and identify it as well. I want to set up for the alternate's approach as if I need to fly it; 99.9 percent of the time you'll never use it, but the one time it happens you'll be glad you don't have the added task of setting up for the approach.

When airborne and away from the terminal area, I revert to the #1/#2 technique used for communications: the #1 nav is primary for the direction I'm going, and the #2 is used for crossbearings or preloading the next frequency for a switchover. I also like to use ADF for crossbearings and heading references toward the nearest airport should the unexpected happen. Loran and GPS will make this system obsolete in time, but for now the vast majority of en route flying, especially under instrument flight rules, will be with VORs. Loran often drops offline at the onset of rain or snow, and GPS signals are sometimes randomly masked by the military, so you don't know when you might have to go back to the "good old days" of VOR and ADF navigation.

As for altitude, I like to keep a running list of assigned altitudes on my lapboard; If I have a question, the altitude on the bottom of my list is the one to fly. Some people like to use the ADF bearing pointer as a "poor-man's altitude-alerter;" others fly airplanes equipped with true alerters or even autopilot altitude preselects. I always use my lapboard as a backup to these technologies, just in case. Whatever you do, come up with some arrangement that helps you remain aware of the altitude that you can safely fly.

Sounds like a lot of work, doesn't it? It most certainly is. The trick is that the vast majority of the work is done before you ever push the throttle forward for takeoff; your job from that point on is primarily one of monitoring conditions to see if they are what you expect. If so, great; if not, you've already done most of the planning to assure a safe return to earth. By preplanning your takeoff targets, selecting a departure alternate, and using consistent techniques to avoid confusion, you'll be able to more easily detect and deal with problems during this and all other phases of flight. That has to make you safer.

6
Phase of flight: Climb and cruise

"CONTACT DEPARTURE." THE RUNWAY FADES QUICKLY BEHIND AS YOU point your airplane upward in climb. You've met all your takeoff targets and safely negotiated one of the most hazardous phases of flight. Now you're ready for an en route climb (cruise climb).

If you're flying a complex airplane (controllable-pitch propeller and/or retractable landing gear), a question often comes up for debate when talking with pilots of similar airplanes: When should you adjust the power for cruise climb? Unless noise abatement procedures or a pilot's operating handbook limitation exists for the time allowed at full power, you're best served to hold off on any power change until you're at least several hundred feet above the ground.

Most pilots will think I'm concerned with the number of engine failures that occur at the first power reduction, but that's not what I'm worried about; the accident statistics simply don't support any assertion that this is when you're most likely to experience power failure. Instead, I'm more concerned with the effect that changing power has on aircraft control and pilot workload while still close to the ground.

What happens when you reduce power? In most aircraft models, the pitch attitude will change. If you really know your airplane, you might know exactly how much it will vary and can actually use that knowledge to help set the cruise climb attitude that you desire. The problem is that the airplane will likely oscillate through a few ups and downs before stabilizing on its final attitude, and that means you'll have to work to keep it steady in the interim. With time, you'll get quite good at this to the point that you can hold attitude without thinking, but my point is to delay this added workload if at all possible until you are well clear of the ground.

What happens immediately after takeoff? You're going to turn to your on-course or assigned heading. If flying in Class B or C airspace, if you've filed IFR, or if you have requested VFR flight following, you'll be handed off to departure control, requiring a radio contact to the tower, a switching panel selector change, and another radio conversation still close to the ground; additional tasks are a possibility. Flying without a headset and boom microphone will add even more to the work of these exchanges because you will have to reach for and eventually put down a microphone. I advise my students to wait until this is all over with and they are established, wings level, on their first heading before adding the additional workload of that first power change.

Climbing just a little longer at full power and V_Y airspeed will net you more altitude in a shorter period of time as well, altitude that you might need in case you really do have a problem shortly after takeoff. Some organizations teach the concept of the "safety window," as a block of airspace roughly 5 miles in diameter from the center of the airport and rising to 2000 feet above the surface. This airspace is characterized by excessive pilot workload (taking off and landing) and the abnormally high percentage of accidents that occur in its confines (nearly 80 percent of all events). Pilots are taught to make *no changes* until clear of the safety window,[1] and that would presumably include deferring that first power change.

ALTITUDE-CRITICAL AREAS

For most general aviation airplanes, 2000 feet above the ground before changing power is probably a bit excessive; I think 1000 feet is more appropriate in most instances. I also like to replace the term "safety window" with what Robert Sumwalt, writing for *Professional Pilot* magazine, calls an *altitude-critical area* (ACA).[2] Mr. Sumwalt wasn't referring to this low-to-the-ground phase of flight when he wrote the article I cite, but I will use his terminology later in the context that he defined, and I think altitude-critical area is a better description of the potential hazard of flying near the surface as well.

How can you use the concept of the ACA to reduce your workload in flight? Your primary concern in the ACA is the physical manipulation of the airplane. You shouldn't be shuffling maps or tuning radios, talking with passengers, or listening to the CD player when flying in the ACA. If you have any task that can possibly be performed before entering the ACA upon takeoff (tuning a VOR radio, for instance), do it before pushing the throttle forward. Don't take off thinking "I'll take care of that once I'm in the air." If you were so rushed that you couldn't square things on the ground, you'll likely be even more swamped once airborne. Make things easy for yourself; be ready before you enter the altitude-critical area, and make as few changes as possible until clear of its boundaries (Fig. 6-1).

If an emergency presents itself, quite likely you'll have at least some time to deal with it. Unless the problem is a total power failure in a single-engine airplane, you will probably have some capability to climb; you'll be much more able to go through the process of making a sound decision if you first put some atmosphere between yourself and the ground. In other words, any situation that changes your plans is best dealt with by first leaving the altitude-critical area.

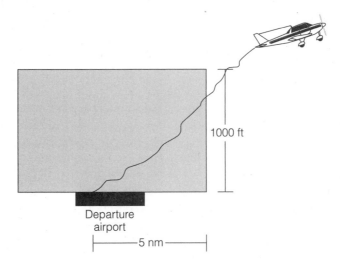

Fig. 6-1. *The takeoff, or departure, altitude critical area.*

Take care of the memory items from the appropriate emergency checklist, but no more. Climb at least 1000 feet above the terrain, if possible, then trim the airplane and set the autopilot, if one is available. Now you can reference your emergency checklists, complete all necessary tasks, and begin the process of making a sound decision. Remember the Lockheed 1011 that crashed into the Everglades while four crew members tried to identify and change a burned-out landing gear light bulb? That was a classical example of no one flying the airplane in an altitude-critical area.

The airlines have a regulation called the *sterile-cockpit rule*. Basically, this law requires that airline crews refrain from all unnecessary conversation (anything not directly related to the physical flying task) within 10,000 feet of the ground. Again, this altitude restriction is excessive for most general aviation airplanes, but the intent of the sterile-cockpit rule is to reduce cockpit distractions at what for heavy jets is an altitude close to the ground.

I recommend something similar to the sterile-cockpit rule for you and your passengers in the altitude-critical area. Prior to starting the engine or engines, advise your passengers that just before you line up for takeoff you'll remind them to please refrain from speaking to you until you tell them that it's all right to do so. If you have an intercom with a pilot isolation switch, this is a good time to use it. Many passengers might interpret this as an admission of lack of piloting skills, that you must not know what you're doing if you're afraid of a few questions.

Calm their fears by telling them the truth: "I am going to be very busy for a few minutes on the ground and in the air tending to the airplane and talking on the radio when someone on the ground is talking to me. The radio conversations will probably be routine transmissions that are nonetheless crucial to safe operation of the airplane. I'd appreciate it if you would refrain from talking to me so that I can concentrate on the radio and flying the airplane. I'll tell you when it's all right to talk to me again."

That should ease their concerns and simultaneously remove unneeded cabin distractions that inhibit your ability to detect problems and to make good decisions. Add a step to your personal before-start checklist to the effect of: "Sterile-cockpit rule explained to passengers." Another step at the end of your before-takeoff checklist should state "Sterile cockpit established; inform passengers."

If you have one of the new and extremely quiet noise-canceling headsets, you might consider turning off the noise-cancellation feature in the ACA. I've been in a number of airplanes where I couldn't even hear the stall warning or gear warning horns with the noise-cancellation turned on. It is possible to wire those warnings through the intercom as a long-term fix; check to determine if you can hear all the warnings in your airplane.

As a flight instructor, I have to regularly violate my own rule and talk to the pilot inside the altitude-critical area. I have to limit my conversation to only the instructional details and not interject extraneous details. I also speak in the ACA with the understanding that this increases the level of risk, requiring me to be more vigilant.

USING CHECKLISTS

When you are clear of the ACA with the wings level and on course, you may transition to cruise climb as prescribed in the operator's handbook. Establish power and pitch, adjust the mixture as necessary, and turn off the landing light and anything else not needed for the trip. Once you have the airplane trimmed for its new condition, pull out the cruise-climb checklist, and run through its steps.

In-flight checklists are probably among the most ignored safety devices available in an airplane. When I first began teaching, flight instructors tended to ignore the use of checklists after the run-up, instead stressing memory techniques and occasionally a mnemonic or two when presenting the art of aviating. Because pilots on the whole tend to be independent and self-reliant types, this reinforces their personality traits; printed checklists come to be regarded as "crutches" for less-than-perfect pilots. A recent poll showed that more than 80 percent of all pilots consider their flying skills to be "above average;" therefore, it's easy to see where inflight checklists can be relegated to the airplane's backseat.

Yet the failure to perform steps on printed inflight checklists can potentially cause mishaps. I once flew a client's A36TC from Wichita to Springfield, Missouri, and back to Wichita transporting a second client to the plane he'd left because of weather. It takes about an hour in each direction; the weather was severe clear, so we went "loran direct" across the plains. Departing Springfield Regional for the return trip, the sky was crowded with airplanes, and cumulus clouds dotted the horizon. My workload was relatively high as I zigzagged between the clouds and around traffic. Leveling at 8500 feet for the trip home, I simply forgot to lean the mixture for cruising flight.

About 20 minutes after leveling off, I finally noticed the fuel flow hovering around 25 gallons per hour. I had burned about 20 gallons on the way to Springfield, leaving about 60 in my tanks. Had I not detected my oversight, I would have run out of fuel approximately 2.4 hours later. This was not crucial for the Wichita run, but it would have meant an off-airport landing on a Denver or Albuquerque trip. How could I have avoided the oversight and potential for an accident? If I were always in the habit of running through the cruise checklist after leveling off and trimming the airplane, I would have discovered my omission right away and corrected it without an increase in risk.

This specific incident was the catalyst for my "crusade" for the use of inflight checklists as a backup to memory technique. The checklist is not to be used as a substitute for training and practice, but as an aid to remembering steps forgotten in the high-workload environment of a light airplane. Transition the airplane to the desired flight condition (cruise climb or level flight, for instance), trim off the pressures and then, as time permits, reference the appropriate inflight checklist on the off chance you might have missed a vital step. Ninety-nine percent of the time you won't have a single thing extra to do. But the one time that human factors prevent you from leaning the mixture, for example, you'll find the few seconds it takes to run through a checklist are worth the effort.

In 1991, I did a study of Beech Bonanza and Debonair accident histories based on the previously cited *General Aviation Accident Analysis Book, 1982–1988*, published by the AOPA Air Safety Foundation. I grouped accidents not in the traditional ranking of takeoff, cruise, and other phases of flight, but instead the accidents were grouped by the pilot operation or equipment malfunction involved. I found that immediately after fuel mismanagement, improper accomplishment of inflight checklist items was the #2 cause of Bonanza and Debonair accidents during the study period. If those pilots had been in the habit of referring to inflight checklists to back up their memory techniques, many accidents might have been avoided.

If you want further proof that checklists save lives, take a look at this NTSB list that is merely a sampling of the airline accidents directly related to checklist misuse:

- December 1968, Anchorage, AK. A Pan American 707 crashes on takeoff; flaps were found to be improperly set.
- December 1974, Thiels, N.Y. A Northwest 727 stalls and spins; pitot tube froze over, affecting instruments; pitot heat was not turned on prior to entering icing conditions; pilot disorientation.
- January 1982, Washington, D.C. An Air Florida 737 fails to develop full power and crashes after takeoff; engine antiice was not turned on in icing conditions, creating erroneous engine power readings.

- January 1983, Detroit, MI. A United Airlines DC8 crashes on takeoff; trim was improperly set.

- August 1987, Detroit, MI. A Northwest DC9 crashes on takeoff; flaps were not set for takeoff.

- August 1988, Dallas-Fort Worth, TX. A Delta 727 crashes on takeoff; flaps were improperly set.

- September 1989, New York, N.Y. A USAir 737 crashes on takeoff; trim was improperly set.

These examples illustrate how even a professional multipilot crew can overlook items that are crucial to flying safely. Are you any better? I can't say that I'll always remember to do everything I need to; that's why I use checklists and recommend that you do as well. Many pilots might think that "reading the book" in flight would give passengers the impression that the pilot doesn't know what he or she is doing; I can't remember how many times nonpilots have commented on the professionalism I exhibit when flying, and how the disciplined manner in which I accomplished tasks and used inflight checklists increased their level of comfort and confidence in an unfamiliar environment.

TRANSITION TO LEVEL CRUISE

Safely settled into climb with the checklist checked and restowed within reach, you anticipate leveling off into cruising flight. Let's say your assigned altitude is 7000, and you're currently climbing through 4000. How will you make certain that you won't bust your altitude?

Many pilots dial the assigned or desired altitude into the ADF rotating card. For instance, if climbing to 8000 feet, I might rotate the ADF card to indicate 080 degrees; if I forget the altitude to which I'm climbing, I can quickly reference the ADF. This works great if you're not using the ADF for any other navigation and if your ADF card is not slaved to the airplane's heading. (Believe it or not, many pilots do more than listen to ball games over this device!) Some people buy little barber-pole altimeter markers that attach to the face of the instrument; they can align the "bug" on their chosen altitude, seeing at a glance when they are getting close to leveling off.

In higher-dollar airplanes, it's not unusual to see an altitude alerter that beeps a warning when the selected altitude is 1000 feet away and then a hundred feet or so before level-off. Many of these devices can be connected to a sophisticated autopilot that actually makes the level-off into cruise for the pilot.

Regardless of your method, in some way record the altitude to which you can safely fly, and check it consistently during climb. I like to make altitude callouts aloud by stating my current altitude, my desired altitude, and the amount of altitude change remaining: "4000 feet climbing to 7000, 2500 to go." I call out passing through each thousand feet of altitude until within a thousand feet; starting at 500 feet to go, I call out each 100-foot increment. I might not speak very loudly, but I do state these callouts out loud; I find it keeps me "in the loop" during a crucial phase of flight and not merely along for the ride.

The last thousand feet of altitude prior to a level-off (either climbing or descending) constitutes what Robert Sumwalt calls an altitude-critical area.[3] This chapter has already expanded his term to include the high-workload airspace near the ground at an airport; similarly to the terminal ACA, you should try to remove as much distraction as possible when within the ACA associated with an assigned altitude.

Air traffic control separation is based upon maintaining your best rate of climb or descent until you're within 1000 feet of your assigned altitude, and 500 feet per minute for the last 1000 feet of altitude change. This is designed to help keep pilots from flying through the assigned altitude. The transition from climb to level-off is one of the most dynamic phases of flight. The airplane, trimmed for a climb airspeed, will continue to nose up, trying to slow back to climb speed as it accelerates into cruise. There is usually a big trim change associated with level-off; the trim change takes place gradually over time until the airplane is established at cruise speed. Why should you increase your workload and risk at this busy time if you can defer low-priority tasks? (Fig. 6-2)

Invoke the sterile-cockpit rule when you enter the level-off ACA. You might not actually brief the passengers at this point, but put off anything you can and concentrate on the task at hand, which is making the altitude transition. Keep an eye on your pitch attitude, either visually with the horizon or by using the attitude indicator; find the attitude that results in about a 500-fpm vertical speed. Leveling off, this allows the plane to begin accelerating; you'll need to trim the nose down gradually to avoid zooming back up at a higher vertical speed.

When you reach altitude, lower the nose for the level attitude. This will again mean that you have to cope with the airplane's trim by changing the airspeed. I've found that pilots who practice this level-off by hand-flying the procedure every time they fly are consistently more precise in all phases of their flying. If you can accurately hit your altitude and heading in a hand-flown level-off into cruise, you obviously can scan back and forth between your horizon reference and the altimeter and heading indicators and make minor adjustments to maintain altitude and heading before either gets away from you. Hand-flying the level-off is excellent recurrent instrument practice, free every time you fly.

To be accurate and to avoid "busting" your altitude, it's important to avoid distractions. Most anything can be delayed for the minute or two that it takes to transition to level flight. I used to present a cockpit management scenario in simulator training that serves to point this out. In this scenario, the pilot was flying a high-performance single or light twin, taking off into instrument conditions out of Wichita. As is often the case in terminal airspace, the pilot's clearance included an altitude restriction:

"ATC clears N0PT to XYZ as filed. Climb and maintain 3000, expect filed altitude in 10 minutes. Departure frequency is 134.8, squawk 4131."

All is normal for the pilot as he or she rolls down the runway and transitions to initial climb. Passing through about 2000 MSL, which is 500–600 feet above the ground,

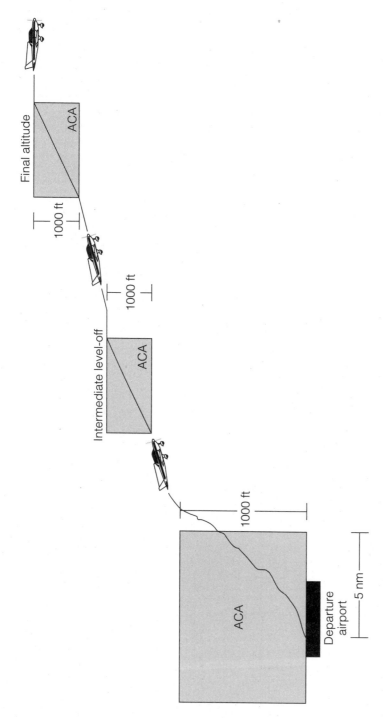

Fig. 6-2. *Altitude critical areas for intermediate and final cruising altitudes.*

Wichita Tower would hand the pilot off to departure. When the pilot checks in on 134.8, this is what he or she hears:

"N0PT, negative radar contact. Check transponder on."

Our valiant pilot is still in his or her departure altitude-critical area and in the level-off ACA as well. At this point, close to an assigned altitude, he or she should be trying to minimize cockpit distractions, and be transitioning to a 500-fpm climb rate toward a level-off. A very small percentage of my students would tell the controller to "stand by" at this point and defer the transponder troubleshooting until in level flight. The vast majority, however, would fall into the distractions trap and visually check the transponder setting. If the pilot said anything other than "stand by" to me as the controller, ATC would immediately reply:

"We're not receiving your transponder. Please cycle and squawk 4131."

Now the workload builds. The pilot is easily within 500 feet of assigned altitude at this point. If he or she had begun troubleshooting the transponder instead of lowering the attitude and reducing climb for the level-off ACA, the plane would be barreling upward at 1000 fpm or more. Our pilot's attention begins to fixate on the transponder problem, diverted from the true goal of this phase of flight, and an altitude bust is imminent. The scenario continues:

"N0PT, still not receiving your transponder. Try new code, squawk 5202, over."

If the pilot tried to change transponder code, chances are pretty good that he or she busted the altitude. Most of my clients went through 3400 feet or higher, and when ATC would suddenly receive the transponder information, the pilot would hear a panicky voice:

"0PT, radar contact, make IMMEDIATE right turn heading 090 for traffic, we show your altitude to be 3600, traffic is a DC9 at your 12 o'clock and one mile, descending out of 4000 feet."

From that point, the flight would proceed without incident.

The lesson of this scenario is that allowing even minor distractions in the altitude-critical area can be fatal. The pilot's first duty is to flying safely, and leveling off on an assigned altitude is vital to that goal. It could even be argued that flying IFR without the transponder is safer because without radar contact the controller must provide a larger "bubble" of airspace around the plane; therefore, the few minutes flown without troubleshooting the transponder are at the worst an irritation for the controller.

Those pilots who told ATC to "stand by" and waited until the airplane was in level flight to fiddle with the problem were commended for their reduction of workload at a crucial time. Those who were lulled into the trap were treated to a videotape replay of their actions in the cockpit, which dramatically showed how the pilot worked fanatically in the cockpit until the usual "altitude bust" resulted.

Significantly, virtually all of the pilots would defer troubleshooting a similar situation on a subsequent simulator flight when presented with an errant engine indication in the final few hundred feet of a descent. They learned that "stand by" can be the two most powerful words in the vocabulary of cockpit management.

ALTITUDE DEVIATIONS

In 1989, the National Aeronautics and Space Administration's Aviation Safety Reporting System (ASRS) received 8965 reports of altitude deviations. The ASRS is the federal government's way of getting real-world data on flight operations in the hopes that trends can be identified and strategies devised to eliminate those problems. To encourage input, the ASRS assures pilot confidentially and promises immunity from FAA action (in most cases) to those who supply ASRS reports.

A tally of nearly 9000 reports of altitude busts in one calendar year is a sobering statistic. Because these are voluntary, unsolicited reports, one NASA official commented that "only one thing can be known for sure from ASRS statistics—they represent the lower measure of the true number of such events which are occurring."[5] In other words, altitude deviations are likely much more common than even the 8965-per-year figure suggests.

Statistics have also been tabulated for the number of reported altitude deviations per 100,000 flying hours in general aviation aircraft:

- 1987 1.04 (per 100,000 hours)
- 1988 0.92
- 1989 0.84[6]

It would seem that the record is improving dramatically; nonetheless, the problem of altitude deviations still exists.

Writing for *Professional Pilot* magazine, Robert Sumwalt pointed out seven categories, or causes, of altitude deviation.[7] I've commented on each category.

Hearback error. A controller assigns an altitude, the pilot reads back a different altitude, and the controller fails to detect the error. This is a classical human-factors problem that is best avoided by warding off complacency and by using standard terminology such as "one-zero thousand" or "niner-five thousand" instead of slang or unofficial terms. According to Sumwalt, this type of error is responsible for 22 percent of all altitude deviations.

Improper altimeter settings. Erroneous instrument adjustments are another human failure that points out the need to check and recheck things you do in the cockpit. Employ a little "healthy skepticism" about everything you do; don't be paranoid, but do realize that workload, fatigue, and other factors can reduce your ability to manage the cockpit, and you ought to double-check your actions. Use of a checklist will also catch those times when an altimeter update might be missed, especially crucial when descending at night, in mountainous terrain, or into an uncontrolled airport under IFR without local weather reporting.

Cockpit distractions. My transponder scenario is an example of how a minor event in the cockpit can overshadow the goal of safety.

ATC error. Controllers are also human beings who are subject to the same human factors failings as pilots. Your job is to work with the controllers to assure safety of flight, not merely to "do their bidding" without question or to operate in an adversarial manner almost in spite of controllers. For instance, descending into Kansas City Downtown Airport in the clouds one day, I was cleared to an altitude 200 feet below the initial altitude for the approach. Kansas City has numerous tall buildings and towers, and I knew that I should not expect to be cleared below the approach altitude until established on the final approach course, yet here I was directed to descend below the initial altitude.

What did I do? I began my descent to fit the flow of traffic and immediately queried the controller about the altitude to which he'd directed me. As soon as I asked (very nicely, I might add), he redirected me to the initial approach altitude, and no lower, while being apologetic in his reply. I read an article once that suggested that the pilot/ATC relationship would be much more amicable and safe if the pioneers of aviation called them air traffic coordinators instead of controllers; regardless of their title, coordination is how you should view the relationship. By the way, only about 16 percent of the "altitude busts" were in any way the fault of people outside the airplane's cockpit.

Improper pilot/crew procedures. Writing for a multipilot-crew airline audience, Sumwalt discussed the crew's interaction and how one pilot might think the other has accomplished a task that actually went undone. One common cause was the failure to set or improper setting of an altitude preselect device. One airline technique to avoid this hazard is to say aloud the altitude when dialing it into the preselect and then to point at the display and reread the altitude out loud before arming the unit. Pilots flying alone presumably won't have the problem of assuming someone else performed a task; however, realize that nobody will remember everything, every time, so use your inflight checklists as a means of making sure that you haven't forgotten some important task.

Other communications breakdown. Again, the author of this article addressed airline concerns. If you use your checklists, imply healthy skepticism, and cooperate with and double-check the controllers, you should avoid communications-related accidents.

Failure of cockpit automation to level off. Malfunction situations are considered in depth in the next subsection of this chapter.

AUTOPILOT USE

Because the transition from climb or descent to level flight is so crucial and because cockpit distractions easily lull pilots away from the task of leveling off, doesn't it make sense to allow the autopilot to make the transition if the airplane is so equipped? Your first impression might be "Yes," supported by the technological leaps in lightplane autopilots and altitude preselect devices in the last decade. Autopilots do fail, however, and more frequently pilots fail when manipulating and monitoring autopilot equipment.

Don't get me wrong; autopilots are wonderfully capable devices and can serve to dramatically reduce workload in the cockpit. If the plane you fly has an autopilot installed, before you launch solo you should know how each and every feature works, what will cause the autopilot to disengage, and what instrument failures also point to failures in the autopilot. The problem I've seen all too often is an overreliance on the capability of the autopilot to the point where a good percentage of the pilots I've worked with in high-performance, autopilot-equipped airplanes had actually lost the ability to fly the airplane without it.

I literally mean that if the autopilot had failed in low-visibility conditions, many pilots could not have even maintained straight-and-level flight while attending to normal (much less emergency) cockpit workloads. A larger percentage of pilots were unable to hand-fly an instrument approach anywhere close to minimums without deviating dangerously from altitude or course. In order to be safe when flying with an autopilot, you have to regularly practice all phases of flight without it. Never let the autopilot take you into a situation you couldn't safely hand-fly yourself.

Unless you fly every day in a wide variety of conditions, you'll find that it's hard to stay proficient in poor-weather procedures. Pilots have often asked me for my recommendations about autopilot use. This is my reply with the understanding that it is a personal opinion and you are free to take it or leave it on that basis.

You should not engage the autopilot in the departure altitude-critical area. You are so close to the ground at this point (within 1000 feet) that you might not have time to recognize and recover from an autopilot malfunction, nor might you be able to detect an error on your autopilot set-up or input before coming dangerously close to a mishap. In my experience, those pilots whose after-takeoff checklist consists of "Gear up, autopilot on" are those who will have tremendous problems hand-flying the airplane if the autopilot fails.

In cruise climb, feel free to engage the autopilot to allow you to reference charts or checklists, adjust headsets or oxygen masks or perform similar cockpit chores, and this will give you a better opportunity to scan for traffic in busy terminal areas; otherwise, hand-fly the aircraft to maintain proficiency. Using your autopilot, however, does not relieve you of the task of monitoring the flight and engine instruments just as closely as if you were hand-flying the airplane. Keep yourself "in the loop" by making periodic altitude callouts, stating your current relationship to the final altitude: "Four thousand climbing to seven thousand, three thousand to go." Remember, the failure of cockpit automation to level off on assigned altitudes is a common cause of altitude deviations; even more common is the pilot improperly setting the altitude preselect equipment. The autopilot is an extremely obedient copilot; it will do exactly what you tell it to do, regardless of whether that was your true intent.

Hand-fly the level-off ACA. With the exception of the final seconds of a landing, the level-off into cruising flight is the most dynamic phase of flight with rapidly changing flight variables that have to be anticipated, detected, and corrected within a short period of time. If you've gone a month without flying, you'll want to practice landings if for no other reason than to feel proficient; the level-off is just as much an indicator of pilot skill, and it serves the further purpose of demanding a good scan between horizon references and the performance instruments (altimeter, vertical speed indicator, heading indicator, and airspeed indicator). I am a true believer in altitude alerters to remind a pilot when he or she has reached an altitude, but I prefer not to use an altitude preselect, which deprives me of valuable and free practice every time I fly and contributes so much to a sense of complacency that leads to altitude deviations.

Cruise flight is the phase where the autopilot comes into its own. The autopilot is a fatigue reduction device more than anything else. You'll spend most of your time in cruise flight, which exposes you to the most potential for fatigue. Two notes about using the autopilot in cruise: First, using the autopilot does not relieve you of your mandate to actively monitor the flight instruments. It's there to help you monitor the flight, not replace you in doing so. Clicking on the autopilot is not a license to read the newspaper or (as one pilot actually admitted to me) set an alarm clock and take a nap. Second, turn off the autopilot and hand-fly the airplane 10 minutes out of every hour or so. As a student pilot and especially during instrument training I had great difficulty learning to fly straight and level while following a navigation signal or folding a map. Flying in turbulence strong enough to disengage an autopilot or setting up for a night landing into a dark and unfamiliar airport in hilly terrain are not the times to relearn how to hand-fly an airplane.

Descent: Your workload will be building in the descent phase of flight, and you might find the autopilot to be a great help during this time. You'll be reviewing approach procedures (whether IFR or VFR), setting up navigation signals, increasing the frequency of your radio communications, and simply preparing the airplane and your passengers for landing. Go ahead and use the autopilot during those times when cockpit chores mount; just be sure that you can take over manually if the autopilot fails. Regularly practice doing it all by hand to make sure that you're not deluding yourself.

Approach: Here's where I differ from most advisers concerning autopilot use, and my viewpoint stems from the basic rule that "you should not allow the autopilot to take you anywhere you can't hand-fly yourself." I don't like "coupled" approaches where the autopilot does all the work. It's not because I'm afraid the autopilot will fail; it's because pilots who don't fly every day rarely make approaches into low ceiling and visibility conditions, and it's extremely difficult to maintain any level of proficiency without practicing on those occasions when harsh IFR conditions exist. Each and every flight represents the opportunity to practice your skills, and if you've set up for the approach before entering the landing ACA, you won't be doing anything besides flying the airplane at this point anyway. I've had two autopilot malfunctions in two different airplanes, both of which led to trim runaways; I wouldn't want to deal with those close to the ground. Regardless of the possibility of failure, I like to hand-fly all approaches simply to help keep myself sharp.

Does your airplane have a flight director? A flight director is a device integrated into an attitude indicator that provides pitch and bank information for either the autopilot or the pilot to follow. It is slaved to heading and altimeter indications to help the pilot smoothly establish or maintain desired performance. A flight director knows the pitch changes (small) required to maintain altitude or vertical speed precision, and the angle of bank (15 percent of the true airspeed) necessary for a standard-rate turn. Unfortunately, the flight director is such a good device for making precise changes in control that it invites fixation on the attitude instrument. You can learn the sort of pitch and bank changes needed to maintain precision without the flight director's prompting. I've seen numerous altitude busts and/or missed interceptions because the pilot had misprogrammed the flight director and failed to scan the other instruments closely enough to anticipate or detect a deviation.

My advice? Just like autopilots, the flight director should be used in moderation. You need to be able to take over using "raw data" (no flight director input) if things go awry. You might alternate flights by using the flight director for today's hop and raw data for tomorrow's; throw the autopilot into the mix, and work without it periodically to keep your skills sharp.

Don't get me wrong; autopilots and flight directors are fabulous pieces of technology that dramatically reduce fatigue and cockpit workload, especially in emergencies. Just don't get so used to using their labor-saving capabilities that the loss of the autopilot or flight director becomes an emergency.

COCKPIT AUTOMATION

In addition to sophisticated autopilots, there is a growing number of computerized navigation and flight management devices available for installation in general aviation airplanes. Most of these devices [Global Positioning System (GPS) displays moving maps, Electronic Flight Information Systems (EFIS), and the like] do much to increase information available to the pilot for position awareness and advance decision making. With their growing sophistication, however, comes an increased complexity that requires a greater pilot investment in training time and experience to master each device. Several highly publicized corporate, military, and airline accidents were the direct result of crew unfamiliarity with computerized cockpit devices.

Proper training in advanced avionics is even more necessary when you consider that there is no standardization to their operation. Tasks as simple as "direct to" on a GPS, for instance, are accomplished in vastly different ways on different brands of receiver. Each manufacturer, independently has developed what its engineers feel is the "best" method of operation, but rarely are the results intuitive, and they almost never match those of competing companies.

As advanced technology becomes more common in even the smallest of airplanes, pilots will have to commit more time to systems checkout and in-flight updating. Not being up to speed on avionics operation is disorienting at best. A massive increase in workload leads to "head in the cockpit" flying to the exclusion of a proper traffic and terrain scan, and incites fixation to the detriment of flying safety. Cockpit technology has the potential to increase the information a pilot has available, but unless a pilot truly masters the particular brand (or combination of brands) that exist in the airplane being flown, advanced automation actually *decreases* the margin of safety.

Just as no airplane checkout is complete without a thorough review of performance targets and airspeeds, no pilot should feel comfortable flying an airplane with an autopilot, GPS, moving map, EFIS, or any other device without understanding normal, abnormal, and emergency operation of that particular brand of equipment. If your instructor can't provide the training you need to gain this level of comfort, seek out others who use the same type of equipment, or call the equipment manufacturer to see if there's someone who can demonstrate its use and answer your questions before you solo behind the spectacular capabilities of computer-driven cockpit automation.

ENGINE MONITORING

Besides watching carefully over the flight and navigation instruments, you need to monitor your engine's health to safely achieve the goals of your flight. Engine monitoring is one of the least-perfected piloting tasks, and many panel layouts make it very difficult to keep engine indications in your scan. The growing trend in high-dollar, computerized systems is to manage by exception, to display engine parameters only when an abnormality occurs. This is great if your airplane has a processor to watch over the powerplant for you; however, monitoring engine health is a manual operation for the vast majority of pilots.

What should you look for when scanning the gauges? Most indicators have a "normal operating range" or a "green arc." Obviously you'll want to see that all indications are normal for the phase of flight; however, you can take this a step further by actively monitoring the trend of the engine instruments. You'll be able to detect a changing trend soon enough to make a precautionary landing, or you might be able to safely complete the planned flight, then have the system checked and repaired as necessary before an emergency ensues. If any temperature indications rise above the expected reading but remain in a green arc, realize the significance of a trend change and have the engine systems thoroughly checked prior to another flight. Trend monitoring affords you the chance to avoid disastrous situations.

Routinely log engine performance; keep a notebook in your airplane, and record data on every flight to find what is "normal" for your airplane. For instance, in cruise climb, log the outside air temperature and the power setting used. This establishes the environment in which the engine is working. Then record the fuel flow, the cylinder head temperature, the exhaust gas temperature, and the oil temperature and pressure. Include any indications you might have in the cockpit, as well as electrical monitoring devices such as ammeters or a bus voltage gauge (Fig. 6-3).

Be as accurate with your observations as possible. When you level into cruise and after you've adjusted mixture and trimmed for level flight, make another separate listing. Soon you'll have a baseline of performance data for both climb and cruise phases of flight. You'll be surprised to find that the figures you write are extremely consistent, that you'll be able to anticipate nearly to the degree, for instance, the cylinder head temperature during climb and during cruise. Now you know what is "normal" for your airplane. I see several benefits from making these sorts of observations:

Operation	OAT	Alt	MAP	RPM	FF	IAS	ADI	VSI	Trim	Gear	Flaps	CHT	EGT/TIT	Oil temp	Oil press

A/C type _____ Tail # _____ Serial # _____

Fig. 6-3. *A sample engine-trend-management log.*

- Confidence. Looking at your engine gauges and knowing that everything is "in the green" is one thing, but scanning performance and seeing that not only are all indications "normal" but they are the same as they were 2 hours before or 2 months earlier is an enormous confidence builder. This is especially important during night flight, on that long overwater hop to the Bahamas, or in instrument flight. Although you can never discount the possibility of sudden engine stoppage, most mechanical failures give some warning beforehand in time for the pilot to make an early landing. If the pilot has the instrumentation to monitor all the engine's cylinders and actively watches the trends of engine performance, IFR or night flying in a single-engine airplane can be as safe as similar operation in a twin.

- Economy. Let's say you notice that the #2 cylinder's head temperature is running warmer than what is normal for that engine. If you took your airplane to the mechanic and said "My number two cylinder is running hot," what would he or she do? Right, he or she would fire up the airplane, perhaps fly it around a while or run the engine long enough to obtain a reading, and look at the gauge. If it were still reading in the green arc, you would be told that it looked "normal," and you would be handed a bill. The mechanic would have no way of knowing that your engine wasn't "normal" from the information available. But if you have been actively "trend monitoring" your engine, you can go to the mechanic and say: "My number two cylinder normally runs at 150°C, but now it's running at 170." You can back up your observation with the data log from your cockpit. Now your mechanic knows that something has changed in that cylinder and has the information to start troubleshooting. For instance, a hot cylinder is often the result of an excessively lean mixture, so the first thing the mechanic might do is to check the injector lines for an obstruction or clean the injector nozzle screens. An hour of shop time wasn't wasted without finding a problem; an easy and comparatively inexpensive fix was made before a dangerous and expensive valve or cylinder failure cut short a flight.

- Resale. Face it, someday you're going to sell your airplane. If you have an accurate log of the engine performance parameters and demonstrate on a trial flight that the powerplant performs as advertised, you might be able to command a higher price and close a sale sooner. Put yourself in the buyer's shoes: if you were trying to decide between purchasing two airplanes, and one seller told you that "the engine runs great" while the other had hard data that appeared to be authentic and accurately stood up under scrutiny in a test flight, which airplane would you want to buy?

How often do you check the engine gauges in flight? Sometimes the pace of a flight is enough to keep you from scanning the gauges, while other times the workload is so low that complacency sets in and engine scan is often one of the first things to go. The instrument panel layout of some airplanes, especially older designs, makes it very difficult to keep engine parameters in your scan. You need some method of reminding yourself to check the engine data regularly.

Poised on the horizon for general aviation airplanes are electronic engine monitors that in many cases don't even display current readings. Instead, they actively monitor the engine for the pilot and create a display and sound an alarm only if the engine is no longer running normally. Until such computerized "flight engineers" are generic to all cockpits, you the pilot still need to regularly check the engine for abnormalities.

How can you "force" yourself to keep the gauges in your scan? A technique I've picked up along the way is to "use the radios" as a means of reminding myself to check the engine. For instance, in busy terminal airspace, the reminders to double-check the engine are the times that you are required to make a radio call or tune a navigation or communication frequency. If you do this, you'll be checking the engine quite often at a time when it's most crucial because in a terminal area you are most likely close to the ground.

When you are away from the terminal area, use the frequency tunings or the sound of anyone on the radio as a reminder to scan the engine indications. Five minutes won't go by without a positive check of engine performance. Of course, if you're flying without a radio or in uncontrolled airspace or simply in a deserted area even under instrument flight rules, you might need to supplement these checks with additional scans; set a timer that reminds you to scan the gauges every 5 minutes.

Whichever of these techniques you use, you'll know that you've checked the engine performance regularly, and if you've been monitoring the trends of the engine over time, you should be able to catch any abnormalities before they become an unexpected emergency.

WEATHER MONITORING

My initial flight training taught me little about interpreting the weather. It was drilled into me to call flight service before every trip out of the local area and to jot down the results of that preflight weather briefing just in case I might want to refer to it later in the cockpit. I don't remember if I ever referenced those weather notes again in the first few hundred hours of my flying, but my guess is that I didn't. I accepted the flight service briefer's report as the final word and scoffed along with everyone else when actual conditions didn't reflect the forecast.

About a year after earning my license, I made my first real cross-country trip. I had purchased a 1946 Cessna 120 and had about 80 or 100 hours in it, and I wanted to fly from my home in central Missouri to see my family in the Detroit area. My father was working as a mechanic for a major airline and flew to Missouri to accompany me on the eastbound trip.

The Cessna had no radios, and this was before the proliferation of hand-held devices, so I was going to "fly deaf." I was entirely dependent upon that flight-service briefing for official weather information, which would be supplemented by my own observations en route to stay out of bad weather. My first briefing, which was for the 2-hour hop to Hannibal, MO, on the Mississippi River, called for the haze and localized fog common to early June mornings. Visibilities were expected to be VFR the entire way, however, so we launched eastward with no surprises.

The subsequent leg northeastward to Dwight, IL, was equally uneventful from a weather standpoint. We were cruising behind a rather strong cold front, far enough removed to not see a cloud in the sky until just before landing. It was ominous to the northeast, the flight service station's briefer told me in Illinois; we sat it out for several hours, enjoying the hospitality of the airport management as the skies over Dwight remained a brilliant blue.

About five in the afternoon, getting a little impatient waiting for "weather" on a clear, sunny day, I checked with flight service one last time. I was warned of heavy thunderstorms to the east with the associated hazards of turbulence and reduced visibility. The briefing was capped with the standard "VFR flight not recommended," although surface reports into southwestern Michigan reported good VFR. With little cross-country flying experience, I made what still seems to be a good decision about continuing. I decided to change my route slightly to follow a major highway that would provide a solid navigation reference for 200 miles. The route also put me over a succession of general aviation airports to land at if the weather ahead became threatening.

I told my father that we'd go due east along the highway and over Kankakee, and then follow ground references to Plymouth, IN. By then it would be getting toward dusk, so we'd stay the night and finish the trip early the next morning. Still a little concerned about the weather briefer's dire warning, we launched into cloudless skies, for one of the smoothest, most pristine flights I've ever enjoyed. The trees were just starting to tinge red with dusk as we touched down and secured the airplane for the night. A highlight of my flying career was when my dad looked at me after a smooth three-point landing and said, "You know, you're a good pilot."

Looking back, that was the first time I ever really made a weather decision. I needed to avoid the hazards of thunderstorms, reduced visibility, and turbulence, so I created a plan for avoidance, along with a set of preplanned options if encountered a storm. Along the way I constantly observed the outside world for some confirmation of the weather threat; when I found none, I continued with my plan until reaching my destination. Had the clouds begun to swarm or the air begun to churn, I could have easily landed at any one of the airports along my way, or made a quick 180 back along the highway to the airport I'd left behind.

As my experience grew and the capability of the airplanes I flew increased, I learned to use the same strategy with the help of a lot of other sources of information. Recently, for instance, I flew a Cessna 172 from Cedar Rapids, IA, to Atchison, KS, which is near Kansas City. The airplane was equipped for basic IFR, and I filed an instrument flight plan to get above the scattered-to-broken cumulus layer. Flight service advised of a slight chance of isolated thunderstorms along the airway from Ottumwa to St. Joseph, but the surface aviation reports along the way reported calm. We took off.

I kept one radio tuned to Flight Watch to monitor what was going on, and I heard several airplanes calling ATC for diversions around buildups almost as soon as I took off. I asked for permission to steer around a dark glob of cumulus at my 12 o'clock during climb. Through the broken layer at 8000 feet I could see darkening skies to the south and a higher layer that might have been an anvil off a distant thunderstorm to the southwest.

With a good bit more experience in cross-country flying to this point, I knew it was time for more information. I asked center for permission to leave the frequency to talk to Flight Watch; after filing a pilot report, I asked for an update along my route of flight. The briefer warned of an isolated supercell over Lamoni, IA, which was a VOR along my route, and a broken-to-overcast layer of cumulus from Ottumwa all the way to my destination. The entire area was gliding slowly to the southeast, away from me, and conditions to the north were quiet. I asked for a Des Moines report, although it was well north of my route. Des Moines reported a scattered layer of fair-weather cumulus; therefore, north was an "out" should I need one.

If I didn't have some obvious way to get myself out of trouble, I would have never proceeded. Conditions were beginning to get worse than flight service had reported, so I needed to start to think in terms of escape. I mentally filed a "right turn" toward the north as the way out of trouble if conditions warranted, and I pressed on.

As I got near Ottumwa and ready for the turn southwest, the sky along my route really began to look black. I wanted to stay in clear air as much as possible to avoid the big buildups, so I called Flight Watch a second time. The isolated cell was becoming a line of level 4 to 5 thunderstorms that were still sliding away from my route but still in the way for the time being. Lamoni was reporting hail and 70-knot winds at the surface— definitely not the place to be—so I retuned the center frequency and made a request: "Cessna 172YA would like to turn about 20 degrees to the right to stay north of the airway to Lamoni." My request was immediately authorized, and I began to fly along the line of storms with a benign scattered layer to my north should I need to make a turn.

Halfway across Iowa, I was zig-zagging between growing plumes of cloud. I was given permission to deviate as necessary and was having little trouble remaining in clear air, but my cumulus canyon was narrowing, and every now and then I had to penetrate a cloud. Each time I entered cumulus, I waited for the "big bump," but most were calm. Each time I broke out in between, I could see the raging dark off the left wing and the calmer skies just to the north. I knew that at the first sign of trouble I could still deviate farther north.

Eventually I plunged into cloud and hit the "moderate" turbulence that lifted me 3 inches off the seat. It was time to turn. I held the heading until I was again in clear skies and then told ATC I wanted to turn about 60° to the right to get out of building clouds; again my request was granted. Soon I was in smooth air 20 miles to the right of my airway, and I was paralleling the line of rising storms. ATC provided a vector that would take me toward St. Joseph.

I was close enough now that I could pick up the ATIS at St. Joe's Rosecrans Airport, which called for gusty winds and reduced visibilities, a thunderstorm in progress. The sky ahead was perfectly clear, but the line of towering cumulus looked endless. Flight Watch told me that it extended west for at least another 70 miles, but that the heavy rain showers ended at about St. Joseph, and airplanes reported gaps in the line.

I adjusted my folded map to include Nebraska and was about ready to request an amended clearance to an airport north of my route when I heard a Bonanza check in for flight following below the clouds at 2500 feet. The Bonanza was following about the same path as I, only his choice was to stay in the clear beneath the clouds, avoiding the rain shafts that indicated most downdrafts. I asked the center controller, "Kansas City Center, Cessna 172YA, do you mind if I query that Bonanza about flight conditions?" I've never had a request like that turned down. Soon I learned that the bases of the clouds were a uniform 4000 feet and visibility was excellent, as is typical behind a cold front. The Bonanza pilot was having no trouble at all identifying the thunderstorms visually and avoiding the rain shafts with small heading changes. Most importantly, the ride was smooth!

Here I was at 8000 feet on an instrument flight plan and unlikely to make it to my destination when a VFR airplane beneath was having no problem at all. I was now within about 30 miles of Atchison, still blocked off to the south by high cumulus, when a large hole opened up beneath. I could see a four-lane highway that corresponded to my known position and my VFR charts; I canceled IFR, descending through the hole, but stayed "on frequency" for flight following. At 3000 feet, the ride was smooth and conditions were exactly as the Bonanza pilot had reported. I did have to pass to the west of the St. Joseph VOR to avoid moderate rain but soon reintercepted the approach course into Atchison on the south side of the beacon for an easy VFR arrival.

Weather is the cause of a good percentage of all airplane accidents. Predicting weather is such that hazards might come and go without much warning. Your job as a pilot is to take that weather briefing as a starting point, a hint of what might come, and plan your flight to include an obvious escape route if things began to go sour. You might be lucky enough to have radar or lightning detection devices (StrikeFinder or Stormscope) on board, but be flexible in your planning; get updates from any available source.

Pilot reports are the best weather indicators, so provide them yourself, ask Flight Watch for other pilot reports, and simply ask for input (with ATC's permission) if pilot reports are not available. You can monitor Flight Watch continuously in bad weather and listen to AWOS, ASOS, and ATIS transmissions along the way. Not the nuisance many think it to be, HIWAS, the recorded weather information broadcast continuously along with many VOR identifiers, is a good source of data about weather hazards as well.

As your skills improve and your confidence builds, you'll be able to tackle more and more weather situations. Just be certain that you're facing the hazards with as much knowledge as possible, and be certain that you always have an easy escape route immediately available.

7
Phase of flight: Descent, approach, and landing

YOU CAN BEGIN PREPARING FOR THE DESCENT, APPROACH, AND LANDING ahead of time to minimize your workload as you get closer to the ground. It's important to reduce your workload as much as possible because two factors conspire to make safety more difficult to achieve:

- The natural increase in workload as you prepare to land
- The insidious effects of fatigue

We've already seen a graphical representation of the levels of workload in various phases of flight. Looking at it again, we'll add another variable: fatigue (Fig. 7-1). At the beginning of your flight, you should be quite rested, and your piloting capability will far out match the demands placed upon it. In other words, you have a margin of safety between the workload and your ability to handle it.

Your capability will continue at pretty much the same level, well above the needs of pilot workload, until the combined stresses of physical control manipulation, status monitoring, navigating, engine vibration, and noise add to a level of fatigue that erodes

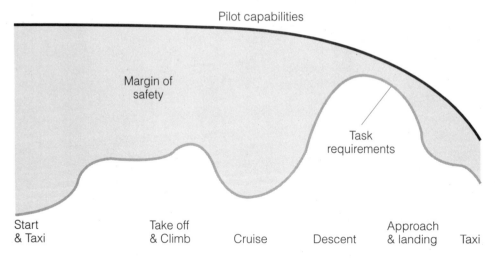

Fig. 7-1. *Fatigue's effects, and the margin of safety.*

your ability to meet the demands of flight. Your capability drops off quickly, reducing the margin of safety between your abilities and the demands of safe flight. Meanwhile, the highest-workload phase of flight, the approach and landing, further reduces the margin of safety you enjoy. Add even a minor emergency or a little extra stress, and the demands of flight might exceed your capabilities as a pilot.

Take a look at Fig. 7-2, which illustrates the phase of flight where emergencies began, and then examine Fig. 7-3, the phase of flight when accidents occurred. Although emergency situations begin in virtually all phases of flight, the natural workload increase of descent, approach, and landing, combined with the reduction in piloting skills brought on by fatigue, mean that those final moments of a flight are the most dangerous. How can you reduce your workload on descent, approach, and landing, and therefore increase your ability to counter the unexpected?

DESCENT

You've been in cruise for some time, and your destination airport nears. When should you start down, and what technique should you employ for the descent? Individuals undoubtedly have numerous perfectly good techniques, but some techniques aren't terribly efficient, others are potentially hazardous, and most make it difficult to decide when to begin the descent. Here's how I like to do it.

I like to make my descents in one of three ways:

- A gradual, 500-fpm cruise descent
- A faster, 1000-fpm steep descent
- A 1000-fpm "penetration descent"

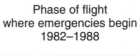

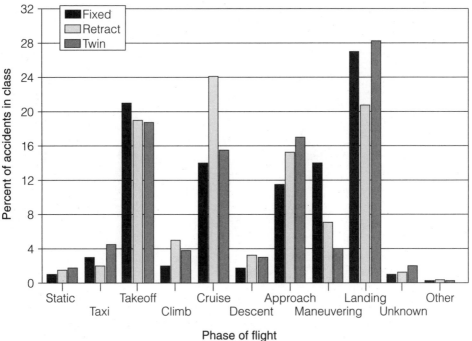

Fig. 7-2. *Fatigue, workload, and the phase of flight where emergencies begin.*
AOPA Air Safety Foundation

The penetration descent is used when ATC, weather, or terrain require that I stay high above the traffic pattern until very close to destination.

My 500-fpm descent requires merely a small power change. Airplanes are basically quite stable, and if you adjust the power, they will pitch up or down to stay at the same trimmed airspeed. You can use this to your advantage to make a gradual en-route descent. Just experiment a little and find a power reduction from normal cruise that gives you a 500-fpm descent at the same airspeed.

For instance, in an A36 Bonanza, changing the manifold pressure (MP) by 1" nets a vertical speed change of about 125 feet per minute. If I'm cruising at 22" MP, reducing power to 18" will cause the airplane to descend at around 500 fpm. There might be a few pitch oscillations that you'll learn to dampen out before the plane settles into the descent; the power change required and resulting descent rate might vary from plane to plane, with aircraft weight, or with the density altitude, but you can easily make small adjustments to fine-tune the performance. In a Cessna Skyhawk, it takes about a 100-RPM power reduction to get a steady-state 500 fpm descent at cruise speed. The

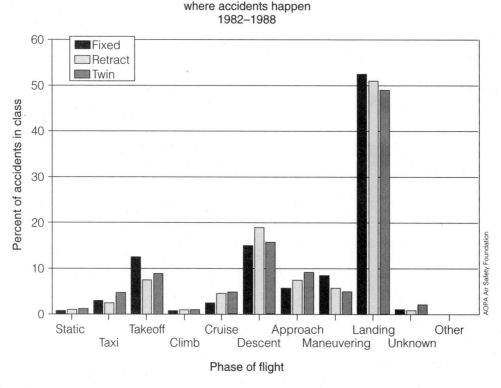

Fig. 7-3. *Fatigue, workload, and the phase of flight where accidents happen.*

small power adjustments in both airplanes also mean that you won't need to worry about cooling the engine too rapidly.

Why not just leave the power set, push the nose over, and get a little more airspeed in the descent? After all, it's "free" airspeed, why not use it? The problem with this technique is that it usually puts the airspeed up into the caution range (the "yellow arc") at the same time that you're descending into the typically greater turbulence of the lower atmosphere. You'll generally have no positive way to know whether you'll hit a layer of heavy turbulence until you're in it, and at these airspeeds, it only takes one big jolt to cause structural damage or even an inflight breakup.

To further argue against this technique, a large number of the "controlled flight into terrain" accidents occur in descent when a pilot is distracted and fails to detect proximity to the ground until it's too late. This distraction might be in part due to all of the changes that the descent technique requires a pilot to make. By trimming nose-down for a faster airspeed, the pilot has created a situation where the airplane will fight his or her efforts at level-off because the airplane will try to continue the descent. If other factors conspire to distract the pilot further, he or she might descend into the ground without ever realizing it.

Using a power-reduction, constant-airspeed descent, the trim remains set, and level-off is merely a matter of returning power to the cruise setting; the airplane will tend to stay level after the reapplication of power with no tendency to descend farther.

Fixed-pitch propellers might increase RPM if the airspeed increases, making for a battle between the engine, the airplane, and the pilot as the variables continually change in descent. The prop might even overspeed in a high-airspeed descent if the pilot isn't careful, which is one more reason not to initiate descent by pushing the nose down.

When do you need to begin the descent? Using a constant-airspeed, 500-fpm descent profile, it's easy to figure out. Let's say you're cruising at 8500 feet and the pattern altitude at your destination is 2500 feet. You've got 6000 feet to go in the descent; drop the zeros and double the remaining digit, and you'll see it will take 12 minutes to make the descent at 500 feet per minute. When you're 12 minutes out from the point that you wish to be at pattern altitude, begin a 500-fpm descent. Remember that the power will gradually increase as you drop into thick air at lower altitudes; therefore, you'll need to make a small power adjustment every thousand feet or so in the descent to keep the power and vertical speed constant.

GPS, loran, and DME make it easy to see when you're about 12 minutes out. If you don't have that capability, you should still be able to figure it out manually. If you think better in terms of miles than minutes, you can figure it that way, too. Let's say your ground speed is 100 knots. That's just a bit faster than 90 knots, which is 1½ nautical miles per minute. In 12 minutes (the time required for the descent), a 90-kt ground speed transports you 18 nautical miles (1½ × 12), so when you're about 20 nautical miles from your destination (accounting for 100 knots, not the 90-knot ground speed), begin your descent. It's just about as precise this way as it is with GPS.

This 500-fpm constant-airspeed descent works well in smooth air, but if clouds, turbulence, or terrain keep you farther up for a longer time, you might try a 1000-fpm constant-airspeed descent. You will have to experiment a little to find the technique that works in your airplane, but a Bonanza, for instance, does this quite well with a 4" MP reduction and a landing-gear extension; a Cessna 172 needs around 2100 RPM to come down at high-cruise speed and 1000 feet per minute.

The advantages of staying at a constant airspeed are all there, with a twist; the higher descent rate means a greater angle of descent, allowing you to stay above obstacles or adverse weather until closer to your destination. Using the same example, with an 8500-foot cruise altitude and a 2500-foot MSL traffic pattern, it will take 6 minutes for the descent at 1000 fpm. Six minutes from the point at which you want to be at pattern altitude, start your descent. Or if you want to do it in miles, a 100-knot-ground speed Skyhawk will need to start down about 10 miles from destination; a 170-knot-ground speed Bonanza needs to begin descending about 17 miles out.

But let's say you have ice-laden cumulus clouds in a scattered layer between you and the ground, or ATC thinks you're flying a Stuka dive-bomber instead of a light twin. You might need to come down at a real steep angle to satisfy the requirements of those descents. You can do it safely not by speeding up, which again exposes you to the hazards of extreme airspeed close to the ground, but by slowing down.

Let's say you're flying that Bonanza again and the controllers have you 6000 feet above the initial altitude for the ILS as you get closer and closer to destination. Your repeated requests for "lower" have been denied because of traffic; a layer of clouds below prevents you from requesting a "VFR descent" to get to a lower altitude. You know you're going to have to drop like a rock to make this approach, but you really don't want to subject your passengers to any more than a 1000-fpm descent in an unpressurized airplane.

Ask the controllers if you can slow down a little before making the descent. Actually, you don't have to ask, you can simply tell ATC you plan to slow down, but let's try to be as cordial as possible with the controllers, okay? Instead of bombing along at nearly 3 miles a minute at cruise speed, decelerate to approach speed, about 110–120 knots. When the time comes to descend, it will take only gear extension and an acceptably small power reduction to yield a 1000-fpm descent. It will still take six minutes to make this descent. Flying at a slower ground speed, however, you'll cover only 10–12 miles, not the nearly 18 you would at cruise speed.

Are you worried about shock cooling? Remember that airspeed doesn't cause shock cooling and rate of descent doesn't cause shock cooling; big power reductions over a short period of time cause shock cooling. These techniques accomplish your goal of a fast descent without "shelling out" the engine in the process.

Why do I spend so much time covering descent technique in a book about cockpit management? To repeat, descent is a fairly high-workload phase of flight, and most accidents occur during high-workload phases. If you have a practiced technique for descents under varying circumstances for the airplane you fly, then you can predict beforehand exactly how your airplane should perform, and you won't have to devote mental and physical power to the task of figuring out how to get your airplane where you want it, when you want it there. The flying techniques that I advocate allow you to concentrate on the "big picture," hopefully increasing your margin of safety and reducing your exposure to the effects of fatigue.

LEVEL-OFF

Let's modify these high-rate descent profiles just a bit. You want to be able to make rapid descents, but you don't want to blow right through the safe altitude while converging with the ground. Remember the altitude-critical area? We have an ACA for the descent as well, which is from the desired altitude to 1000 feet above it. Make altitude callouts during the descent to help keep yourself fully aware of the airplane's altitude and the altitude's relationship to the final, safe height: "6000 descending to 2000 . . . 4000 feet to go."

Getting close to the level-off ACA, if at all possible, defer approach setup, navigational tuning, or radio communications. Concentrate solely on the process of leveling off because that's by far the most important thing you have to do at this point. Entering the level-off ACA, adjust power, drag, and pitch to reduce the rate of descent, if necessary, to 500 feet per minute. Just as on level-off into cruise, we want to (and are expected by ATC to) moderate the rate of altitude change, precisely to keep us from busting our altitude. If you're still a ways from destination, you might reduce drag and start a transition back to level cruise. If turbulence is a factor or you're getting close to destination, you might instead reduce vertical speed with a pitch change, starting to trim the airplane for the slower approach speed at altitude (Fig. 7-4).

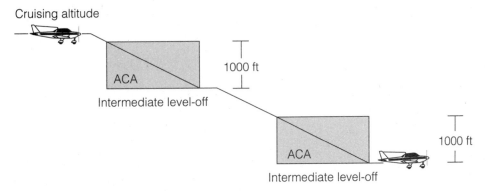

Cruising altitude

ACA

Intermediate level-off

1000 ft

ACA

Intermediate level-off

1000 ft

Fig. 7-4. *Altitude critical areas for leveling off during a descent.*

Regardless of your goal at this point, taper off the descent rate until smoothly leveling out on altitude at or near your desired airspeed. To do this, you'll need to add about a minute or a couple of miles to your computed point of initiating the descent. Now you're ready for the approach.

APPROACH AND LANDING

Another altitude-critical area is associated with the arrival airport. If you're within about 5 miles of the airport and/or closer than 1000 feet to the ground, you need to be deferring as many nonessential tasks as possible and instead concentrating on what it really takes to fly. I've seen more than one highly experienced pilot drift off an instrument approach course while dialing the ground control frequency into the #2 radio (Fig. 7-5).

You don't need to talk to ground control until you've completed your landing; so if you haven't tuned that radio before entering the arrival ACA, don't worry about it until you're on the ground. Remember the old cliché "aviate, navigate, and communicate"; that's always the order in which you should prioritize pilot tasks, but especially so in an altitude-critical area.

Most of my discussion about approach and landing centers on techniques for instrument pilots making IMC letdowns. The concepts are equally valid for visual approaches and VFR traffic patterns; the only difference is that the pilot flying visually substitutes outside references for course guidance and descent glidepath.

Be sure that you've got everything set before allowing yourself into the altitude-critical area. You can use entering the ACA as a final check to make certain you're

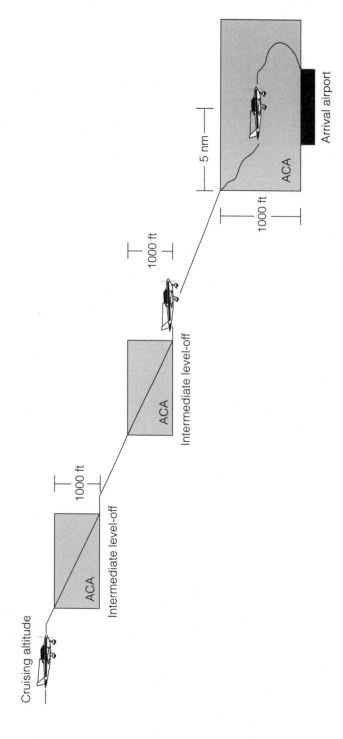

Fig. 7-5. *The arrival altitude critical area.*

Cruising altitude

1000 ft

ACA

Intermediate level-off

1000 ft

ACA

Intermediate level-off

1000 ft

5 nm

1000 ft

ACA

Arrival airport

ready for approach and landing; if you're not ready for the final descent, don't enter the ACA until you are. Likewise, if you find yourself inside the ACA and experience a malfunction, major distraction, or disorientation, climb out of the altitude-critical area, sort it out, and then get set up for another approach.

Approach checklist. If you haven't had a chance to complete the descent and approach checklists on the way down, now is the time to assure yourself that all is complete, then double-check with the printed checklists. You want to be doing all of the major before-landing checks (especially setting/verifying the heading indicator/compass and altimeter, and switching fuel tanks as appropriate) while you still are outside of the approach or the airport traffic pattern with ample time and altitude to recover if moving a switch or dialing in a value makes something go wrong.

That's why you might want to create an "approach checklist" in addition to those printed in the pilot's operating handbook to help you accomplish all those prelanding steps that you don't have a lot of time for on short final or after breaking out at minimums on an instrument approach.

Such an approach checklist might contain steps ensuring correct configuration of such items as:

Fuel selectors—set
Fuel boost pumps—set
Fuel mixture—set
Landing lights—on
Seat belts and shoulder harnesses—on
Seat backs—up
Avionics—set
Approach—briefed

See the pilot's operating handbook to verify the proper positioning of these and other controls and accessories.

A note about that avionics step: Setting up for an approach is an individualized task. The only rule is to use every piece of equipment you possibly can to help with orienting yourself during the approach and to use them properly. When the radios are set the way I want, this is how I double-check to ensure that I didn't miss anything. As I go through the steps, I physically touch each piece of equipment to help me check. I'll say out loud as I go down the stack from top to bottom:

"Marker beacon set, tested
"Number one nav tuned, identified, number one OBS set
"Number two nav tuned, identified, number two OBS set
"ADF tuned, identified, bearing card set
"GPS set"

Now I know I'm ready to navigate the approach.

Approach briefing. Before entering the ACA, you need to brief yourself for the approach. If your arrival is VFR, the briefing is usually simple; however, prepare a fill-in-the-blanks checklist for your lapboard to remind yourself to review everything prior to the approach. A sample VFR approach brief might sound something like this:

"This will be a visual landing on Runway 18 at Sedalia Memorial Airport. Wind is 210 at 7 knots, giving me a right crosswind on landing. I have 5000 feet of runway available, much greater than the 1200-foot ground roll I've computed for landing. Runway 18 has a left-hand traffic pattern, which I'll enter on a downwind leg. Field elevation is 909 feet with a traffic pattern altitude of 1900 feet; altimeter is verified at 29.90. There are no significant obstructions on either end of the runway."

The approach briefing for an instrument approach might get a little more complicated. Because there is so much more information required to safely fly an instrument approach, you need to review it in a formal, almost ritualistic manner. A sample IFR approach brief might sound like this:

"This will be the ILS 1 Right approach for Wichita Mid-Continent Airport. Wind is 310 at 10 gusting to 15 knots, giving me a gusting left crosswind on landing. There is 5000 foot of runway available, much greater than the 800-foot ground roll I've computed for landing. ALSF-1 lighting is operational.

"Field elevation is 1320 feet. Once cleared for the approach, I can fly at 3000 feet until established inbound and within 10 miles of the marker, then 2700 feet, then down the glideslope to a decision height of 1520 feet. I'm entering on radar vectors from the southeast; altimeter is verified at 29.89.

"This approach requires 200 foot ceiling and ½ mile visibility. ATIS reports a measured ceiling of 600 overcast and 10 miles visibility; I should break out at around 1900 MSL. If I need to miss the approach, I'll fly runway heading to 3600 feet, and then make a left turn directly to the Wichita VOR and hold."

That's a ton of information to try to remember for an instrument approach. It's vital that you know all the factors that go into flying a safe approach, but it's not necessary to use "memory space" on most of those facts when actually on the approach. In fact, there are only three things you need to remember once established on the inbound course:

- What *altitude* is correct for each segment of the approach
- What *distance* you'll fly between segments of the approach
- What the initial *missed approach* procedure calls for

ADM: altitude, distance, missed. This is really all that you should be thinking about when you are inbound on the approach because all else is extraneous to your goal of trying to put it on the pavement. First, how low can you go? What **A**ltitude is safe for each segment of the approach? Your approach briefing reviewed the whole procedure, but now you're on the approach, so all you need to know is when you can go down to each altitude.

Some people like to highlight or circle the altitudes on the instrument approach plate. That's fine, but circumstances (availability of certain navaids, category of airplane, local versus remote altimeter settings, FDC notams) can change the particulars of an approach, and if you plan to use a plate more than once, having highlighted or circled data might cause you to fly it improperly on a later day. Besides, if the approach plate isn't positioned close to your line of sight, you'll distract yourself from the approach by looking in your lap or on the seat beside you for the information during your descent. You might be different, but virtually every pilot I've ever seen try to reference an instrument approach plate during an approach ended up off pitch or heading or in some other way off the approach; this is particularly dangerous down close to minimum altitudes.

A technique I've learned is to write the particulars of an approach on an adhesive-backed note and to stick that paper on the panel as a reference without looking away from the instruments during your approach. Furthermore, I like to do it in a simple, pictorial format with a line showing level flight and my assigned altitude to the final approach fix, then a descent down to MDA or the decision height with step-downs depicted along the way. You can make up an approach "quick reference" note as soon as you hear what approach is in use. For that matter, you can usually anticipate what approach you'll be using before you even take off by comparing forecast weather at your destination for the available approaches. Don't forget also to make up a reference sheet for your departure alternate and have it posted on the panel during takeoff if needed. Figure 7-6 shows the altitude drawing I make for an approach.

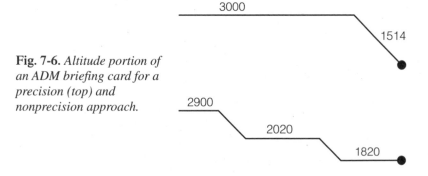

Fig. 7-6. *Altitude portion of an ADM briefing card for a precision (top) and nonprecision approach.*

How long are you going to fly at each altitude? What **D**istance determines your step-down points and your missed approach point? The points are determined by:

- A navigation fix, such as a waypoint.
- A beacon.
- A cross-bearing.
- A radar fix.
- A distance, in terms of DME from a navaid.
- Time, as listed on the instrument approach plate and based upon your best estimate of ground speed.

Those values go on the "quick reference" note also, as seen in Fig. 7-7.

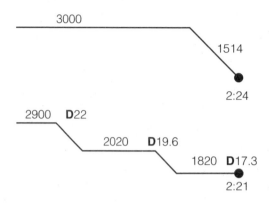

Fig. 7-7. *Distance portion of an ADM briefing card for a precision (top) and nonprecision approach.*

Lastly, which way are you going to go if you reach the missed approach point and the runway environment is not in sight? What is the **M**issed approach procedure? I like to draw an overhead view of my course with the altitudes written in as appropriate. If the missed approach takes me in a turn to a navaid, especially if I need to reference something other than an approach-course beacon for the missed approach, I also write down an approximate heading that will take me to the holding point. I've seen pilots literally fly in circles while trying to retune a nav radio during a missed approach. Figure 7-8 shows a sticky note that I prepared for a typ-

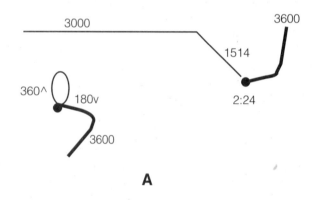

A

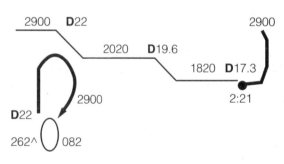

B

Fig. 7-8. *Full ADM briefing cards for a precision (A) and nonprecision approach (B).*

ical precision and nonprecision approach. I've also included the holding pattern and, in a move to further reduce my workload in this hectic phase of an instrument flight, the type of hold entry I'll use plus the initial entry heading on the rare chance that I need to fly the missed-approach holding pattern.

This technique allows me to see a lot of information that I need to have—**ADM**: altitude, distance, and missed—up in my instrument scan where I can refer to it during the approach without diverting my attention from the flight instruments. It's kind of like the Aresti symbology that aerobatic pilots use to describe the sequence of their maneuvers. Be sure to experiment with locations on or near the panel that work for you and accept the glue on the adhesive-backed paper without causing it to drop off in the midst of an approach.

Beginning the approach. What criteria do you use to decide whether to accept an approach? I'm often asked "What do you mean?" when I pose the question to a student or in seminars. Most private pilots will begin any approach that they've been assigned, without thinking too much about it. True, FAR Part 91 allows you to "go take a look" if you want, but to blindly launch down the approach course without giving the weather conditions some thought might invite disaster.

First, evaluate the weather conditions on the approach course. Think in terms of the four aviation weather hazards: thunderstorms, turbulence, reduced visibility, and ice. If you can detect thunderstorms along the approach course, divert or delay until the storms have passed. It's better to hold at 9000 feet above the cloud layer dodging the buildups as necessary for the 20 minutes that it takes for a thunderstorm to die out or move on than to try and outrun the cell only to be hit by the gust front close to the ground. Do you have reports of severe or extreme turbulence, or wind shear, or pilot reports of rapid airspeed shifts close to the ground? This is another time to think about diverting or delaying. Are conditions likely to get better soon, perhaps caused by a frontal passage or a dissipating cumulus cloud? Hold and wait it out. Is the turbulence more entrenched and expected to last for some time beneath a jet stream core or with strong surface winds? You might want to go elsewhere.

Have other pilots reported icing on the approach course? If your airplane isn't certified for this "known ice," you can't legally begin your descent. If your craft is equipped for ice, remember that means it is equipped to fly through short periods of moderate or less ice accumulations, and then only at the airplane's published ice penetration speed, which is usually faster than the normal approach and missed approach speeds. Check the limitations section of the pilot's operating handbook for details.

And what about visibility? Approaches have minimums. If the visibility is below minimums or the cloud ceiling is lower than the final altitude of the approach, why bother? You're not going to legally (read that "safely") land if either is true, and if you can't land, you'll need the fuel reserves to go someplace else. Why waste the time and fuel flying an approach you know you'll have to miss. Hold for a while if you have reason to believe conditions will improve, or go ahead and ask for clearance to an alternate.

Remember to consider weather along the missed approach path; if you have to fly an approach, there's always the possibility that you might have to miss it as well.

The precision approach. Perhaps a "precision approach" is a misnomer because all approaches should be flown precisely, but by definition a precision approach has rate-of-descent guidance as well as an over-the-ground navigation reference. Everyone is familiar with the instrument landing system (ILS) approach; another type is the precision approach radar (PAR) system that has an air traffic controller tracking the airplane and providing the pilot with verbal commands concerning heading and altitude. The microwave landing system (MLS) was supposed to rival the ILS, but MLS floundered and is essentially dormant. Advances in Global Positioning System (GPS) technology may soon bring precision-approval capability to almost all public-use airports.

Don't expect a PAR approach unless you're flying into a military airfield. I flew an MLS approach in a Bonanza into Wichita Mid-Continent Airport, but the straight-in approach path was indistinguishable from an ILS, not the curving MLS approach path that is supposed to increase airport capacity.

The one thing that all precision approaches have in common is that they are designed to lead the pilot gradually down to a point very close to the surface, aligned with the runway centerline, and aimed for a point usually 1000 feet from the approach end of the runway, assuming a "normal" rate of descent. Your job upon beginning the descent stage of this approach is to initiate a gradual descent that keeps you aligned with the glideslope or the controller's verbal call-out altitudes. It helps a lot if you have the airplane stabilized in an approach mode prior to beginning this descent.

Techniques vary widely, and airplane handbooks often include type-specific recommendations, but if you can be set on your desired approach airspeed and have flaps configured before you intercept the vertical portion of the approach, then all you'll need to do is to make a small power or pitch change or lower the landing gear and nose simultaneously to hit the proper descent rate.

From this point on, the primary reference isn't the glideslope needle, it's the airplane's pitch attitude, backed up by the vertical speed and airspeed indicator. For instance, in a Bonanza or Baron on approach speed, lowering the landing gear at the intercept pretty much makes the airplane pitch to 3° below the horizon on the attitude indicator; this 3° descent pitch yields a 500 to 600 fpm rate of descent that, with about 100- to 120-knot ground speeds, creates the 3° descent slope common to most ILSs. A Cessna 172, on the other hand, requires about a 100-RPM power reduction to settle onto the glideslope. The pilot who has stabilized his or her configuration prior to intercepting the glideslope has a very slight and predictable change to make to begin the descent and a set of defined targets (pitch, airspeed, and vertical speed) to aim for to get desired performance. From there, it's a matter of slight corrections in pitch and heading to remain aligned with the localizer and glideslope.

On the way down, continue to make altitude call-outs aloud, along with the altitude's relationship to decision height: "1700 feet descending to 984, about 700 to go" might be a call-out early in the ILS descent. I like to make call-outs every 500 feet until within 500 feet of the final altitude and then each 100 feet from that point on. Remember that you're well into the altitude-critical area, and you've already extracted the

ADM from the approach plate. Your only job now is to fly the approach, so you'll have plenty of time to make these call-outs. You might have a radar altimeter or an altitude alerter or some other means of detecting the decision height mechanically, but don't trust any device without monitoring the altitude yourself.

How close to decision height can you keep the needles centered on an ILS? Based upon my experience as a simulator and flight instructor, many pilots have difficulty in the last couple hundred feet of the approach due to needle-chasing instead of basic attitude flying backed up with the navigation indicators as I've described. If you can't fly an ILS to minimums, you can't fly an ILS at all. To back up this holier-than-thou statement, consider this: Most ILS approaches have a decision height 200 feet above the runway threshold. When you look at the notes at the bottom of the approach plate, you'll find that you can also fly this as a localizer-only approach if for any reason you're unable to receive the glideslope. The localizer-only minimum descent altitude (MDA) is usually 350 to 400 feet above field elevation.

Even if nobody had ever invented the glideslope, you could get within 350 feet of the ground on this approach. The glideslope does you no good unless you can accurately track it during the last 150 to 200 feet of the approach. At altitude, practice precise pitch and heading control in a constant-rate descent to get the feel for how you should fly an ILS, and then resist the urge to "chase the needles" on the approach.

Remember, your job as a pilot is always basic attitude flight; the navigation radios merely tell you which direction to point the airplane.

The nonprecision approach. Some people feel that localizer, VOR, loran, GPS, and especially NDB approaches are called "nonprecision" because they only put you in the general vicinity of an airport. Not true. Flown precisely, a nonprecision approach puts you in a position to make a normal landing usually from about 500 feet above the pavement. The approaches are called "nonprecision" because they do not employ a glideslope reference. That's it.

If a nonprecision approach is identified by name with a runway number (VOR Runway 3, Hutchinson, Kansas), then the final approach course is aligned within 30° of the runway heading; therefore, you should see the runway roughly straight ahead when approaching the missed approach point. A nonprecision approach identified by a letter (Jabara Airport VOR-A) means that the final approach course is not within that 30° tolerance from runway heading. Look at the runway diagram in the lower right corner of the instrument approach plate to determine the approach's lateral angle to the runway. This is especially important if you don't want to accidentally line up with the wrong runway or a road while making that approach at night or in poor visibility.

Take a look at the chart and decide beforehand where you will look for the runway environment after you establish visual contact with the ground: "It should be out the right side of the windshield, angling northwest away from me." Knowing the type and pattern of runway lights will also help you distinguish the runway from a road; look at the light pattern identifier in the overhead view of the airport on the approach plate, and compare that designator to the picture of the light patterns elsewhere in the charts (Fig. 7-9).

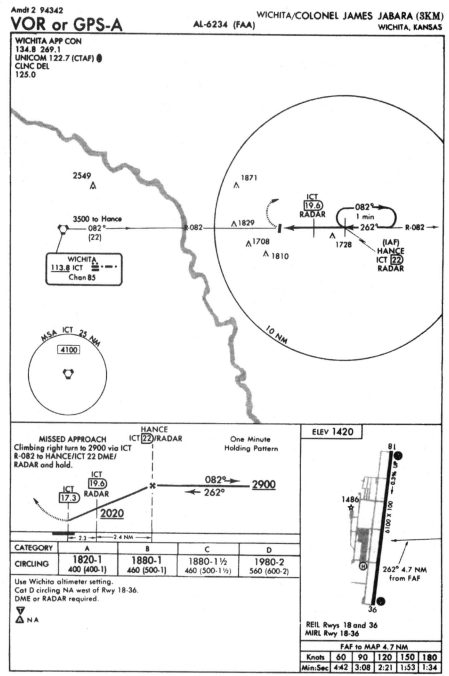

Fig. 7-9. *The approach plate illustrates the angle at which you'll approach the run-way on a nonprecision approach.*

Knowing the light pattern might be more important than you think. There was a near-tragedy involving a Boeing 737 at Kansas City International several years ago. Although I don't remember seeing a formal write-up on the incident, as the television press reported it, this is approximately what happened, with a few embellishments. (This is not an official account of the incident, and it is not meant to judge any entity.)

The airliner was inbound from some point east and was making a night approach into MCI. Thunderstorms cracked in the night air; visibility was near minimums in fog, low cloud, and rain showers. As was customary for the airline involved, the captain was flying the approach while his first officer monitored the approach. According to the cockpit procedure, when the first officer sighted the runway environment, he would take the controls from the captain and make the visual landing. This technique is designed to minimize the hazards of a single pilot making the transition from instrument to visual flight. The crew was inbound on the approach for Runway 27 at Kansas City.

Straining to see through the rain-soaked windscreen, the first officer caught sight of first one light, then another, and then a string of lights ringing the active runway. Apparently the first officer was not alarmed by the absence of approach lighting or runway end identifier lights, nor did he realize that the airplane was not quite aligned with the runway despite the near-perfect flying of the captain. Nonetheless, the first officer called visual contact and took control of the descending Boeing.

Turning slightly to line up for landing, the crew shuddered as a bolt of lightning flashed in the cockpit. The airplane lurched, then continued downward, but the bolt had been so intense and the rocking of the airplane so acute that the crew wisely decided to miss the approach. They powered up and climbed to altitude, eventually diverting to the 13,000-foot runway at Salina, Kansas, for landing. Only after touchdown did they realize what had really happened.

The pattern of lights the copilot used to line up for landing, which didn't match what he should have expected based upon the instrument approach chart, was not the runway at all, but the rows of bright street lamps that illuminate a stretch of Interstate 29 around the airport. The bolt of lightning wasn't lightning at all, but the discharge as the plane snapped a high-tension electrical wire, tearing out several electrical poles and damaging the nose gear of the Boeing.

This is an excellent example of why it is important to know which pattern of lights to expect during an approach to verify that you are in that runway's landing environment, especially at night or in low visibility.

A nonprecision approach is designed differently than one with a glideslope. With precision approaches, the intent is to line the pilot up with the centerline, then gradually guide him or her to a point just above the runway. A nonprecision approach, on the other hand, is designed to align the airplane on any known course, not necessarily directly down the runway, so that the pilot can descend to a minimum safe altitude as far away from the airport as possible. This allows the pilot to get below clouds in a position where a normal landing can be made. If visibility is poor as well, the pilot can continue until the prescribed missed approach point, often directly over the airport.

Your job while flying a nonprecision approach is to descend as quickly as you can at the appropriate step-down points. Like any other altitude change, make verbal call-outs as you near your final altitude. Some instructors teach that you should compute a constant rate of descent that puts you at the correct altitudes at the exact time you reach each step-down fix and at the minimum descent altitude at the same time you reach the missed approach point. There are three problems with this technique.

First, how do you determine the correct rate of descent? The vertical speed that will get you to each altitude exactly at each fix is a function of ground speed. As you descend, the wind's effect on your airplane will change, which will change the ground speed; this requires you to constantly monitor ground speed and adjust your vertical speed as it varies.

Second, if the altitudes and/or step-down fixes are not at consistently changing values of distance and altitude, you'll need to engage in this trial-and-error ground speed/vertical speed game between every one of the step-down fixes. The technique required in both of these instances will phenomenally increase your workload when flying a nonprecision approach, potentially so much so that you'll miss other indications that the approach is not going well.

Third, this often-taught technique puts you at the minimum descent altitude just as you reach the missed approach point. Have you ever looked outside just as you've reached the MAP on a nonprecision approach? Where were you? In most cases you were actually over the airport, sometimes even at the far end of the runway headed away from the touchdown zone. This is even more common in timed approaches, which assume a constant, known ground speed. You're probably at least 500 feet above the runway at the minimum descent altitude; convince me that you can make a safe arrival using a "normal rate of descent" (in the FAA's words) from a point 500 feet above the midpoint of a runway in low-visibility conditions.

Instead, I believe that the safest way to conduct a nonprecision approach is to maintain a constant airspeed and vary drag and power to make rapid descents at each step-down fix. For example, I've taught in Beech Bonanzas to fly the approach at the same 110-knot approach speed used on the ILS; one tenet of cockpit management is to reduce the variables by doing things the same way every time as often as possible. At 110 knots, it takes about 18" of manifold pressure to keep a Bonanza level at 110 knots, assuming gear up and approach flaps set. Upon reaching the final approach fix, extending the gear would cause the same 500- to 600-fpm descent used on an ILS, but we need to come down more rapidly than that; reducing the manifold pressure to 16" after extending the gear creates a roughly 1000-fpm descent rate, which is about the fastest you'd want to do in an unpressurized airplane.

Use this 1000-fpm descent to get down to the next authorized altitude, and level off by adding power. If you leveled by pitching the nose up, the airspeed would decay;

the natural trim of the airplane would cause it to pitch down, trying to regain lost speed, and you've made controlling the airplane a battle (assuming you maintain altitude) or you could easily allow it to drift below a safe altitude. By adding power (about 22" of manifold pressure in the Bonanza example), the airplane returns to level flight on the proper airspeed and in the proper configuration (flaps and gear) for the landing.

Remember to apply power a little before reaching each altitude to avoid blasting through. When you reach the next step-down fix, repeat the procedure, all the way to the missed approach point. There is no need to increase your workload by trying to match vertical speed to a varying ground speed, only to end up at a point from which you can't make a safe landing anyhow. Do it the same way every time, and on the rare occasion you fly a nonprecision approach to minimums you won't have to make it up as you go along.

Missed approach. Rain streaks off your windshield as the plane bounces in the low-altitude turbulence. Your eyes are occasionally jarred by the bumps, but for the most part the localizer and glideslope needles remain near the center of their scales; you're doing a good job of flying the approach. You make altitude call-outs as you near the decision height, glancing up every now and then in the hope of seeing the runway in the murk: no such luck. The middle marker is shrieking, you're at decision height, and nothing but gray is visible out the windscreen. You need to miss the approach.

It's amazing how many times that I have repeatedly put pilots in this situation in the simulator, and they weren't prepared for what came next. I've seen numerous students fly the simulator into the ground trying to locate the missed approach procedure. If you have properly prepared for the "missed" portion of the ADM technique, you know exactly what do do. But if you have any doubt, remember that "climb" is always part of every procedure; climb straight ahead if you're lost, but get out of the altitude-critical area, and then sort things out.

According to AOPA's Air Safety Foundation, improperly executed missed approaches and VFR go-arounds accounted for roughly 4 percent of all general aviation accidents in the years 1982–1988. Four percent of all fatal accidents in the period were caused by human factors in the approach or landing abort.[1]

Missing an approach should not be a throttle-slamming, yoke-yanking event. It needs to be a smooth transition back into a climb configuration and attitude. You'll make the missed approach more easily if you fly approaches as though you expect to miss, having to change trimmed airspeed only if you sight the runway and prepare to land. I've used 110 knots as a recommended approach speed for the newer models of Beech Bonanzas in my examples because that speed is very close to the cruise-climb airspeed.

If a pilot flies an approach at that speed and needs to miss the approach, the process of smoothly applying full power will cause the airplane to pitch up to a climb attitude while trying to maintain trimmed airspeed; cleaning up the gear and flaps returns the airplane to its cruise-climb configuration at the cruise-climb airspeed, which usually is more than adequate for a missed approach, except when the airplane is at near-maximum weight and/or the airplane is flying in conditions that cause high density altitude.

I also fly approaches in that type of airplane with the mixture "full rich" or as needed for best power, and the propeller is set to climb position because that's the most efficient setting for this cruise-climb/missed approach. At the missed approach point, it only takes movement of one lever, the throttle, to establish power needed for the climbout. Many instructors teach flying "by the numbers," which is good, but make sure that the numbers by which you fly are chosen for a good reason and not just arbitrarily picked because they match a speed listed in the time portion of the instrument approach plate.

You might comment that the airplane won't be trimmed for the landing doing it this way. My answer would be that you're setting yourself up for potentially the most dangerous phase of an approach, the transition back to climb from a low altitude, and you want to make that transition as easy on yourself as you can. Besides, you have to practice the transition from high-speed flight to flare speed every time you fly, so you should get pretty good at it. But when was the last time you practiced a lot of VFR go-arounds and IMC missed approaches? Flying by the appropriate numbers prepares you for that less-practiced event.

Okay, you've reviewed the "missed" of the ADM technique before even entering the altitude-critical area, you've posted the information on the panel so that it is in your scan if you need it, and you've flown the approach in a configuration that helps you make the transition if you need to abort the approach. When you get to the missed approach point, it's obvious that you need to miss, so you successfully make a smooth transition back into a climb on a heading that takes you to safety. What next?

"What are your intentions?"

"Power up, pitch up, positive rate of climb, gear up, flaps up, cowl flaps open . . . ." You've initiated the missed approach procedure, and the airplane is settling into a healthy climb away from the obscured runway. Now it's time to talk.

Modern pilots are radio-happy. Pilots are often taught that they need to "get permission" in the form of a clearance for everything that they do. It's so prevalent that pilots flying in and out of the uncontrolled airport where I used to teach routinely called on unicom for "permission" or "instructions" to land or "clearance" to take off; we who manned the ground-based microphone sometimes had to expend a lot of effort to explain that the pilot could do pretty much what he or she wanted. Sometimes we gave up and played "pseudo controller" with a phrase similar to "At pilot's discretion, you may take off."

Where radio confusion can be most crucial is in the beginnings of a missed approach. I've seen an incredibly high number of pilots in the simulator fly excellent approaches to the missed approach point and have everything ready for the missed approach only to continue downward and fly into the ground trying to make radio contact before powering up to go around. I'd like to do a study some day of the missed-approach accidents that were probably caused because the pilot "failed to maintain positive rate of climb." I'd bet that a good percentage of those pilots, if not all of them, radioed "missed approach" before flying into the obstruction.

What's my point? When you're cleared for an approach, you're also automatically cleared for the missed approach procedure, whether as published on the approach plate or as amended by the air traffic controller. You don't need to ask permission to use that airspace because you already "own" it. Think about the rapid-fire communication exchange that calling "missed approach" initiates.

Pilot: "Metro tower, Arrow 12345, missed approach."

Tower: "Roger, Arrow 345, fly the published missed approach procedure, contact Metro Departure 134.5"

Pilot: (switches to departure frequency) "Metro Departure, Arrow 12345 missed approach Metro Airport, one thousand five hundred climbing published missed."

Departure: "Arrow 345, ident, what are your intentions?"

If you're initiating that string of radio calls before or during the time that you're also configuring your airplane for a climb toward a holding fix that might require turns or retuning navigation radios, you are needlessly increasing your workload dramatically. I am not telling you to delay unduly your required reports to ATC; what I do advocate is to follow the old axiom "aviate, navigate, communicate." Get the airplane in a stable climb, steer it in the correct direction, and *then tell ATC about it.* You don't have to ask to use the airspace, so nobody should be in your way.

Regarding "your intentions," you have to make some decisions. Do you go to your alternate? Do you fly to an airport not listed on your flight plan? Do you try the approach again? You need to engage the DECIDE model, and to do so you need to gather some information. Do you need to be doing this at the same time that you are closing in on a holding pattern? No. The purpose of a missed approach procedure is to get you out of the arrival altitude-critical area and in a block of protected airspace where you and ATC have the time to figure out what happens next. Your reply to ATC should be something like "I'll enter the published hold and get back to you."

Engage the autopilot, if you have one, after leveling off at the holding airspeed (usually the same configuration you use for approach prior to final descent), and maneuver your airplane onto the racetrack course. It's "options time." Most compelling is to try the approach again. Be very careful with this choice because it was "missed approach" the first time for a reason. The weather was below minimums, or something distracted you enough to prompt leaving the ACA to figure it out, or you botched the attempt and drifted far enough off course that you were required to execute the procedure. Unless the reason has gone away, don't even think about flying the same approach again.

Maybe the fog is reported as "patchy" and others are landing successfully. Perhaps the visibility was reduced because a departing airliner kicked dry snow into the air; the snow might settle by the time you circle around. Maybe you've replaced a landing-gear light bulb while in the holding pattern, and now you can verify "three-green." Maybe you admit that you weren't as careful as you could have been the first time and you'll concentrate more on pitch and heading to keep the needles centered on your next attempt.

These are cases where you might choose to try the approach again; however, be cautious about the second attempt because the temptation is to "go a little lower" or "fly it a little farther" on a subsequent attempt. Choosing to try the approach a second time reinforces your natural "landing expectation," which is the mind-set that you'll be able to land because others are or simply because that's where you really want to land. That mind-set can interfere with your decision making and your physical flying skills because you "will" yourself to make it to the runway. Force yourself to fly this second approach "by the book," and start the procedure with the expectation that you'll probably have to miss the approach. After all, you had to miss it just a few minutes ago.

If you need to miss the approach a second time, forget about landing at that airport that day. The accident reports are rife with stories of multiple approaches eventually ending in accidents, such as the NTSB account of this Beech Travel Air twin.

The commercial pilot, who held multiengine and instrument ratings, was attempting an early evening trip from Alabaster, Alabama, to Atlanta's Fulton County Airport. With over 2000 hours total flight time and 200 in his Travel Air, the pilot was fully qualified to safely make the flight. The airplane had almost three hours' worth of fuel on board, which was more than necessary for the flight.

Atlanta's weather wasn't helping. Flight service had briefed the pilot before takeoff, citing a 200-foot overcast and ¾ mile visibility in light drizzle and fog. The temperature and dew point both measured 52°F. The forecast was rosier: 400-foot overcast and half a mile with an occasional 800-and-2 condition. The pilot decided to try.

He reached the Atlanta area at around 7 p.m. The temperature and dew points were still locked at 52 degrees (an indication that conditions shouldn't be expected to be any better than earlier), and Fulton County was reporting an indefinite ceiling of 100 feet, obscured, and ¾-mile visibility. Nevertheless, the pilot accepted clearance for the ILS Runway 8 approach, which required at least 1 mile visibility and a 273-foot ceiling with the minimums published at the time.

As expected, the pilot missed the approach. He asked for vectors to try again, and he missed a second time. After the second missed approach, the Travel Air pilot began to ask questions. The tower reported a continuing visibility of less than 1 mile but also reported that other airplanes had successfully landed before the Beech. "No problems before you," the controller put it.

The Travel Air pilot elected to try the approach again, which again required a missed approach. "It looks pretty bad out here," he radioed the tower. "I can't see a thing." Nonetheless, he claimed to have "caught a glimpse" of the runway lights on the third attempt, so he asked to try it again. While on vectors for his fourth approach, he told approach that if he had to miss once more he would divert. The controller recommended nearby DeKalb-Peachtree Airport, where some airplanes had been able to land despite the weather. The pilot replied: "That's a negative, sir. If I can't make it in, I'd really rather just go home."

On an amazing fifth attempt to complete the ILS into Fulton County Airport, 1 hour and 15 minutes after first checking in with the approach controller, the Travel Air strayed south of the localizer course. When queried by the controller, the pilot advised that he was getting a lot of yaw but he was correcting. Soon afterward, he reported a loss of engine power. There were no further transmissions from the Beechcraft before it crashed into the woods west of the airport killing the pilot. Again from the cited source, investigators later could find no evidence of mechanical failure prior to impact. The NTSB concluded, "The loss of engine power resulted from the pilot's failure to properly use carburetor heat. The pilot (then) failed to maintain flying speed during the emergency descent, which resulted in a stall on final approach."

To speculate further, the lack of carburetor heat might have resulted from the pilot's landing-expectation mind-set. The multiple approach attempts might have so consumed his thinking that he failed to accomplish basic steps of an approach checklist, such as applying carb heat for the descent.

If the pilot had adhered to some basic tenets of cockpit management, perhaps the outcome would have been different. First, with current weather of 200 and ¾ and a forecast of 400 and ½ at destination, he should have seriously considered delaying the trip. The FSS had thrown him some bait, though; the weather was forecast to be "occasionally" 800 and two. The pilot bit and was hooked.

With that in mind, he should have expected the possibility of a missed approach. This is especially true because of the time of day; it was early evening by the time he arrived in the Atlanta area with no additional daytime heating to widen the temperature-dew point spread. Only a frontal passage or strong surface winds could have cleared the approach course, and apparently neither of these were imminent.

To his credit, the pilot seemed to be pretty good at flying approaches and missed approach procedures. Perhaps that he was "spring-loaded" in an "I-missed-the-approach-I'll-try-it-again" mind-set. Unfortunately, typical IFR training tends to reinforce this belief, whether consciously or not.

For instance, if you're working toward an instrument procedures review, what would most instructors do with you? You'd jump in the plane and fly a few approaches, missing again and again, and finally landing out of the same approach you'd been missing all along. This might just plant the seed in your mind that if you try enough times you'll be able to land out of any approach. Maybe this unintended training result was a factor in this wreck as well.

After the second attempt, the pilot wisely started gathering information. Going directly to the source, he asked the tower controller about conditions. ATC replied that conditions were slightly above minimums, at least in visibility, and added that the Travel Air pilot was the only one who hadn't completed the approach with a landing. ATC's statement might have triggered a need in the pilot to prove that he could do it.

One thing that strikes me about this accident report is that the pilot's age and experience mirror mine at the time of this writing, except that my multiengine time is in Barons, not Travel Airs. I could see myself being talked into a third try at the approach "because everyone else is making it" unless I was very careful. Remember, the other pilots might have been lucky or might even have been busting minimums, or maybe it's just the difference between altimeter tolerances that's causing one plane to miss when others aren't. You have no way of knowing; the only information you have at decision height is what you see out your own windscreen. Don't let others tell you otherwise.

What can we learn from this? If he had considered that taking off almost certainly meant missing the approach and landing elsewhere, he could have safely begun his trip; if he had decided beforehand not to try an approach a second time unless conditions were measurably better, and that under no circumstances would he try a third approach, he'd probably be alive today. The "probable cause" of this Travel Air accident was the failure of the pilot to use carburetor heat and subsequently a failure to maintain airspeed with a dead engine, but the real cause of this accident seems to be poor decision making.

When you've decided not to try an approach again, are you stuck with going to the alternate that you filed on your flight plan? What if conditions didn't require an alternate when filing, but you still had to miss an approach? Filing an alternate airport is for your personal planning purposes only. The regulations require an alternate in certain weather conditions simply to force you to consider the possibility of a missed.

Look at the "1-2-3" rule governing the filing of an alternate. If plus or minus 1 hour from your estimated arrival time the ceiling is forecast to be less than 2000 feet and/or the visibility under 3 miles, you have to declare an alternate. Two thousand feet and 3 miles is fairly good VFR weather. The rule is that if there's even a chance you'll have to fly an instrument approach, there's the possibility you might have to miss it; you need to make sure you have enough fuel to get somewhere else before you ever take off. How do you know you have sufficient fuel? You have to pick an alternate airport and determine how much fuel you'll need to get there legally after the miss. Filing an alternate is the FAA's way of telling you to double-check your fuel reserves.

Once you've missed an approach, you are not committed to your filed alternate. A good example of this is a common situation I had while instructing out of Beech Field or Colonel James Jabara on the east edge of Wichita. Both airports are served by only VOR approaches with fairly high minimums, and it wasn't too uncommon that we'd have to file an alternate outside of the Wichita area and miss the approach at the end of a training flight because we couldn't get in to our departure airport. For purposes of planning, we often filed Hutchinson or Salina as an alternate because conditions were much better there, but at the time we flew the approach, Wichita Mid-Continent Airport, which is 10 miles away on the west side of town, was reporting weather above ILS minimums. After missing the approach, we told ATC we'd divert to Mid-Continent. (We'd give Beech or Jabara one shot, if for no other reason than real-world training.) It was that easy.

Crosswinds. Everything I've said about instrument approaches and the missed approach holds true in conditions of strong crosswinds as well. If the wind is gusty or doesn't quite line up with the pavement, there's always the possibility that conditions are beyond the airplane's or your own personal capabilities.

Landings in gusting winds and crosswinds account for nearly 40 percent of all weather-related general aviation accidents, according to the AOPA Air Safety Foundation. On the whole, airplanes are quite capable of handling the extremes of wind. It's generally the pilot who hasn't maintained crosswind-landing currency that finds that conditions are beyond his or her abilities only after it's too late.

Just as an instrument rated pilot puts together a regimen for maintaining IFR skills, all pilots need to think about the current state of their crosswind ability. Here's an exercise. When a good 10- to 15-knot wind is blowing more or less straight down the runway at your "home 'drome," jump in the airplane and do a few full-stop takeoffs and landings. Then fly to a nearby airport with a runway that is a little out of kilter with the wind, something with a computed crosswind component of about 5 knots or so. Make a few takeoffs and landings in this comparatively small crosswind component until you've got the feel of it, and then move on to a runway with a 7- or 8-knot crosswind and practice some more.

Keep working your way around the local runways until you've practiced crosswinds in the 15-knot range. Also practice go-arounds at each airstrip to get the feel of drift correction at the beginning of your climbout. If at any point you feel uncomfortable or that you're not going to be able to maintain runway alignment, go around and fly home. You've found a "personal crosswind limit" as it exists in that airplane on that day (Fig. 7-10).

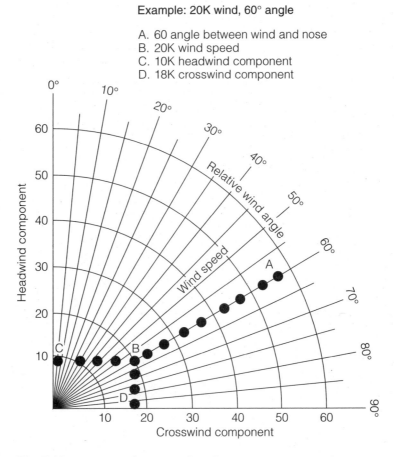

Example: 20K wind, 60° angle

A. 60 angle between wind and nose
B. 20K wind speed
C. 10K headwind component
D. 18K crosswind component

Fig. 7-10. *A crosswind computation chart.*

Let's say the greatest crosswind component you could comfortably handle was computed at 12 knots. That's your absolute, which you arrived at only after practicing up to that level. Knock a couple of knots off your personal-best to make 10 knots the final calculation of your personal crosswind limit. Before takeoff, be certain that conditions are within your capabilities; if not, depart on a different runway with a smaller crosswind component, if a runway is available, or wait until the wind alignment improves. Getting ready to land? Compare the reported wind speed and direction to the runway in use. If the crosswind is within your limits, fine; otherwise, divert to another airport with a runway that is within your ability to land safely.

Do you crab into the wind or fly the wing-low method? Both techniques are valid, and at one time or another I have taught crosswind landings both ways. I present both methods in flight training and decide along with the student which seems to work better for the individual. The wing-low method has one clear advantage, however; if you establish a wing-low attitude on final approach that compensates for the wind, you'll know before you begin your flare whether you and the airplane are capable of compensating for the drift that is present that day. If you have a lot of trouble maintaining runway alignment on final approach using the wing-low method, you'll probably have even greater difficulty during the flare and on rollout when the slower airspeed makes the control surfaces less effective. If you can't stay lined up on short final, go somewhere else. Using the crab method, you won't be able to make this evaluation until you've actually begun the flare.

The descent, approach, and landing phases of flight are historically the most dangerous. Pilot workload naturally increases as you near the surface. Fatigue is at its greatest just when you need to be at your best. Although the factors that cause accidents often originate in other phases of flight, it's when the pilot attempts to land that he or she often comes to grief. Practicing good cockpit management will allow you to reduce as much as possible the workload in these crucial phases of flight, and you will be more able to concentrate on the unusual and the unexpected factors that threaten the safety of your flight.

8
Risk factors

ALL HUMAN UNDERTAKINGS ENTAIL RISK. SOME, LIKE SKYDIVING OR BUNGEE jumping, are purely recreational activities; the risk level is very high, but the necessity is low (at least for most people), and few therefore are willing to take the risk. Others, like driving a car, seem to be almost a basic human need in our society, and despite the horrific deaths and injuries that occur on the highways each year, virtually everybody drives. We accept that risk because in our minds the rewards are worth it.

The possibility of an automobile accident lurks in the back of the mind. To reduce the risk of driving, standard right-of-way rules have been adopted, taxes are paid to build and maintain roadways, and safety-related devices such as seat belts and air bags are mandated. In this way, we've done what we can to reduce the risk of an accident and reduce the chances of injury if an accident does occur. We have tried to manage the risk of driving in order to realize its benefits.

We do the same thing in aviation. Rules and regulations can obviously be restrictive and impersonal sometimes, but the rules allow us a freedom virtually unknown anywhere else in the world. Our fuel and other taxes help pay for the National Airspace System plus research and development, which brings the benefits of general aviation to the public whether they know it or not. Great strides have been made in equipment reliability and airplane crashworthiness. General aviation is safer now than it ever has been.

Chapter eight

Aviation nonetheless is inherently risky, and to be safe you need to consciously manage that risk. Sometimes managing the risk is obvious. No sane pilot would do certain things, for instance taking off in the middle of an ice storm. It's when the risk factors are not quite so apparent that pilot decision making breaks down. Risk is cumulative, if not multiplicative; the *effect* of individual risk factors becomes greater than the specific factors themselves, a form of negative synergy, or a "the-whole-is-greater-than-the-sum-of-its-parts" combination that can seriously degrade safety. Consider this flight from Florida to Texas that was related in the December 1993 issue of *AOPA Pilot*.

I had been planning the trip to Texas for weeks and was anxious to see my girlfriend in Houston Friday night. Prior to my departure from Boca Raton, Florida, a check with flight service confirmed my suspicions that it would be difficult, if not impossible, to circumnavigate a cold front across my route with IFR conditions and embedded thunderstorms stretching from the Gulf of Mexico to Illinois.

The first task was to find a VFR passage through the Florida panhandle, which was pretty well socked in behind the well-defined front. After flying north to Jacksonville and southwest to Tampa without finding a hole in the weather system, it seemed the only way to reach Houston that night was by flying a couple of hundred miles in the soup. Since earning my instrument rating nearly five years earlier, most of my actual instrument experience was limited to popping up through low scud on departure to fly VFR-on-top or flying an instrument approach to an airport reporting conditions well above minimums.

I hate flying in the soup. It gives me butterflies; every unexpected sound raises the specter of some mechanical emergency. Nonetheless, my 1983 Turbo Saratoga was well maintained, and all systems appeared functional. My girlfriend was impatiently waiting, and I really didn't want to spend the night in a strange town with the possibility of an IFR departure the next morning. After landing at Gainesville to check with flight service, I learned that instrument conditions extended only to Pensacola, with excellent VFR from that point all the way to Houston.

It was getting very close to dark when I departed Gainesville, quickly disappearing into a solid cloud deck at 500 feet. By the time I was approaching Tallahassee, outside illumination was almost nil, and those old butterflies were busily flapping their wings in my stomach. Radio checks on the weather revealed that most airports within a 100-mile radius were reporting near-minimum conditions, and I was encountering moderate turbulence and heavy rain. Nothing showed up on the Stormscope, but the airplane felt like a roller coaster at times.

I suddenly noticed my transponder display was completely dark. There was no way to tell what code I was "squawking" or if the transponder was working at all. About that time, Tallahassee Approach also notified me of my transponder problem. I mentally reviewed how seriously I had compromised my personal safety standards on this flight. The risk factors included: single-pilot, single-engine, IFR, moderate turbulence, night, and near-minimum conditions.

Now I couldn't tell if my transponder was working properly. That finally awakened me to the fact that I had far exceeded my comfort level as a pilot. I wasn't just uncomfortable—my insides were like an overtightened guitar string. Would the string break during my "performance?" It wasn't until I picked up my microphone that I saw my hands shaking as I asked Tallahassee for an ILS approach. Even if it was IFR the next day, at least I would be flying in daylight.

Runway lights have never looked as good as they did when I finally broke out of the clouds 300 feet above the ground, with about 1 mile visibility in fog and rain. I taxied up to the FBO, tried to act cool as a cucumber, and asked for a ride to the nearest motel (while wondering if I had been cowardly to cut my flight short just because of a transponder problem).

I awakened to a chilly, foggy morning on Saturday, but flight service promised VFR conditions by 10 a.m., and it didn't let me down. Soon, I was wheels up and flying across the panoramic forests of the Florida panhandle with a beautiful view of the Gulf of Mexico out my left window. I settled back in my seat, put the airplane on autopilot, and marveled at how wonderful it felt to be piloting my Saratoga on such a gorgeous day. While blissfully cruising along, I casually glanced at a small airport just outside the small town of De Funiak Springs.

One minute later, my engine began to cough severely, and it was obvious that it was rapidly losing power. I sat bolt upright in my seat, my heart pounding, and called Eglin Air Force Base to report the problem while banking into a 180-degree turn. My eyes, squinting into the direct sunlight, began a search for that little airport. Eglin asked if I was declaring an emergency, and I told them no because the propeller was still spinning, and the engine noise, although sporadic, gave me some sense of security.

By the time I crossed the threshold and touched down on De Funiak Springs' 3000-foot runway, it was obvious that my engine problem was serious. The Saratoga sounded like a circus jalopy as it backfired all the way to the hangar. I left it with the FBO, flagged down a farmer refueling his Cessna 150, and hitched a ride to Pensacola to finish my trip on Continental Airlines.

Later, I learned the engine had experienced a catastrophic failure, causing substantial damage to the cylinders, crankshaft, and the like. A major engine rebuild was required.

I don't push it so close to the limits anymore. If that transponder had not acted up, I could have lost my engine over the Florida panhandle the previous night in the soup and would have faced an emergency landing in thick forests. It is doubtful I would have walked away. Since that flight, I have raised my "personal minimums" to improve the margin of safety. My girl-friend would rather have me arrive late and in one piece.[1]

The author of this account nearly learned the hard way the hazards of assuming too much risk on a flight. Through a stroke of good fortune, a minor annoyance (the transponder failure) caused him to eliminate the risk by landing early, thereby avoiding a probable crash. How did he know that enough was enough, that the risk was too great to continue the flight? How can you evaluate the risk of a flight, determine personal minimums, and manage the risk to make valid go-no-go decisions?

EVALUATING RISK

To accurately evaluate the risk of a flight, you have to assess the impact of a horde of variables. To make sense of it all, and to make an informed decision about beginning or continuing a flight, it helps to group the variables into four categories: the plane, the pilot, the environment, and the situation.[2]

The plane

The type of airplane you're flying and the equipment that it has on board are going to determine the level of risk involved in a flight; however, more equipment does not always mean less risk. For instance, flying a marginally IFR-equipped airplane like a typical Cessna 172 or Piper Cherokee might be riskier than operating its VFR counterpart because the IFR airplane might lull a pilot into a false sense of security about bad-weather flying.

Similarly, an extra engine is not always a good thing. Using information from the AOPA Air Safety Foundation, NASA, and NTSB I did a study of the fatal accident rates of Bonanzas and Barons, which are essentially identical airplanes except for the number of engines. I found that predictably the Baron pilot had about twice the chance of experiencing an engine failure than his or her Bonanza counterpart. Twice as many engines means twice the chances of losing an engine, considering the number of hours flown.

The fatal accident rate resulting from loss of an engine in a Baron, however, was almost exactly twice that of fatal engine failures in Bonanzas. In the single, the choice is easy; an engine failure means a landing, usually straight ahead. In a twin, however, sharp piloting technique is required to keep the airplane under control if an engine quits, and historically pilots don't do a good job of managing a failed engine in any twin. The Baron pilot was four times as likely to die from an engine failure in the course of a flying career. Of course, recent training will manage this risk; we'll look at human factors in a moment.

Brainstorm some airplane-related risk factors. You might come up with a list like this:

- Single engine
- Twin engine
- Conventional gear (tailwheel)

- High performance
- Well maintained
- VFR only
- Basic IFR
- Full IFR
- Deice equipment
- Icing-certified
- Radar-equipped
- Stormscope/Strike Finder

You'll undoubtedly come up with more.

Each separate risk factor is neither good nor bad; however, any combination of these and other risk factors will help you make go-no-go decisions. For instance, a tailwheel airplane is generally more risky than a tricycle-gear type; if you have any doubt, ask your insurance agent for a quote on a Cessna 170 versus a 172! However, tailwheel airplanes are the mount of choice among back-country operators for the greater prop clearance when rolling on rough surfaces; an Idaho bush pilot might tell you landing a 172 is riskier than landing a 170. Look at this list and see how the airplane you fly relates to the other categories of risk when making your decision whether to begin or continue a flight.

The pilot

As we've seen before, human factors are the most crucial variable in decisions that impact the safety of flight. How can you evaluate the risk you have as a pilot when the factors affecting that risk change from day to day? I modified a pilot self-evaluation checklist put out by the FAA; it's called the "I'M SAFE" model. Each letter of the model is related to a checklist item.[3]

I: Illness. Is there any illness that affects your ability to fly today? If you've ever tried to fly with a sinus head cold, for instance, you know that the pain can be excruciating. As you climb in altitude, gases trapped in your nasal and ear passages naturally expand, but swollen tissues prevent those gases from venting into the atmosphere. The result is extreme pressure against the inside of your skull, your sinuses, and your eardrums. Do you feel feverish? This is a sign of some illness that might at the very least affect your decision-making ability and at the most prevent you from competently manipulating the flight controls. Gastrointestinal distress can be especially debilitating. If you don't feel well, you can't fly well.

M: Medication. Are you taking any drugs that limit your ability to fly safely? Just about any prescription medication for a nonchronic illness will prevent you from passing a flight physical. If you're taking medicine for a short period of time, it's usually a no-go item. Remember, the flight surgeon certifies you as fit to fly for the long haul, but it's your responsibility to determine your own fitness on a day-to-day basis. If you have any question about whether a particular over-the-counter or prescription medicine will "ground" you, ask your flight surgeon. If you're nervous about bringing it up with a person who has the authority to deny you a medical certificate, that alone should be enough to tell you not to fly.

S: Stress. I've alluded to this factor quite a bit already in this book. Stress can be a positive motivational factor, to a point. An individual desire for excellence, for instance, might drive you to concentrate on your flying precision and force you to stay within one dot either way on the localizer and glideslope, and that's going to make you safer when flying an approach. When this ego-driven stress becomes so great that you fixate on the needles, however, it erodes safety; you might be the sort that keeps the needles centered all the way to impact because your "need" to maintain precision was so demanding that you forgot to monitor altitude as well. You have entered the realm of "negative stress."

Many forms of external pressures vie for your attention. You might have an important job presentation to make after landing, or you might have argued with your spouse or companion before takeoff because this trip makes you miss a Little League game. The weather might be closing in at destination, and your passengers can't understand why you're sitting under blue skies delaying your departure. Your accountant might have warned that you'll have to sell the airplane if you don't use it more. Any one of these or a hundred other situations has the potential to affect your flight-safety decision making; the trick is to leave the stressors behind and concentrate solely on the task at hand, completing a flight safely. If you can't stop worrying about the job presentation or the family argument, find some other way to travel.

A: Alcohol. Alcohol has absolutely no place in or near the cockpit. Accident statistics clearly show that alcohol-affected pilots almost always crash; the accidents are almost universally fatal.

The good news is that society's view of alcohol use has changed such that the instances of alcohol-impaired aviating seem to be lessening. People have come to realize the dangers of driving drunk, and that emerging attitude has carried over into airplanes as well. Unfortunately not everyone has stayed in line, and people still occasionally drive and fly drunk. And they die, often taking innocent victims along with them. There is a strict 8-hour bottle-to-throttle rule in the Federal Aviation Regulations, but this represents a minimum sobering-up period. Either 12 or 24 hours between the last drink and the beginning of flight planning would be a safer standard. Notice that I said "flight planning," not "flight," because a large portion of aviation mishaps can be traced to a poor decision made during the flight-planning process. It stands to reason that pilots should be completely free from the effects of alcohol while planning, not just conducting, a flight.

F: Fatigue. Weariness is another hard-to-measure component of pilot safety; fatigue's effects are actually quite similar to alcohol impairment. Garbled decision making, impaired motor skills, and lack of concentration are all symptoms of the lack of rest that can kill a pilot.

I've already mentioned a personal rule I have about rest and flying, but it bears repeating here. I tend to be at my best in the mornings; therefore, if at all possible, I'll plan a trip to leave early and arrive at the destination early in the day. This keeps my flight time aligned with my periods of peak personal effectiveness. If I'm forced into flying in the afternoon, I try to have at least half an hour "quiet time" alone before making the flight; this opportunity to rejuvenate is a go/no-go item if the flight is to start after 4 p.m. If I have to take off after 6 o'clock in the evening, I require at least a half-hour nap that afternoon, or I don't fly. If I need to be some place else at the start of business in the morning, I'm better off to check into a hotel the night before and get up around 3 a.m. to make the trip in the morning.

Consider the entire flight, not just the takeoff. Fatigue will increase during the flight due to the stress of piloting the airplane and the noise and vibration of the airplane; therefore, you'll be much more fatigued at the end of a trip. Recall the cruciality of the landing phase of flight; you need to plan your trip so that you are not too tired when reaching your destination. Do anything that can reduce the onset of fatigue. Intelligent use of the autopilot, while still monitoring the flight and with enough "hand-flying" practice to remain truly current, will stay the effects of fatigue. A good headset or at least a well-fitting pair of ear plugs likewise will reduce fatigue. Isometric exercises in the cockpit have been shown to improve the performance of long-distance pilots; the exercises might also help you.

E: Experience. The Federal Aviation Regulations spell out rules of experience required for a pilot to legally command a flight. Remember that most FARs are the result of an accident; these regulations on experience are an attempt to avoid the causes of actual accidents in the past. Remember also that the regulations represent absolute minimum safe standards.

First, in order to operate as pilot-in-command, you're required to hold at least a recreational or private pilot certificate. Of course you can fly solo on a student license, but under the direct supervision of an instructor. I have, however, seen a few cases where a person is afraid of taking the written exam or unable to pass a checkride and continued to renew student pilot licenses. I even know of a particular case where a man flew on a student license for several decades, owning among other things a Mooney and a Bonanza along the way. I'd like to think he knew that he was not only breaking the law, but also that he was violating a tenet of flying safety. He didn't even meet the barest minimum experience requirements, yet he launched cross-country regularly.

Once appropriately licensed, pilots need to have a flight review (FR) to practice the privileges of their certificates. Instituted in the early 1970s, the FR is a way of encouraging recurrent training by making refresher training mandatory on at least an infrequent basis. True, many holdouts feel that they don't need or want a review, but most of the pilots that I have worked with far outdo the minimum requirements.

Do you fly a complex or high-performance airplane? (Recall that a high-performance airplane will have retractable landing gear, a controllable-pitch propeller, and/or an engine with more than 200 horsepower.) Is it a tailwheel design? Unless you logged pilot-in-command time prior to the effective dates of the rulings, you have to get specialized training in the class of airplane, and a logbook endorsement from a CFI stating you're qualified to operate the type.

If you have a license, a current FR, and the appropriate sign-off, you're free to do whatever you want solo in an airplane, within reason of course; however, if you want to carry passengers, you must maintain some minimum standard of currency. Three takeoffs and landings in the last 90 days are required to carry passengers; this requirement is met by aircraft class (single-engine land, multiengine land), so it's possible to be legal for passengers in a twin but not in a single if you haven't kept your logged landing count up. If the airplane is a tailwheel design, all landings have to be to a full stop; the differences between tricycle and conventional gear are most obvious when taking off and landing. Similarly, night currency requires full-stop landings at night. Meet these minimum standards and you can carry passengers.

You can earn a license, sit for 1 year 11 months and 29 days, and then legally jump in an airplane solo and fly. You're legal, but are you safe? Some people actually think so. Like your medical certificate, however, the license and/or flight review are just a snapshot indication of your legality to fly at the starting point. It's your responsibility to ensure that you are truly safe from that point on.

In my case, I just changed jobs and bought a new house. I have not had time to fly in the last month or so, and I have only logged about 15 hours in the last 90 days. I am still current by every measure; my instrument currency (addressed in a minute) is even still "up" by logged experience alone. I am not going to go rent an airplane, throw in my wife and child, and launch into instrument conditions or night flight without a little practice first. I'm legal, but there's enough doubt in my mind that I'm probably not totally safe at night or in the clouds.

What do I do? It's time to find a safety pilot or an instructor and work on retaining currency. How can you use currency in making your go-no-go decision? It's up to you, but if you've kept your VFR experience within regulatory limits in the last 90 days, but haven't flown in the last month, it's time for some flying. Practice stalls, steep turns, and takeoffs and landings, which are the basis of the private pilot checkride. The maneuvers and tasks are designed to prepare you for the worst an airplane might throw at you. Have a night cross-country coming up? Wait for a calm and clear evening, and make several trips around the traffic pattern. Then flight plan, file, and make a short "round-robin" cross-country trip. It doesn't have to take more than an hour, but get away from the bright lights of a city, practice a little en-route navigation in the dark, and find a different airport for a practice landing along the way. Now you're ready to load up the family and go.

What if your trip is to be in actual instrument conditions? Obviously you need to hold an instrument rating for the class of airplane (single or multi) that you will be flying. There are also several ways to legally retain currency for instrument flight.

First, you're good for six months after the checkride. Get as much experience as you can, slowly expanding your envelope. If you log at least six actual or simulated instrument approaches, including navigation tracking and holding procedures, you've maintained the minimum currency standard. "Actual" instrument time, according to federal guidelines, means time physically in the clouds, not just on an instrument flight plan; "simulated" time is flown solely by reference to instruments (though not necessarily requiring a view-limiting device) with a CFII or other qualified safety pilot acting as observer. "Actual" or "simulated" instrument approaches are those where at least one published segment of the approach is flown without outside visual reference.

If you fail to stay IFR current by experience in the first six months following your checkride, a second six-month period begins when you can log the minimum approaches, tracking and holding to regain currency. You can't do this without a CFII in "actual" conditions, because you're no longer current to fly IFR as pilot in command, but you can find a safety pilot and log the procedures in VMC as "simulated" time.

If you've not been "current' for over a year, or if before that time you wish to work with a certified instrument instructor, you have the option of logging an Instrument Procedures Check (IPC) to restart your six-month currency counter. An IPC is a logbook endorsement from an authorized instructor, stating you have taken dual instruction and met at least the minimum standards established in the practical test standards for the instrument rating. There are no specified limits or number of approaches or procedures called for in an IPC, and it's the instructor's call whether you meet at least the minimum standards.

Of course, you always have the option of calling up the FAA and arranging to take the instrument rating practical test ("oral" and "flight" checkride) over again; however, there's a catch. If you opt for this method and don't meet standards, the FAA has the right to take away your instrument rating. That's why very few pilots choose this route to maintain instrument currency, despite their confidence in their abilities.

Are you really IFR ready? "Meeting minimums" does not translate into a "yes." Meeting minimums means that you have the option of deciding whether or not you're safe; if you're not legally current, the decision has been made for you. If a month has gone by without some sort of actual or simulated instrument flight, maybe you need to go out and practice a little IFR navigation under the hood with a safety pilot and log a few approaches of various sorts to judge for yourself whether you're safe. Use this as your guide: Would you feel comfortable riding in the back seat of the airplane if the pilot were flying to the same level of proficiency that you're exhibiting? If you can truthfully say "yes," then you're safe to fly in the clouds.

Strong gusts or crosswinds are another type of currency factor. Although there are no federal rules about recency of experience in crosswinds, this environmental factor is one of the most common elements of takeoff and landing accidents in tricycle-gear craft as well as taildraggers. Like your instrument currency, you'll need to practice crosswinds as much as possible to set limits for yourself.

Currency is yet another variable in making the go/no-go decision. A subsequent subsection of this chapter examines how experience combines with other factors.

The environment

The environment includes all those risk factors external to the pilot and the airplane. Typically two parts of the environment affect a flight: weather and time of day.

Tomes have been written about weather factors in aviation, yet according to some sources, meteorology is a factor in as many as 40 percent of all general aviation accidents. When regarding the weather as a risk factor, use the flight service station "categorical outlook" model as a guide. Ask yourself which of the following best describes the weather for your trip:

- VFR: Visibility exceeds 5 miles and ceiling is higher than 3000 feet.
- MVFR: Marginal VFR. Visibility is between 3 and 5 miles and/or ceiling is between 1000 and 3000 feet.
- IFR: Visibility is between 1 and 3 miles and/or ceiling is between 500 and 1000 feet.
- LIFR: Low IFR. Visibility less than 1 mile and/or ceiling is lower than 500 feet.

Now compare the categorical weather description to your license and experience. For instance, if you do not have an instrument rating, or if the airplane you're flying isn't certified and equipped for IFR operations, simply don't fly anywhere the weather is reported or forecast to be less than marginal VFR. If the weather was okay on takeoff but conditions change to worse than marginal VFR up ahead, divert around the bad stuff or make a precautionary landing at the closest suitable airport. Sure, the weather might look all right where you are at the time, but the old adage goes that you'd rather be on the ground wishing you were flying, than flying and wishing you were on the ground.

If you're an IFR pilot, within currency, and in an airplane equipped and certified for instrument flight, you of course have greater flexibility in making go/no-go decisions. It's a good idea, however, to view "low IFR" reports and forecasts as automatic no-go items unless you're certain that you have significantly better conditions as an alternate well within the range of your airplane. Don't take off into bad weather without a firm idea of which direction will take you toward improving conditions, just in case the weather worsens along the intended route.

Treat thunderstorms the same way you would marginal VFR conditions if you're a VFR pilot and similarly to low-IFR reports if you're flying IFR. You may give it a try, if you want, but not without a solid idea of which way will take you away from the threat if you come up against a thunderhead. Forecast ice in the clouds warrants a similar plan for the IFR pilot; freezing rain or sleet that is forecast or occurring are definite no-go items for anyone.

Is your flight going to take place at night? Take the actual forecast (VFR, MVFR, IFR, or LIFR), and adjust it downward a notch, then plan accordingly. For instance, marginal VFR conditions should be approached just like IFR conditions if the flight occurs at night; therefore, night MVFR is a definite no-go item for the VFR pilot or airplane and should require an instrument flight plan and clearance for the properly rated pilot. The horrendous accident rate at night in marginal conditions mandates this strategy.

The situation

It is time to take the risk factors and link them together into a go/no-go decision. You can, if you like, make yourself a list of the aircraft, pilot, and environmental factors that affect you, and then see how much risk an individual flight entails. For example, let's say I'm going to fly a Beech Bonanza on a cross-country trip with the family to a holiday gathering. Here are some of the factors potentially affecting my flight:

- Single-engine airplane
- IFR conditions
- Possible ice in clouds
- Short daylight hours
- Family-induced time pressure
- Lack of recent night flight
- Lack of recent IFR flight
- Aircraft maintenance
- Physical fitness
- Fatigue
- Minor medications
- Job pressures

Jotting down the possible factors affecting a safe flight, I can now "tick off" any that actually apply to that flight. Let's say I'm hoping to make the flight after work to get to the family homestead in time for dessert. I check the weather, and all's clear the entire way. Maybe these actually hold true for this trip:

- Single-engine airplane
- Night flight
- Family-induced time pressure
- Lack of recent night flight
- Fatigue (after a day's work)

Five "risk factors" are in place for this trip. If the flight is short and the weather is good, I can probably still make the trip safely. But let's say a sixth factor crops up during flight when some of the instrument lighting goes out. Now I'm starting to have more working against me than perhaps I would like, and it's time to sit down and wait for morning when my risk factors will be fewer. Or perhaps my destination weather is slipping into IFR conditions. Again, it might be time to reevaluate the decision to fly. Five risk factors might be an arbitrary selection on my part and might be a bit pessimistic, but whenever I use this exercise, it seems that six risk factors are enough to make me nervous about making a trip.

Let's try another one. Let's say you're planning a trip to Gatlinburg, Tennessee, to take in the shows and the scenery. You wake up on the first day of vacation and find these factors await you:

- Single-engine airplane
- Mountainous terrain
- Sinus head cold

- Minor medication
- IFR conditions

Do you go? It's your call, but if your airplane is properly certified and you hold the rating and have the experience to fly in the clouds, you can certainly try. But what if you fire up Old Reliable and find that the number two navigation radio is on the blink? Do you fly? It's legal to do so (if you make the appropriate logbook entry and placard, unless you're operating with an approved minimum equipment list), but it might not be wise. Do you really want to be flip-flopping the number one nav to identify an intersection while flying a bumpy approach in the mountains?

The situation is the sum total of the other risk factors: the airplane, the pilot, and the environment. Your job as a "risk manager" is to consciously identify what factors affect your flight and decide if the benefits of going indeed are worth the risk you're taking. Furthermore, you need to reevaluate this decision as factors change during flight and be ready to make a diversion or an early landing if the risks begin to mount beyond your threshold of safety. Remember that it all goes back to the goals you set for your flight, and you should never sacrifice safety for the lesser goals of convenience, economy, or satisfaction.

9
High-risk situations

CERTAIN PHASES OF FLIGHT ARE INHERENTLY RISKIER THAN OTHERS. WE'VE already looked at the takeoff and especially the landing as being more dangerous than any other segments of a flight mainly because of the relatively slow speed and proximity to the ground, which gives pilots little time or kinetic energy to extricate themselves from the unexpected. Other operations entail a great deal of risk. Some sources claim that if we could eliminate these causes of mishaps, we would avoid 95 percent of all "pilot error" accidents. This list of high-risk flight situations consists of:

- Taking off with a known problem
- Midair collision
- Inadequate terrain separation
- Unstabilized approach
- Deviation from standard operating procedures
- Runway incursion or landing at the wrong airport or wrong runway
- Weather
- Complacency[1]

Let's take a more detailed look at each of these situations.

TAKING OFF WITH A KNOWN PROBLEM

A good percentage of mechanically related accidents take place because the pilots take off despite knowing that a problem exists, such as a maintenance discrepancy. I've related the poor decision that I made to fly a Cessna 120 over eastern Kansas into the approaching night only to end up with a total electrical failure and eventually an unlighted night landing. I should have foreseen that some electrical failure was possible when the engine wouldn't start electrically and I was forced to find someone to "prop" the airplane to get it started.

I also mentioned a client of mine who was a bit impulsive with the auxiliary fuel pump in his B55 Baron. At the end of our flight, after finally getting back to the tiedowns, he elected (despite my urgings otherwise) to go ahead and fly home before getting the engine-drive pump fixed, using the auxiliary pump in its place. He made it without incident, but I nervously watched his takeoff and disappearance into the low-lying cloud base.

I also remember a classic misfueling scenario when a Douglas DC-3 was contaminated with jet fuel at Spirit of St. Louis Airport in Chesterfield, Missouri. According to witnesses at the scene, the pilots noticed nothing out of the ordinary during start and while on the ground (this isn't unusual in misfueling situations), but the engines would not develop enough power to get the tailwheel off the ground on the takeoff roll. The two-man crew aborted the takeoff and performed another engine runup at the far end of the runway; all was normal, so they elected to try it again.

On the second takeoff run, in the opposite direction (the winds were calm), the big transport again failed to achieve takeoff speed, so the pilots taxied to the the ramp to consult a mechanic. Again no problems were evident during the engine checks, so the crew confidently maneuvered the cargo-laden Douglas to the runway, then applied full throttle and gave it another go. Perhaps resigned to the fact that they had to take off because no problems could be discerned during normal checks, the crew forced the lumbering twin into the air when its engines coughed, backfired, and sputtered to a detonating stop. The aircraft struck the ground and burst into flames, killing both on board.

Maybe your problem isn't as dramatic as these. Perhaps the only known defect on your airplane is a malfunctioning radio. Maybe it's as simple as a tire that's a little bit low. Maybe one of the fasteners on the cowling has worked itself loose. Most likely these little sorts of defects won't cause an accident, but how long would it take to fix them before a flight? Should the absence of a backup radio be a no-go item for a night flight or an instrument flight? It's up to you to decide (Fig. 9-1).

If you should ever notice a problem with electrical generation, however, you should decide against night flight or flight into the clouds. If anything structural is less than secure, the airplane should be grounded until it's fixed. And if there is ever anything amiss with the powerplant of your airplane, don't even think about flying.

MIDAIR COLLISION

Pilots are more scared about midair collisions than just about anything else. Maybe it's the thought of careening toward the ground with absolutely no feeling of control, but I

Fig. 9-1. *What instrument failure or combination of failures would constitute a no-go decision?*

know I worry more about midairs than perhaps their frequency of occurrence warrants. Midair collisions do have some patterns, however, so you can recognize when you're in a high-risk situation and take steps to avoid the threat.

The last time that I attended a flight instructor refresher clinic, one of the aviation safety specialists from the local flight standards district office gave us a short presentation on midair collisions. He provided us with some statistics and then discussed some ways to avoid running into other airplanes in flight. One thing that struck me, if you'll pardon the pun, is that flight instructors and their students are at a greater risk of having a midair than the average pilot, and it's not because they tend to fly more.

According to the FAA, 52 percent of all midair collisions involve dual flight instruction. Instrument instruction is particularly risky; it seems that CFIIs are watching their students a little too closely and ignoring their primary function of seeing and avoiding other airplanes while the student pilot is "under the hood." Part of the problem, in my opinion, is that CFIs don't do a good job of educating other pilots about where these approach procedures take place.

For instance, if a pilot reports "final approach fix inbound" or "Hance intersection on the VOR approach," the average VFR pilot won't have a clue where to look. Instead of using IFR terminology when practicing approaches, pilots and instructors should express their positions as direction and distance from the airport. FAF inbound might become "five miles north of the airport at 3000 feet" and Hance intersection would be "seven east of the field, aiming for midfield and descending to 1800 feet." Cumbersome, perhaps, but preferable to crashing into someone who doesn't know where to look.

Speaking of education, it seems that 49 percent of all midairs involve pilots with fewer than 1000 total flying hours, and another 19 percent happen to pilots in the 1000- to 2000-hour total time range. In a whopping 90 percent of the cases, neither airplane had filed a flight plan, and 95 percent of the midairs were in day VFR conditions near an airport. In fact, 77 percent of the accidents happened below 3000 feet and within 5 miles of an airport, and 49 percent—nearly half of all midairs—happened in the airport traffic pattern. Of those, only 2 percent took place on the downwind leg, 18 percent on base, and the remaining 80 percent occurred on final approach. Eighty-two percent involved a faster airplane overtaking a slower one from behind, while only 5 percent were head-on collisions.

Several factors conspire against pilots when trying to see and avoid other airplanes. One is airplane configuration. Most airplanes, especially older designs, have some blind spots. My 1946 Cessna 120 was particularly bad for this; visibility was good looking forward and down my side of the airplane, but in the opposite direction (looking out the right while seated on the left, for example), I couldn't see much behind the trailing edge of the wing. I tried to compensate for this as much as possible by making a short heading change and then leveling the wings in a right turn to check for traffic and only then turning to my desired heading. I also "picked the wing up" a little for a look before making a turn in either direction in case there was another airplane just above my altitude in the direction that I wanted to fly.

Second, our eyes aren't really built for distant vision, except when looking straight ahead. Relying again on FAA information, an average adult can see a general aviation airplane straight ahead at about 2.7 miles. If the other airplane is but 5° off the centerline of the pilot's eyes, however, it's invisible until about nine-tenths of a mile from the viewer. At 10° off center, the pilot won't detect the other airplane until it's within half a mile; when 15° off, the other airplane will get within four-tenths of a mile before detection, and at 20° or more off the pilot's vision line, it might get within three-tenths of a mile before the pilot sees it.

This is why so many midair collisions occur at around 500 feet above ground level on the final approach course; the pilot on the straight-in is concentrating on the runway while the other pilot on base turning to final is looking everywhere *except* on the final approach course. Typically they'll be half a mile apart before either pilot will see the other unless both pilots are actively scanning beyond their directions of flight.

Other human-factors problems include eyes that tend to focus on near objects and avoid those farther away. You might think you're looking outside when your focus is still on the instruments. Also, the brain might ignore objects not seen with both eyes, so if a windshield centerpost partially obstructs your view, you might miss a converging aircraft. Lastly, objects on a collision course have no relative movement across the windshield; our eyes pick up moving objects much more quickly than stationary objects, so a collision threat might go unnoticed.

Once you have actually detected a potential collision threat, you still need time to react to avoid it. Tests show that the average pilot will take about 12.5 seconds to identify and avoid a threat—one-tenth of a second to see the hazard, 1.0 second to recognize it as an airplane, 5.0 seconds to become aware that a collision is imminent, 4.0 seconds to decide what course of action to take, four-tenths of a second for muscular reaction once a decision has been made, and 2.0 seconds for the airplane to respond to his or her commands. If the pilot is flying a 90-knot final approach, traveling one and a half nautical miles a minute (0.025 nm per second), the airplane will cover about three-tenths of a mile before any corrective action is effective. If the opposing airplane is also converging, there simply might not be enough time for a human being to see and avoid another airplane.[2]

Does this mean collision avoidance is more a matter of luck than skill? Of course not. Pilots can take steps to become more visible to others and to see other airplanes in time to react. Remain alert, and scan all around the horizon, not just in your direction of flight. Plan ahead of the airplane; employ good cockpit management, so that you have more time to look outside of the airplane. Keep the windows clean so that other airplanes will be more obvious. Adhere to standard operating procedures, such as complete traffic patterns in the proper direction. If possible, avoid the crowds; fly around, not through, airport traffic patterns, and be especially watchful near navigational facilities. Compensate for the airplane's design, as I did when making clearing turns in my Cessna 120. And use as much safety equipment as you can, including a radio and landing lights, even in the daytime.

Don't think that flying into a controlled airport absolves you of the responsibility to see and avoid other traffic, either. The closest I ever came to a midair collision was at a controlled airport with both airplanes under positive ATC control. I was instructing in a new Baron, flying left-hand VFR traffic patterns to Runway 31. Approaching from the southwest, practicing a VOR approach to Runway 3 at the same airport was a spanking-new Cessna CitationJet on a test flight prior to delivery to a customer. The C-jet had told the tower it was going to make a low approach, so I thought I knew exactly what he was going to do (Fig. 9-2).

The VFR pattern altitude at that airport is 2500 feet, and my student, an excellent pilot, had the altitude nailed on the downwind. The minimum descent altitude for the VOR Runway 3 approach is 2080 feet, which meant that the CitationJet would pass beneath us on the downwind, and then climb straight ahead, away from the airport, after reaching the airport boundary. No problem. I had the jet plainly in sight as I monitored the Baron pilot and commented on procedure. The Citation was cleared for the low approach, and we were cleared to land.

Suddenly, upon reaching MDA a couple of miles short of the threshold, the jet powered up and began to climb. The pilot had done one of two things: elected not to complete the approach or made the common IFR error of beginning the missed approach portion of a nonprecision approach immediately upon reaching MDA instead of flying level at MDA to the missed approach point.

Regardless of which was the case, the little white jet was now climbing toward us, and it looked like we'd collide over the downwind leg of this controlled airport. Because I had the jet in sight and my student did not, I took the controls and hauled into a steep turn toward the jet and across its path, taking us out of danger. The Citation

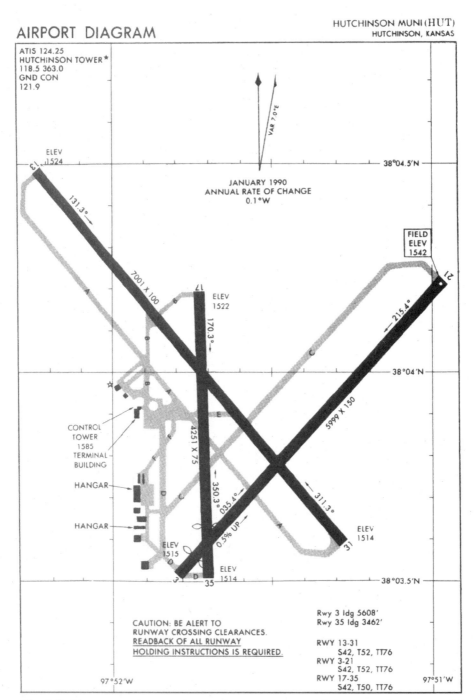

AIRPORT DIAGRAM

HUTCHINSON MUNI (HUT)
HUTCHINSON, KANSAS

ATIS 124.25
HUTCHINSON TOWER *
118.5 363.0
GND CON
121.9

VAR 7.0°E

JANUARY 1990
ANNUAL RATE OF CHANGE
0.1°W

ELEV
1524

131.3°

7001 X 100

FIELD
ELEV
1542

21

215.4°

ELEV
1522

170.3°

38°04.5'N

38°04'N

CONTROL
TOWER
1585
TERMINAL
BUILDING

4251 X 75

5999 X 150

311.3°

350.3°
035.4°

HANGAR

HANGAR

ELEV
1515

ELEV
1514

0.5% UP

ELEV
1514

38°03.5'N

CAUTION: BE ALERT TO
RUNWAY CROSSING CLEARANCES.
READBACK OF ALL RUNWAY
HOLDING INSTRUCTIONS IS REQUIRED.

Rwy 3 ldg 5608'
Rwy 35 ldg 3462'

RWY 13-31
  S42, T52, TT76
RWY 3-21
  S42, T52, TT76
RWY 17-35
  S42, T50, TT76

97°52'W

97°51'W

Fig. 9-2. *The airport diagram for Hutchinson, Kansas. A left pattern for Runway 31 was in use; the VOR approach course comes straight in from the southwest.*

passed through our altitude about where we would have been; the jet's flight path never wavered, and I doubt he ever even noticed us. The moral: Don't expect ATC to keep you out of each other's way, and if you're practicing an instrument or VFR approach procedure, do it exactly as published or prescribed because other pilots might be maneuvering based upon an expectation of what you will do.

CONTROLLED FLIGHT INTO TERRAIN

Controlled flight into terrain (CFIT), or running into an obstacle or the ground, under control in a near-level attitude continues to be a leading cause of accidents. The National Transportation Safety Board attributed 232 general aviation accidents to CFIT in the years 1982 through 1988; nearly two-thirds of those accidents were fatal. Not surprisingly, most of these mishaps take place on approach and landing, especially at night or in instrument conditions.

The key to avoiding controlled flight into terrain is altitude awareness. I've already outlined one technique to avoid altitude excursions, the altitude call-out. Especially in descent, the habit of verbalizing your current altitude, the height at which you'll level off, and the relationship between the two will help you avoid losing track of your altitude and possibly descending into the ground: "Three thousand descending to fifteen hundred. One thousand five hundred feet to go." Combined with good use of moderate climb and descent rates in the level-off altitude-critical areas, this should help you avoid most CFIT accidents.

Many CFIT collisions take place in the mountains. Ironically, most rising-terrain CFIT accidents happen within a few hundred feet of the mountaintop. Especially for pilots with little or no experience with rising terrain, flying in the mountains entails some additional planning. One thing you need to do is check the minimum safe altitudes at which you can cross ridges or mountain passes. Look at the IFR en-route charts and see if you can maintain at least the minimum en-route altitude (MEA) for each segment of your trip. MEA assures you of 2000-foot obstacle clearance, as well as positive reception of the navaids that identify a Victor airway for the entire length of each segment.

If flying VFR, you might not need the navaid reception; you can, if you wish, fly at the minimum obstacle clearance altitude (MOCA), which is identified with an altitude preceded by an asterisk on the airway depiction. MOCA assures that same 2000-foot obstacle clearance, but might not be high enough to pick up the primary VOR navaids when more than 25 nautical miles away from the transmitter. Be sure that you can positively identify your track along the ground if you plan to fly at MOCA because the VORs won't help you keep aligned with the course that the depicted altitude is designed for.

Take a good look at the VFR charts for your route. Make sure you can positively identify landmarks that will keep you lined up with the pass you've chosen. It's easy to get confused and follow the wrong canyon upslope; you might find yourself at a dead end with no room to turn the plane around. If you even begin to feel lost navigating your way up a canyon, turn around while you have the chance and find an unmistakable landmark to verify your route, then try again.

Don't try to fly VFR in mountains under a cloud layer unless you're absolutely certain the entire pass is clear. Open skies at your departure airport and at destination don't mean that the route between the peaks will be clear. You might have to wait, but don't go until you have a reliable pilot report of conditions en-route. Cloud layers tend to have fairly uniform bases, so an overcast that is 2000 feet above your departure field might obscure the passes that are another 2000 feet higher in elevation.

More and more, pilots use loran and GPS for accurate point-to-point navigation in good weather as well as in bad. Traditional sources of IFR safe altitude information (en route charts, etc.) generally don't provide safety data for off-airways routes. If you're flying "direct," or by way of great-circle routing, you'll need to look at the sectional charts to derive your own minimum obstruction clearance altitude (MOCA); because altitude versus navaid reception presumably won't be a problem with GPS, MOCA is a more correct term than minimum en route altitude in this case. This will be a major player with the growing concept of "free flight," the scenario for the future where all pilots chose their own altitudes and routes using GPS for navigation and some sort of cockpit traffic alerter to detect other airplanes, even in IMC.

Plan your own flight, including minimum crossing altitudes, on the basis of VFR charts, and remember to plot the locations of changes in your MOCAs. Remember also that these altitudes might not always guarantee communications radio reception. When I fly from Wichita to Santa Fe, a once-a-year trip, I usually get this report as I'm handed off to Albuquerque Center: "November 12345, contact Albuquerque Center 123.5. You're below the base of radio coverage; attempt contact every 15 minutes." This is at the 10,000-foot MEA, on airways! Undoubtedly, then, off-airways navigation might often put you in unusual situations, especially west of the Mississippi where ATC facilities are less numerous.

Check the minimum obstacle clearance altitude against your airplane's performance charts. Most nonturbocharged airplanes have service ceilings (where they cannot climb more than 50 fpm at V_x speed) and absolute ceilings (where no climb at all is possible) at altitudes from 13,000 to 18,000 feet. Look in the pilot's operating handbook to determine the maximum altitude. My Cessna 120 "manual" that was typical of the day was little more than a sales brochure with pictures of an airplane pulled alongside a swimming pool, and it didn't list a service or an absolute ceiling. I thought one day it would be fun to see what the ceilings might be.

I loaded the airplane as close to gross weight as I could and took off, climbing into a stiff southwesterly wind. Up and up I went, knowing I couldn't top 12,500 feet for more than half an hour nor cross 14,000 feet for want of supplemental oxygen. It was summer, however, and the air was warm; at about 9000 feet, holding V_x speed kept me in level flight, while going slower nibbled at a stall, and the added drag of faster airspeeds netted a descent. I had found my absolute ceiling.

That 9000-foot mark seemed a little low until I realized that service and absolute ceilings are measured in air density; therefore, density altitude should be used to evaluate whether an airplane has the "oomph" to make it over a mountain pass. Looking at accident records, it's not unusual to read about airplanes that just wouldn't climb even though well below published service ceilings; the pilot was probably using actual altitude and not density altitude when the decision was made to try. Reduce the weight of the airplane, or better yet wait for temperatures to cool so that you can accurately predict airplane performance at the pass height before trying to cross mountains in a naturally aspirated airplane.

What about scud running? Low-level VFR flight in poor visibility or low cloud decks accounts for a good percentage of CFIT accidents. You have already learned how to factor in variables such as weather and pilot ability to make a go/no-go decision. If you do elect to fly underneath a low cloud base or in reduced visibility, take a few precautions. Spend some "quality time" with your sectional chart to memorize the locations and heights of obstacles along your path. Plan to use prominent landmarks to plot your course; radio navaids might not be usable at low altitudes, loran might drop offline because of precipitation static, and GPS tells you where you are in relationship to airports and such, but not hills or radio towers.

Make the flight at a slow cruise speed because the faster you fly, the harder it will be to see an object in time to maneuver around it. Also, flying slower means that you have a tighter turning radius if you need to turn around to stay in visual conditions. Prepare for this by practicing a lot of minimum controllable airspeed maneuvering on a good day, just like you did when working on your private pilot license.

Plot your course across as many airports as possible so that you will have lots of options if the weather turns sour; however, remember to fly around traffic patterns and not through them. Keep all the aircraft lights on to make sure that the airplane is visible to the other pilots who are out "running the scud."

What about the IFR pilot who "busts minimums" on an approach? This is another type of CFIT accident. In all fairness to pilots, a good number of altitude deviations are probably not intentional. How do unintentional "altitude busts" occur?

Altitude deviations are generally the result of complacency, the sort of mind-set that develops from over-familiarity and perhaps boredom and lulls a pilot into overlooking minor details that can add up to a mishap. What do the NASA Aviation Safety Reporting System and NTSB databases have to say about the causes of altitude deviations and controlled flight into terrain (CFIT) accidents?

The biggest portion, nearly 70 percent of all CFIT accidents come from communications errors: incorrect altitude readbacks, lack of adequate "hearback" on the part of a controller, when a pilot reads back an improper altitude and the controller fails to correct him or her, and improper altitude assignments that fail to provide traffic or terrain separation.

Pilots are also often guilty of misreading their altimeters or setting them improperly. It's not difficult to dial in an altimeter setting a thousand feet off if a big front has blown through between flights or the pilot flies through a rapid change in air pressure.

Improper approach procedures, especially nonprecision approaches flown without benefit of radar, lead to some CFIT accidents. Over half of the air-carrier approach accidents in the 1980s occurred during the step-down phase of a nonprecision approach. It's worth mentioning, however, that nearly all of the CFIT crashes that happened during an instrument approach took place along the runway's extended centerline.

Cockpit automation is a boon to safety but can create an unsafe condition. I've already laid out some recommendations about the use of autopilots and altitude-preselect devices. More often than not, autopilot-related CFIT accidents happen when the pilot improperly inputs the altitude to which he or she wants to fly; the capable-but-nonthinking automatic copilot flies the airplane where it's told, not where the pilot wants it to go.

"Scud-running" often causes a controlled collision with obstacles or the earth. Be especially wary of low ceilings and/or visibilities in mountains or at night, when your visibility is limited further and your options are few. Instrument-rated pilots seem to have as many (maybe even more) of this sort of accident than those pilots limited to visual flight only; perhaps the IFR pilot presses on with the mind-set that "I can fly this thing on the gauges; therefore, I can certainly duck in safely under the clouds."

What steps can you take to avoid the controlled flight into terrain sort of accident?

1. Be very careful about altitude assignments and readbacks. Try to anticipate the altitudes to which you'll be directed by talking with controllers beforehand or simply by studying the IFR and VFR navigation charts. If a controller gives you an altitude assignment you don't expect, query it. If the assignment didn't make sense but ATC doesn't seem to disagree with your readback, ask again. Controllers are people too and suffer from their own mind-set expectations; they expect you to read back correctly, and perhaps they miss an incorrect readback or the correct readback of an improperly assigned altitude.

2. Double-check your altimeter settings and use that "healthy skepticism" when reading your altimeter after you have dialed in the setting. If you're practiced in making altitude callouts to yourself on climb and descent, you'll be much more likely to catch a misread altimeter somewhere between the beginning and end of your altitude change. On takeoff, make it a practice to compare your altimeter reading to the published field elevation. Not only is this smart, it's also a legal requirement prior to IFR flight.

3. Practice your approach procedures, especially full-procedure nonprecision approaches. Take some dual instruction on a regular basis using approaches that you're not familiar with beforehand to develop a sense of ease with setting up for a "strange" procedure. Although you may not be able to log the time, consider flying the approaches you plan for a trip a number of times on a PC-based flight simulator. This will help you find the pitfalls and nuances of the approaches you'll be called upon to fly before your life is truly on the line. Make use of the ADM method to prepare for the approach and avoid distractions.

4. Be very careful when using cockpit automation, especially altitude preselect devices in a descent. Be sure to double-check your work when you've activated such a device, and remember that you are still fully responsible for monitoring the autopilot's control while it's flying the airplane.

5. Don't "scud run" if you can help it. If you're instrument rated and the airplane is so equipped, file and be done with it. If you have to fly underneath a low deck

or in poor visibility, spend some time familiarizing yourself with ground features, terrain elevations, and landmarks before launching. Be especially wary of towers and high-tension wires that will be virtually invisible in marginal weather conditions. Practice "slow flight" maneuvers, including a 180° level turn, often enough that you'll have a good feel for these maneuvers if conditions deteriorate while on a low-level mission.

UNSTABILIZED APPROACH

The purpose of having the airplane properly set up for an approach is threefold: first, to relieve the pilot of the workload required to wrestle the airplane around at the same time he or she is trying to fly an instrument procedure, second, to fly instrument letdowns the same way every time, so the pilot isn't experimenting with techniques each time an approach is flown, and third, to keep the airplane from continuing to settle into the ground if the pilot becomes distracted by some other cockpit demand. If the pilot does not stabilize the approach, get the airplane trimmed in a proper configuration prior to the final approach fix and hold that configuration until the missed approach point, the risk of an accident is much greater.

Approaches are some of the most demanding procedures a pilot can fly. There's no secret to the fact that instrument approaches are the staple of initial and recurrent training for IFR pilots because during the approach a pilot's skills are all brought to the test at the same time. If a pilot can't maintain a good instrument scan and make small corrections to correct minor deviations in pitch, heading, and vertical speed before a big correction is needed, then that pilot is going to be concentrating so hard on the physical demands of flying the airplane that he or she might fly right through a minimum altitude without realizing it.

If the plane is so out of trim that a glance at the approach timer or out the windscreen in hopes of seeing the runway throws the airplane off the pitch and heading targets, the pilot is fighting and not guiding the airplane down the approach course. If the pilot changes flap or power settings midway to the missed approach point in hopes of making a landing, he or she has done three things to reduce flight safety:

- Destabilized the approach and will have to refight the trim battle at a low altitude while continuing to navigate
- Reinforced a "landing expectation" that might make it difficult to execute a timely missed approach if the need arises
- Trimmed the airplane for a speed so slow that an application of power, if a missed approach is called for, causes the airplane to nose up into a departure stall

How can you avoid these hazards? To the extent that traffic flow permits, get the airplane on the airspeed and in the approach configuration prior to reaching the final approach fix. Choose an airspeed based upon what will be needed if you need to miss the approach; slowing down to final approach speed won't take place until you've visually acquired the runway. And hold that speed and configuration all the way to the missed approach point. With a little experimentation on a clear day, you'll be surprised at how easily most airplanes will negotiate an instrument letdown if you work out the power settings and fly trimmed airspeeds. More than one pilot has marveled at my demonstration of this concept and asked "Why did I buy an autopilot?"

DEVIATION FROM STANDARD OPERATING PROCEDURES

If I've tried to impress upon you any single tenet of good cockpit management, it should be standardization. Do everything the same way each time to the extent possible, and you'll expend as little brain-power as possible on the physical task of flying the airplane, which will free you up for the cross-checks and go-no-go decision reviews that should eliminate the vast majority of aviation accidents. Even high-speed ILS approaches and excessive descent rates to capture a glidepath should be standardized and practiced regularly so you won't have to make them up as you go along in the "real world" the first time that you're asked for such gyrations.

Standard operating procedures go well beyond these sorts of maneuvers, however. We've talked about checklist use and how running checklists as a backup to memory procedures can help you miss the "little things" that sometimes add up to tragedy. If you're too rushed to run the checklist, you're doing something wrong and setting yourself up for additional "wrongs" that never add up to "right." If you think you don't need the checklist because you've flown the same airplane for a dozen years without incident, you should consider that thought as a warning sign that you have actually increased risk by letting a personality trait erode your decision-making ability.

Standard operations include regular training. Every excellent pilot I've ever worked with trained well beyond the minimum prescribed by law. By excellent, I mean a pilot who can fly as well with an engine shut down, or an attitude indicator failed, or ice building on the wingtips as he or she flew with everything working perfectly. "You can have a thousand hours of experience," the old saying goes, "or you can have a single hour of experience a thousand times." If you have not practiced an engine failure or an instrument malfunction or a short-field landing lately, you haven't prepared yourself for the first time that it happens, even if you have a thousand hours in your logbook.

Standard operating procedures include checking the weather for every flight away from the traffic pattern and reviewing airplane performance and weight and balance before each takeoff. You don't necessarily have to pull out the loading tables and performance charts before every flight if conditions are what you're accustomed to, but you should at least review the approximate performance targets you hope to see so you'll know when things are going right and when they aren't. If you're doing anything out of the ordinary with runways, environmental conditions, or airplane load, get out the charts and verify what you can expect.

In flying, rules are not made to be broken.

RUNWAY INCURSIONS AND
WRONG AIRPORT OR RUNWAY

It actually happens. I was working the rental line at Sedalia, Missouri, one bright sunny day when suddenly without warning an Air Force KC-135 Stratotanker came screaming through the traffic pattern aligned with the runway; it was only a few hundred feet above ground and powering up to go-around. I had a good idea what happened and managed to verify the story with a former squadronmate of mine who just happened to be riding as a passenger on that plane that day. It seems the crew had never flown to Whiteman Air Force Base, which is about 20 miles west of Sedalia, and was inbound from the east.

It was a clear day, and Kansas City Center had handed the airplane off for a non-radar visual approach to Whiteman while the craft was still 30 miles out and several thousand feet in the air. Navigating visually without a radar backup, the crew started searching for the 15,000-foot airfield, aligned north and south, only to find the white pavement of Sedalia, a 5000-foot 18/36 strip on the east edge of a town of 30,000 inhabitants. Ignoring the proximity to the small city, the crew "expected" that the airfield would be Whiteman and began a visual descent.

Whiteman Tower reported the airplane NOT in sight, but cleared the tanker to land anyway because Whiteman at the time enjoyed about three airplane movements a day and there wasn't any other traffic in the terminal area. The inevitable was avoided when the crew realized on short final that Sedalia's airport wasn't quite as long as they expected; they powered up the airplane in time to go around. Luckily, none of my students were nearby in a Cessna 152 to flip over in the wash or to collide with the tanker, which then landed at Whiteman without further incident.

It's not too uncommon for airplanes to land on the wrong runway at the right airport. Whether from failure to check the winds, blatant disregard for wind direction at uncontrolled airports, or disorientation that causes a pilot to enter a pattern in the wrong direction, "wrong runway" accidents set the pilot up for a wind-related runway excursion or a collision with other airplanes on the runway.

I was at the Experimental Aircraft Association's 1993 Oshkosh convention and witnessed two near-tragedies one behind the other. Wind was out of the southwest, probably at 10 knots or so, but with an occasional gust beyond that speed. To maximize capacity, the frenzied Oshkosh controllers were recovering aircraft on Runway 27, which was aligned more or less into the wind, and the intersecting Runway 36, which had a gusting quartering tailwind.

A beautiful Taylorcraft was on final approach, bouncing in the breeze to the northbound runway. Tailwheel airplanes are naturally unstable on the ground, tending to turn around and go the other direction if the pilot doesn't actively prevent the "end-swap." Ask any conventional-gear pilot and he or she will tell you that it's much easier to push the airplane backward than to pull it forward on the ground; it took a healthy two-handed tug to pull my old Cessna 120 taildragger forward, but I could move it backward with one hand.

Back to the Taylorcraft: Because of the direction of rotation of American-built engines, a tailwheel plane turns most readily to the left. Because all airplanes will tend to "weathervane" into the wind, a quartering tailwind from the left is the most dangerous for a tailwheel pilot. Smooth pavement exaggerates this trait, and this is exactly what the Taylorcraft pilot had allowed himself to be set up for: a left-quartering and gusting tailwind on a paved surface. Add the significant "audience" factor and the excitement about arriving in the thick of things, and it's easy to see why this pilot didn't decline the clearance and ask to be routed to Runway 27.

So here he came, planting onto the pavement in a showcase wheel-landing with the tail high in the air. Wheel landings are designed to keep prop-blast airflow over the rudder, supposedly improving a taildragger's directional control in a crosswind, but wheel landings eventually turn into three-pointers when forward airspeed will no longer support the tail's weight. That's when the Taylorcraft swerved to the left, then toward the right as the pilot countered the gust, and then hard around left, reversing direction 180° and digging a wingtip into the pavement. Luckily no one was hurt, and there was little visible damage to the vintage craft.

Immediately behind the T-craft was a North American T-6 Texan, another tailwheel design. It too made a beautiful wheel landing on the northbound runway, swerved in the breeze, and suddenly cocked into the wind and drove into the grass. The plane rode down into a ditch and up the other side, pointed at the crowd; the pilot was able to reverse course and bump back up onto the pavement.

It must have been a wild ride as he rolled across the width of the runway and into the ditch on the other side; deciding the better of it, he applied full power for a go-around. At his slow forward airspeed and with the increased left-turning tendencies of high power and the quartering tailwind, the T-6 again crossed the pavement to the air-show side of the pavement, propeller barking supersonic, and then once more to the other side as the pilot fought to regain control.

With a mighty tug and still low on airspeed, the warbird driver tugged the old trainer into ground effect. I was sure that I was going to see a departure stall and crash, but to his credit the pilot shoved the stick forward and stayed close to the ground long enough to regain true flying speed. He circled the field for some time before he tried again, going around prior to another possible touchdown, and eventually asked for the westbound runway and made an uneventful landing.

These pilots apparently ignored the runway, weather, and airplane limitation conditions and accepted clearances that put their lives, their airplanes, and perhaps the lives of those in the crowds in jeopardy. Landing with a tailwind or in gusting wind conditions is a frequent causal factor in crashes of tricycle gear airplanes as well as taildraggers. Had either of these incidents resulted in a crash, part of the accident report might have read: "Pilot chose runway inappropriate for conditions."

What other sorts of runway incursions take place? If you fly into controlled airfields, you likely are reminded several times during each flight that "pilots are required to read back all hold-short instructions." Taxiing "into position and hold" is not supposed to be requested by ATC after dark, and all intersection takeoffs are discouraged.

These are all the result of a runway-incursion accident at Los Angeles. A Boeing 737 airliner landed atop a commuter airplane that was holding on the arrival runway. There was apparently some confusion in the tower cab as to which airplanes had been cleared to where, and the accident report states that the controllers thought the turboprop was somewhere else when the collision occurred.

It's still your responsibility as pilot-in-command to see and avoid other airplanes while on the ground and in the air. If you're given a "position-and-hold" or "cleared-for-takeoff" instruction, you still need to visually check for traffic on final or on the runway, and the same goes when cleared to land. You can always decline a "position-and-hold" clearance if you want to (that's your option with all clearances); you might consider easing the controller's capacity woes by accepting a "position-and-hold," but position yourself on the pavement aligned in such a way that you can still see the final approach course until you're given the go-ahead to fly.

Remember that traffic already on the runway has the right-of-way, so look hard before taxiing out. Remember also that "taxi into position and hold" is no longer a proper ATC command at night, another result of the 737/Metroliner collision in Los Angeles. And nothing approximating "position and hold" should exist at uncontrolled airfields, where you'll have no help at all watching for traffic behind you.

When you fly out of uncontrolled airports, you'll need to be even more wary of airplanes on approach to landing. Many airplanes fly perfectly legally without radios. When I owned my little Cessna, I learned to make a complete 360° turn on the taxiway just before taking the active runway to check for airplanes in all quadrants. Pilots sometimes do not announce their positions on the radio, or they have the wrong frequency and are inadvertently deaf and mute to others using the same field. Pilots sometimes get lazy or forget to do their homework and fly "backwards" traffic patterns or no pattern at all, so look *everywhere* before you taxi out onto the pavement.

You can make intersection takeoffs if sufficient runway remains. There is an old cliché about "the runway behind you" being useless on takeoff and in an emergency, and attempted intersection takeoffs all too frequently cause an accident, especially during times of high-density altitude. Intersection takeoffs can be declined like any other clearance, and I always feel a little uneasy when I see airplanes make intersection takeoffs at all except the largest airfields. If you don't have time to taxi to the end of the active runway, perhaps you're too rushed to safely start a flight.

WEATHER

Whole books can be written about meteorology's effect on flight planning, decision making, and accident statistics. You can recall the examination of the "categorical outlook" method of determining safety of flight, considering weather as a major risk factor when deciding whether or not to fly. Be very wary of marginal VFR conditions at night if you are not instrument rated or the airplane is not properly equipped for instrument flight. Plan such a trip with lots of time for delays and along a route with favorable terrain and numerous alternate landing sites if the weather "goes down."

If IFR, don't go unless you have at least MVFR weather somewhere within range of the fuel remaining in all phases of flight so that you will have a visual "out" if equipment, weather, or instrumentation forces a diversion. If at least "minimums" don't already exist for an approach, there's no need to waste fuel and tempt your "landing-expectation" mindset by flying the approach at all. If you do fly a procedure and are required to miss, don't try the approach again unless you have a positive indication that the weather has improved since your first attempt or you can identify something you did wrong that caused you to miss the approach and know that you have the ability to do it correctly the next time. If a second attempt at the approach fails, there is no decision to make; just go to your alternate.

Simply stated, use your head, and don't try to fly beyond your capabilities or those of the airplane.

COMPLACENCY

Have you ever been driving along a familiar stretch of highway only to come to the realization that you don't remember passing a known landmark or you can't recall the last 10 minutes of your journey? No, you haven't been abducted by extraterrestrials; you've simply experienced one symptom of complacency. You're so familiar with the operation at hand that you can do it pretty much by instinct, and your conscious mind is therefore free to contemplate business or family or that Mexican vacation.

In a car, you can usually get away with that sort of daydreaming. In an airplane, the same level of detachment has a much greater potential to create disaster. Complacency encompasses the entire spectrum from familiarity with the airplane or the procedure to mistakes that result from expecting one thing and missing another.

Sophisticated autopilots, even on very light airplanes, add to a level of complacency that erodes pilot ability and can actually increase risk. Recall that about 10 percent of the instrument-rated pilots I worked with while providing Bonanza and Baron factory pilot training could not pass an instrument competency check at the end of a hard week's training; the check was based upon practical test standards for the instrument rating. I attribute almost all of those incompletions to an overreliance on the autopilots commonly found in that class of airplane.

I've mentioned before how autopilots are incredibly nonthinking copilots. They'll do exactly what you ask them to do, regardless of your true intent. And most often they'll do absolutely nothing to warn you that your input was flawed.

The more sophisticated the autopilot, the more complacent that a pilot who uses it might become. Don't get me wrong. Autopilots are wonderful workload reducing devices, capable of helping you fight the causes of fatigue, and generally much smoother and precise on the controls than any human could be. Autopilots have specific uses, but acting as pilot-in-command is not one of them.

It's worth repeating: Don't ever let an autopilot do anything for you that you couldn't do yourself. Stay out of the trap that's set when you accept worse weather conditions or longer trip lengths than you'd be willing to handle by hand-flying just because the autopilot can do the job for you. I've had at least two autopilot failures and another two brought on by the failure of the airplane's pneumatic pump and the subsequent autopilot impact of the failure of the attitude gyro. That averages to about one autopilot-related outage per year for the last four years. That's often enough that I don't trust an autopilot to do the job for me.

Autopilot failure and flawed autopilot data input and verification continue to cause a good percentage of altitude deviations and accidents. This is especially true in the airline world where many more flying hours and better recordkeeping and reporting than general aviation tends to skew accident and incident data. Consider that airliners are flown by professionally trained multipilot crews and you're all alone in the cockpit with no one to catch your mistakes. With the continued advancements in autopilot design and function reaching into lightplane cockpits, the frequency of such errors and failures might well actually increase.

How do you avoid complacency? As I've said before, employ "healthy skepticism" about everything you and ATC do. Double-check everything. That sounds like the model of using a checklist for all phases of flight as a reminder to catch those little things that you might have forgotten. This is especially important when engaging various modes of the autopilot because you need to check whatever annunciation system exists to verify that it was set the way you meant. And never relinquish command to the black box; autopilots are there to assist, not replace your efforts as pilot in command. Using "George" actually requires greater vigilance from you than hand-flying the airplane because the airplane will not necessarily maintain the performance for which you have trimmed.

If you feel that you're okay without using the checklist or you decide to make one more leg tonight because "the autopilot will keep me out of trouble," be advised that you're becoming complacent, and complacency has many times proven fatal.

There are eight high-risk categories of aviation accidents. Avoid the hazards and you'll avoid 95 percent of all general aviation accidents: taking off with a known problem, midair collisions, inadequate terrain separation, unstabilized approaches, deviation from standard operating procedures, runway incursions and landing on the wrong runway or at the wrong airport, weather, and complacency.

You can take affirmative steps to greatly minimize those risks; the next chapters reveal how you can monitor and manage the risk factors during flight and recognize when action is required to avert disaster.

10
The safety equation

INFORMED DECISION MAKING IS RELATIVELY EASY: THE MORE INFORMATION you have to work with in the cockpit, the more intelligent (and safe) will be the choices that you make.

Pilots are, as said before, an independent lot. You probably wouldn't have earned your pilot's license if you didn't have a strong streak of self-reliance; however, as also noted earlier, this trait can sometimes get in the way of safe decision making by limiting the amount of information available to use. Let's look at several sources of information that you have at your disposal in the cockpit and some techniques for utilizing all sources of knowledge to ensure a safe flight.

THE PILOT

Of course, you are the most important part of the safety equation. Everything hinges on your abilities as a pilot; if you are severely lacking, there's little other sources of support in or out of the airplane can do to make up for your shortcomings. It's your most important job as a pilot to make sure that you can perform at the standards of the certificate and ratings that you hold. Just as other professionals (engineers, physicians, insurance agents, etc.) require periodic study to stay abreast of their disciplines, you should consider flying a "profession" in its own right, whether or not you're being paid to fly.

This is where I draw the distinction between *refresher* and *recurrent* training. The function of the first is to "refresh" to bring a pilot back to the minimum standards of the privileges he or she enjoys. Recurrent instruction is a regular meeting meant to knock the rust off latent skills but challenging and frequent enough that the pilot doesn't have to be brought up to minimum standards; pilots instead can actually advance their competence to the next level. In my experience, pilots who train at the minimum times required (biennial flight reviews, etc.) tend to need "refresher" training, while those who go the extra mile and seek out instruction annually or even every six months generally get better with each added session.

Unfortunately, few lightplane pilots feel the need for this sort of recurrency training. This seems to be especially true of those who learned (regardless of their age) from the "old school," the World War II method of extreme machismo and self-reliance against all elements. (I'm not making this up. My first instructor pilot, an ex-Navy dive-bomber pilot, wouldn't even let me use the elevator trim in the Cessna in which I logged my first few hours. The trim should be set for takeoff, he felt, and a "real pilot" didn't need it beyond that point. It's amazing he had the muscle to haul around a U.S. Navy Skyraider presumably without realizing the benefits of trim.)

In another example of the reluctance (and perhaps fear?) of regular training, several independent industry sources tell me that only about 5 percent of Beech Bonanza pilots ever seek out type-specific training, such as that offered by the American Bonanza Society, FlightSafety International, and the like. To be sure, many of the remaining Beech pilots are certainly logging time with local instructors, but how many simply fly these high-performance airplanes with the minimum instruction required, when (again in my experience) the legal minimums generally don't even allow a pilot to maintain the skills required to pass the private or instrument checkride if it were suddenly required again?

A third illustration: An informal poll of companies offering high-performance homebuilt airplanes revealed that very few would even consider creating a detailed pilot checkout syllabus. I've heard "My airplane flies like a Cessna 182" from half a dozen kit manufacturers. I got a feeling that if a company offered a training program to pilots of its design, customers might interpret that to mean the airplane is difficult to fly and take their kit monies elsewhere. Again, my experience as a flight instructor—teaching pilots who already had their certificates and ratings, who came from all over the country and even overseas, and who are regularly flying VFR and IFR in the system—showed that few students could adhere to the standards of their certificates without some effort to get back up to speed.

A significant exception: Canadian pilots in general tend to have excellent instrument flying skills. The difference? Canadian pilots are required to periodically retake their instrument checkride to retain their instrument rating. I'm not advocating that stance by the United States Federal Aviation Administration, but the regular, recurrent training that this requirement forces upon Canadian pilots certainly shows in the level of their flying competence. There's no reason you can't voluntarily be as safe as the average Canadian pilot without a federal requirement to do so.

The form that recurrent training takes is entirely up to you. You're already engaged in a part of regular training by reading this book. One hard part of any profession is keeping up with the literature. Published materials certainly allow you to benefit from the experiences of others, perhaps changing your behavior in the process. Certainly, you should seek out experts on the type of flying you do (instrument, mountain, whatever) as well as the specific make and model of airplane you fly. You will learn more from their experiences and to pick up elements of operation that you might have missed or learned and then forgot somewhere along the way.

You might find useful data from other disciplines that make flying easier or safer. Don't rule out a mountain flying or aerobatics course even if you never plan to use that knowledge. FAA Wings programs and other seminars are usually close to home, offering the benefit of information. Even "hangar flying" with the gang at the airport on Saturday morning has a measurable benefit in the level of knowledge that you take to the cockpit. No one is above the need for recurrent training.

I flew to Kansas City with a good friend of mine, a trip of about an hour in an A36 Bonanza. Both of us have a high level of expertise in that airplane, and I helped train this friend when he first came to work in Wichita. I'd been away from flying for a couple of months, and half jokingly told my friend to keep a close eye on me during the flight. It was IFR to near minimums at the destination, and I wasn't as current as I'd like to be in the airplane. I asked my friend to treat me like any other student receiving dual instruction on the trip.

At the end of our day, he commented about our relative level of knowledge (his is much higher than his modesty will allow), even writing something about "the student teaching the master" in my logbook. I told him that I appreciated the acclaim, but that if the day ever came that I felt I didn't need some instruction now and then, that it would be time for me to stop flying. And to be sure, I picked up a few pointers from my friend that day. You can always learn something from others that will support you, "the pilot," as the most significant part of the safety equation.

THE AIRPLANE

A great deal of information can be gleaned directly from the airplane that will help you make important decisions. Does it sound and feel right? Abnormalities, as subjective as they might be in detection, can point to the possibility of hazard before the threat truly exists. A rough-running engine can warn of failure in one instance. A heftier tug on the yoke might reveal ice on the control surfaces in another. The more familiar you are with a particular airplane, the more you'll be able to use the airplane itself as a source of decision-making input.

Other knowledge sources are inside the airplane. Someone went to a great deal of effort to create a pilot's operating handbook if the airplane is of a certified design. Keep "the book" handy in the cockpit to help you make decisions if things go wrong in flight. I was just beginning a training flight in a Beech Baron one day, climbing east out of the low-level scud over Wichita and poking into the blue skies above when my client and I noted that the right-engine "alternator-out" light had illuminated. Setting the plane on autopilot for the continued climb and now in clear air above the morning fog, we determined that the right-side alternator was still carrying a load by referencing its alternator load gauge and momentarily turning off the left-side alternator to see that the right-side load increased. We had a faulty light.

Should we continue the flight? After leveling at our assigned altitude and again engaging the autopilot, I asked my student to make the decision. He was 90 percent sure that we could safely and legally continue. I asked him to find some data to back up that assumption. When he questioned what I meant, I pulled out the airplane's pilot's operating handbook and looked through section 2, regarding limitations, until I found the list of required flight instruments and indicators. A note beside the "alternator-out" light entry stated that day and night VFR and IFR flight was still permitted with the failure of a single alternator-out light, provided the associated alternator load meter was operable. The flight was legal.

The information provided comforting input that continued flight would also most likely be safe, especially considering the relatively benign and improving weather for our local flight. Did the pilot's operating handbook make the decision for us? No, we did that ourselves. The POH provided additional input that in this case supported our decision, calmed our fear of being incorrect, and reduced stress that might have degraded some other decision downstream. It also emphasized that we needed to watch that right-side alternator load meter closely for signs of malfunction because a failure of the device would be much less obvious without the lighted warning.

If the limitations section of the POH had stated that flight was not approved without the broken indicator, or that day-VFR-flight-only was authorized, then that would have caused us to reconsider the decision to continue. In either case, the pilot's operating handbook was a source of information available to increase the level of knowledge available in making a safety-related decision, in effect putting the certification test-flight engineers in the cockpit with us to determine the level of increased risk.

Another source of information in the cockpit is the in-flight checklist. I've already expounded on the use of checklists in flight as a verification that you haven't forgotten something when configuring for some phase of flight. In the Baron alternator-out scenario, we did not begin blindly playing with the switches to troubleshoot the problem. Instead, we relied on our memory of the abnormal-procedures checklist.

Before being completely satisfied that we had done all that we could do, I asked my student to reference the checklist for a "Single Alternator-Out Light Illuminated" to make certain that we hadn't forgotten something vital. In this case, we had not forgotten anything; if we had, using the checklist would have allowed us to include its designer in the decision-making loop, silently suggesting "why don't you try this . . ." from the printed pages.

Do you have any other sources of information in the cockpit? You undoubtedly have some type of aeronautical chart. Engine roughness? The charts point toward lower and flatter terrain and provide safe altitudes if you are following a GPS or loran receiver's "nearest airport" signal. Do you have an *Airport/Facility Directory* or commercial equivalent onboard? You can determine frequencies for ATC assistance or weather information near a given airport or pick a "preferred routing" if you have to file IFR in the air or divert from direct routing because of an equipment outage.

Are headwinds stronger than forecast? The directory will help you find a suitable airport with services near your route, simplifying the decision-making process. Even a copy of the *Airman's Information Manual* might come in handy eventually. As I say in seminars, "If you've got it, use it." If you have a communications failure or some other abnormal incident, make use of all the information you have on board.

When looking at the safety equation, remember that the airplane and the information you can find within it can either add to or detract from your level of risk while in flight. Being unfamiliar with an airplane, for instance, can increase stress and therefore reduce your margin of safety. If you don't know where to look in the pilot's operating handbook or other printed materials, you might get so fixated on finding the information you want that you ignore the very critical task of flying the airplane. Put succinctly,

Safety = Pilot + Airplane.

PASSENGERS

One autumn weekend I was assigned to work with the owner of a turbocharged Baron. I had developed a rapport with this gentleman over the years as his instructor and was looking forward to working with him again. When he arrived early Saturday morning for his simulator session, he brought a friend who wasn't a pilot but usually sat in the right front seat alongside the Baron's owner. My client-pilot asked if his friend could also ride in the right-side seat of the simulator during the instrument procedures refresher. I welcomed the observer.

Setting up for the simulated flight, my client began assigning tasks to his "copilot," things like finding the appropriate instrument approach plate, organizing materials to the pilot's satisfaction in the cockpit, and reading the checklist as the pilot prepared for takeoff. I sat back and watched, noticing that the pilot retained control at all times, always double-checking the work of his friend but certainly finding it easier to work in this "two-pilot" cockpit. It was a good example of crew resource management, even though one member of the "crew" was not a pilot.

The goal of this training session was simply to let the pilot fly a few simulated instrument approaches, some with and some without the requirement to miss the approach, and to throw in a few malfunctions along the way to keep things interesting. Playing air traffic controller, I cleared the pilot for takeoff, noticing that his crew procedures continued even into the air, although once airborne my client made less use of his partner. Based upon my earlier work with the pilot, when I was convinced that he could fly like a pro without his "copilot's" assistance, I wanted to see how he would perform with his friend onboard. After all, that's the way he usually did it in the "real world," so why not train that way? I gave the pilot a minor malfunction after takeoff, nothing dramatic, but enough that the simulated god-awful weather conditions demanded a return to the takeoff point.

Like a training videotape, the two set up for the approach, the pilot always checking his right-seater's work as they were vectored around for the ILS into Wichita's Mid-Continent Airport. It was obvious that they flew together often and practiced this technique in their everyday flying. Intercepting the glideslope, the pilot lowered the landing gear and began a three-degree descent.

In this phase of flight, the pilot was solidly on the gauges. The "copilot's" job was to look outside for signs of the runway. I had set the cloud base at around 400 feet, but the visibility was set at half a mile, so a couple of hundred feet above decision height the friend could make out ground details on the visual display ahead of the simulator. This is where their well-practiced cockpit coordination broke down. At the first signs of green and brown wisping by beneath, the friend called "I see it."

"You see what?" asked the pilot, diverting his attention from the gauges. Ground detail was becoming more focused.

"I see the ground," the right-seater replied hurriedly.

The pilot looked up, confused that he could not see the runway lights, and the airplane began to drift to the right of course and low on the glideslope. The needles were still well within the parameters of a "good" approach when the approach lights hove into view and the pilot set up for an uneventful landing.

I stopped the simulation after touchdown to complement the "crew" on its division of cockpit chores and the way that the pilot accepted all the help while retaining responsibility for the outcome of the flight. Then we talked about the approach. "Yes, we fly IFR all the time," the pilot responded to my query, "but rarely to minimums on an instrument approach."

"How could you have avoided the confusion on short final?" I asked. The "copilot" offered that he not be included in the approach at all; the pilot didn't have an answer that would maintain the "crew" technique even on a tight approach. "What are you looking for when you fly an approach?" I asked the nonpilot friend. It was soon clear that he wasn't certain exactly what the pilot needed to see to effect a safe landing.

It took about two minutes to reposition the simulator to about 500 feet above decision height in varying levels of visibility and cloud ceiling to show the right-seater different styles of approach lighting. From there it was a quick matter of defining terminology. Pretty soon we had this nonpilot holding comment to three standardized callouts on a low-visibility approach: "I see the rabbit" (the sequenced strobes leading to the runway), "I see the runway end lights," and "I see the runway." For the rest of the session he stuck with these standard callouts, and the "crew" maintained the same level of cockpit coordination throughout low IFR approaches and missed approaches that were displayed in other phases of flight.

What's the point of all this? This experience was a good illustration of the effect of having a second set of hands and eyes in the cockpit. When the "crew" is well practiced in every phase of normal and emergency operation, having a passenger perform some cockpit duties greatly enhances the pilot's safe operation of the airplane. When the nonpilot does not know what the pilot is looking for, his or her input can actually reduce the level of safety as demonstrated by the drift away from a perfect approach in my simulator example. In all cases, the pilot retains total authority and responsibility for safety and should double-check the work of his or her "crew," just as does the captain of a jet airliner. Right-seat passengers can add to safety if well trained and practiced but increase risk if they are not well trained.

What about "untrained" passengers or those in the back seats? What use are they in increasing the level of safety on a flight? You should encourage your passengers to look for other air traffic. I have a friend and former client who travels quite a bit with his wife and two children. Before each flight he cashes a check and gets a number of $1 bills, which he gives to his wife. He also gives $5 to each child before takeoff. The game he has established with his children is that if one of them spots an airplane before the pilot does, then dad gives that passenger $1. If the pilot spots an airplane before his passengers, he collects $2 from each of the others. Sitting in the right front seat, mom verifies the spotted traffic and makes the payouts. It's a fun way to get the whole family involved in the flying, he told me, and he's been amazed at how many airplanes his kids see that he otherwise never would have seen. The children always come out ahead, he said.

How else can passengers help the pilot? I've read numerous accounts of the crash of a corporate jet into a hillside in instrument conditions. It seems that the crew of this jet was anxious to deliver its charges, seven or so high-level executives of a grocery-store chain, to the next stop. Conditions were marginal VFR at the airport that they were leaving, which has an instrument approach but is nonetheless an uncontrolled field. Either there was no radio link to flight service or ATC on the ground at their departure airport or that link was not operational.

Obtaining a clearance before takeoff meant a telephone call from the airport terminal followed by a harried start-up and taxi to try and get airborne before a notoriously short "clearance void time" window would close. Instead, the crew elected to take off into lowering visibilities, hoping to pick up an IFR clearance from ATC when in the air. Aloft and scud-running beneath the lowering clouds, the jet crew found that there was other IFR traffic in the area, and that their clearance was to be delayed. Orbiting the area at an altitude that was too low to receive navaids, the crew became lost and eventually flew into the side of a mountain. No one survived.

How could the passengers have helped? It's not a certainty, but I bet that at least one of those high-level executives in the back of the airplane had a cellular telephone. If the crew had asked, they might have found a phone to use in the cabin to obtain a clearance (or word that it would be delayed for other IFR traffic in the area) while on the ground before takeoff or perhaps before engine start and taxi. A significant possible option, one that might have saved lives, was apparently overlooked.

Unless your passengers are well trained in techniques to assist your flight, then try to limit their input, especially in altitude-critical areas. To continue the safety equation, remember that the input of passengers can often detract from safety, but that your fellow travelers have the capacity to increase your level of knowledge as well:

Safety = Pilot + Airplane + *Passengers*

OUTSIDE SOURCES

Plainly there are myriad sources of information available outside of the cockpit that can help you make safety-related decisions while in flight. Most obvious are the fine folks at air traffic control. ATC has the capability to vastly expand the information you have available with which to make a decision (Fig. 10-1). Let's look at another favorite simulator scenario that I used to employ.

Fig. 10-1. *Air traffic control is a great source of information for your decision making.*

The pilot of the high-performance single or light-twin is on a flight from Wichita to Kansas City. Weather for the trip is lousy. There's a warm front paralleling the route with IFR to low-IFR ceilings at takeoff and destination and sporadic reports of marginal VFR and IFR ceilings and visibilities at the few reporting points along the way; however, the cloud tops are at relatively low altitudes. Most client-students filed for an altitude of 7000 or 9000 feet, which put them on top of the overcast layer for the hour-long flight. Although unreported, a little rime ice accumulates upon climbout and melts away when clearing the clouds.

About 10 minutes after departing Wichita, I'd introduce a minor problem, like a failed slaving mechanism in the electrical HSI compass card. This would also impair the autopilot heading function, making the autopilot nearly useless. Now the pilot is faced with a decision to make:

- Continuing the flight to Kansas City using the magnetic compass for heading reference for a low IFR approach.
- Returning to Wichita "partial panel" and with the prospect of ice building up during the descent.
- Continuing to a third location.

As I mentioned when discussing the concept of a "departure alternate," most pilots seem to be locked into a mind-set of returning to the departure airport or continuing to the intended destination without much consideration of other likely diversion points. Many of my clients were again of this mind-set during this simulator session, and I (from the back of the simulator) would play along with the decision that they made.

If the pilot continued to Kansas City or Wichita or even an intermediate point like Emporia or Topeka, I'd let him or her try it using the magnetic compass with no serious ice accumulation or other incident. Flying an instrument approach to minimums using the magnetic compass is enough valuable training by itself; I would rather not spoil the experience by heaping on more trouble. The pilot could dramatically reduce the risk and increase his or her level of safety by simply asking ATC for some information.

I wouldn't volunteer it, but available for the asking was the knowledge that a twin Cessna had just missed the approach into Emporia, signaling that option as a poor choice, and that conditions just 20 miles to the northwest of Wichita improved to marginal VFR conditions with a 1000-foot ceiling and good visibility. Sometimes the simulator pilot would ask for help, and I as "ATC" would provide it. Occasionally a client would declare an emergency, and I'd reinforce that safety decision by providing all the information I had without further query. In any event, the pilot would remain in clear air most of the way to Salina or Hutchinson north and west of Wichita, with only a little time in the clouds during letdown before breaking out in conditions that were well above minimums (Fig. 10-2).

ATC can be of help in a much less dramatic way, as well. It's a good idea to check in with controllers every now and then—even when not participating with ATC services on a VFR flight—for updates about special-use airspace such as MOAs or low-altitude military training routes. It's been the rare trip when my preflight briefing included accurate information about special-use airspace more than a hundred or so miles away from my departure airport. Controllers are good for a "Where am I?" check if you feel a little lost and for altimeter updates on those longer trips or when flying through a steep pressure gradient. It's even possible that you can get some technical information from a controller on staff who is also a pilot if things start to get away from you and ATC workload permits (short of declaring an emergency).

Approach control and air route traffic control center facilities can usually provide radar vectoring information to help you navigate, if necessary. Airport tower controllers usually don't have radar, but can act as an intermediary to provide vectors in an emergency.

And what about flight service specialists? Over the charted frequencies or through flight watch, you have available to you the most up-to-date weather information if conditions are not shaping up as expected. Flight service also has the capability to provide position information and "vectors" to a suitable airport by plotting your position with direction-finding equipment (a *DF steer*). You'll be asked to make a few 5-second or so transmissions on a couple of different radio frequencies. The specialists can triangulate your position based upon a plot of the transmissions and then provide steering and even recommended altitude information to get you to a landing in poor visibility, at night, or if you're just plain lost. Call flight service in advance via telephone and set up a time to

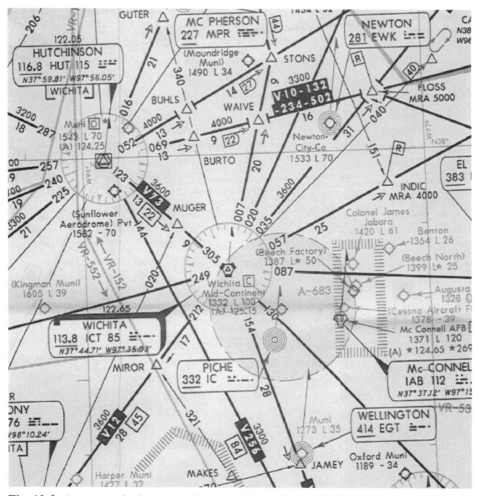

Fig. 10-2. *A portion of a low-altitude en route chart for the Wichita area.*

practice this technique when the workload is low; it will be good practice for all involved.

Are there other sources of outside information available? Sure. Anybody you can reach by radio is a possible provider: an airport operator or mechanic via unicom or an instructor pilot in another airplane. If you have questions, don't be afraid to ask. In an example common in air carrier operations but fairly unique in the general aviation world, I once heard the cockpit crewmembers of a corporate turboprop call their instructor at FlightSafety International via "flight phone" for help in troubleshooting an unusual problem while en route. Be creative if you have to; there's almost always somebody under less stress outside of the airplane who probably has more safety-related information than you.

Look at the Safety Equation again:

Safety = Pilot + Airplane + Passengers + *Outside Sources*

Notice that each factor can either add or detract from the total level of safety in the cockpit. Each factor can be a valuable source of information if properly used, but each factor can also be a distraction or prompt unsafe fixation if not properly applied. Your job as pilot-in-command is to balance the equation by soliciting information that you can use, evaluating the information using the goals of your flight as a benchmark, and employing the DECIDE model to choose information that is indeed valuable and subsequently using that knowledge to make crucial safety decisions.

11
Situational awareness
and the judgment chain

"SITUATIONAL AWARENESS" IS THE OVERRIDING BUZZWORD OF THE CREW resource management concept. Several definitions of situational awareness are used in the industry. I propose a less technical definition of situational awareness to be "The sum total of the aircrew's *perception* of the facts and conditions affecting the safe outcome of a flight."

Note my emphasis on the word "perception." Situational awareness is the result of accounting for, to the extent possible, all those factors we've discussed in this book so far. We've covered how you can set and evaluate goals of your flight and to use those goals and the DECIDE model to make informed decisions that affect flight safety. The extent to which you review your goals and make timely and accurate decisions in turn affects your situational awareness and your perception of the risk factors inherent in a given flight segment.

If you have a high level of situational awareness (your perceptions are accurate and all-encompassing), then your level of risk is low, or at least you have the tools to deal with that risk; however, if your measure of situational awareness is low, the risk level increases and might actually exceed your ability or the capability of the airplane itself to overcome a problem.

We've looked in detail at factors that can impair your ability to make good decisions. Fatigue, stress, medication, alcohol, and health are human factors that often are not easily measured, but they certainly change your ability to evaluate hazards and to make a good choice. Personality traits (machismo, invulnerability, impulsiveness, antiauthoritativeness, defeatism, and a "go" mentality) always affect your decision-making ability and tend to become more dominant and destructive when the physical human factors such as stress or fatigue are increased. Other external factors—the weather, your level of piloting proficiency and currency, familiarity with the particular airplane you're flying, and the situation in which you're flying (the "mission," as it were)—serve to vary the levels of fatigue and stress and to create challenges that your personality traits cause you to shrink away from or to "prove" that you can overcome.

"Situational awareness" is just a fancy way of saying "seeing the big picture," which is a function of human factors, personality traits, and the sum of all external forces. Unfortunately, while human factors, personality traits, and external stressors serve to make up your total situational awareness, they also tend to keep you from seeing all of what's going on around you. You need some way of measuring your level of situational awareness and knowing when that awareness is starting to break down.

CLUES TO YOUR LEVEL OF SITUATIONAL AWARENESS

Thankfully, definite clues or indicators can help you measure your level of situational awareness. It's a list of exceptions; if certain items on the list are not happening, then your level of situational awareness is high; if certain items on the list begin to crop up, then the "big picture" is beginning to get a bit clouded for you.

In its crew resource management seminars, FlightSafety International (the industry leader in CRM training) lists 11 clues to the level of situational awareness:

1. Failure to meet targets
2. Use of undocumented procedures
3. Departure from standard operating procedures
4. Violating minimums or limitations
5. No one flying the airplane
6. No one looking out the window
7. Communications breakdown
8. Ambiguity
9. Unresolved discrepancies
10. Preoccupation or distraction
11. "Bad feeling"[1]

Let's look at each one of these indicators in turn.

Failure to meet targets

We've already touched on this indicator of situational awareness. One of your tasks in preflight preparation is to review the expected performance of your airplane. In doing so, you'll derive a set of performance expectations, or targets, that you hope to achieve for each phase of flight. For instance, you hope the airplane will develop maximum available takeoff power, and you have several ways to measure attainment of those goals: manifold pressure gauge, tachometer, fuel-flow indicator, the "feel" of acceleration, and actual versus expected takeoff distance.

You have other performance or flight targets that tell you that all is going well if you achieve these targets: you should reach a certain altitude before crossing a ridge on climbout; the pitch attitude, indicated airspeed, and vertical speed readouts should all confirm normal operation; you should be able to contact ATC at a certain point. When one or more of your targets are not reached, things begin to go awry. Does this mean that a crash is imminent? Of course not! Not reaching a performance target means that you need more information if the flight is to progress safely.

Think back to our example of the airplane that took off with an excessively rich fuel/air mixture that led to power loss and a potential accident. The instructor pilot in this case detected a failure to meet established targets (in this case, anticipated climb rate) after takeoff and correspondingly adjusted pitch and airspeed to net best angle-of-climb until he had enough altitude to maneuver for landing. If the instructor had not been monitoring actual versus expected performance—if he had not detected that a target was not being hit—the aircraft might well have ended up in the trees.

Performance targets will help you maintain situational awareness by instantly telling you whether all is going well. Your level of risk has correspondingly increased if you find that you are not using targets in all phases of your flying, if you detect that your situational awareness is not what it could be, and if you are missing part of the "big picture."

Use of an undocumented procedure

Airplane performance manuals are full of checklists and procedures. Some are well thought out using flow patterns across the cockpit and logical step-by-step checklists to help the pilot accomplish tasks completely with a minimum of exertion. Other manuals, especially in older airplanes, have sketchy data at best, and it's up to the pilot to fill in the gaps from memory or with personalized procedures.

Regardless, there are usually at least a few manufacturer's recommendations regarding how to accomplish routine and emergency tasks. If you follow the recommendations, the airplane will perform to "book" specifications for the most part. Using the techniques found in the publications will help you establish those performance targets we've talked about, which will in turn increase your level of situational awareness.

It's when you start to deviate from the norms that you risk losing situational awareness precisely because you don't know what the airplane is going to do until it has already done it. When you use an undocumented procedure, no matter how well thought out, you are a test pilot in every sense of the word.

Chapter eleven

Several years ago I had the honor of addressing the employee flying club of a large general aviation manufacturer. My topic was the historical accident trends for the type of airplane that the club members most commonly flew, a low-wing retractable-gear high-performance single-engine airplane.

After my talk and the questions that followed, one flying club member wanted my opinion. "I fly one of these airplanes into a farm's grass strip," he said, "and it's only about 1800 feet long with power lines on both ends. I can get in and out of the field if I'm lightly loaded, but I want to be able to fuel up nearby, load my family in at the farm, and take off fully loaded. I think if I try something, I can take off in a shorter distance."

I tried to avoid looking skeptical as he continued. "I figure that the airplane will accelerate faster in ground effect than it does on a "book" short-field takeoff. If I can get the airplane off the ground and into ground effect in the shortest possible distance, like in a soft-field landing, and then immediately retract the landing gear while still in ground effect, I should be able to accelerate to V_X speed a lot quicker, then pull up and clear the wires by a wider margin."

I thought a moment before commenting, first citing the mention of "use of an undocumented procedure" in my presentation as a major source of accidents in this type of airplane. I then restated my stance that pilots using undocumented procedures are test pilots in every sense of the word and asked the pilot if he really wanted to try this technique with his family onboard the airplane. "It may well work," I concluded, "but I wouldn't want to be the first person to try it." The querying pilot decided to stick with his policy of picking up and dropping off his family at a nearby municipal airport.

Have you ever known a pilot who people call "an accident waiting to happen"? Such types are usually those who do things others don't, such as fly an airplane as it was never intended to be flown (rolling a nonaerobatic airplane) or make up procedures where none existed. Most of the time things work out fine for even these folks, for the sky is a pretty big place and experience is a good teacher. If you play test pilot long enough and with enough altitude beneath your wings, I suppose you could recover from a lot of situations other pilots could not. This brand of machismo probably helped spawn the cliché that "there are old pilots, and there are bold pilots, but there are no old, bold pilots."

Take for instance a pilot who owns a light piston twin operating out of a rural airstrip on which he runs a business. He has a lot of incentive to get back to his home airfield, for there is work to be done and money to be made. There is a VOR approach into his home airport, but the minimums are quite high. Despite the fact that there are several airports with ILS approaches within half an hour's drive of this airport, the pilot is known to have "made up" a loran approach to his home base (with a non-IFR certified loran installation) with "minimums" far lower than any nonprecision approach I've ever run across. I hear stories of his airplane droning overhead in the fog and suddenly appearing at power-line height when the throttles are chopped, and the airplane glides onto the ground.

I'm sure self-preservation drove this pilot to try his procedure several times in VFR conditions before blindly trusting it in the clouds, but whenever the sky thickens and snow fills the air, local pilots perk up a little when their radios blare the news, subconsciously expecting to eventually hear of a crash. This sort of procedure is the ultimate in undocumented-procedure flying and obviously elevates a pilot's level of risk well above acceptable levels.

How do conscientious pilots use the clue of "using an undocumented procedure" to measure their level of flying risk? When you are doing something different than the usual way or you anticipate maneuvering the airplane in a way it is not intended to be flown or you begin to plan a way "around" procedures or regulations that prevent you from getting to your destination on schedule, you've discovered that you're artificially increasing the risk level in the cockpit when you might have the ability to maintain a lower level of risk. If there's anything you can do to stop the escalation of risk (decide not to try a new short-field technique, for example), use your ability to do so.

If your procedure is undocumented because an emergency or unforeseen circumstance forced you to try something new (using a hand-held GPS to navigate when faced with a total electrical failure, for instance), then realize that your lack of familiarity with the procedure has reduced your ability to "see the big picture" quite so clearly. The potential for situational awareness has decreased and risk has increased; merely recognizing this fact might help you take steps to reduce your risk level elsewhere (establish a course for known-VFR weather instead of proceeding toward an airport that at last report was near minimums).

Departing from standard operating procedures

Virtually all disciplines employ standard ways of doing things. Individuals might modify these standard operating procedures somewhat, but after a while they usually settle into personalized brands of the SOP: their way of doing things the same way every time.

When people start to do things differently from the way they usually do, situational awareness can suffer. Making things up as you go along takes a lot of concentration that can rob your attention away from crucial safety-related facts. An example: A friend of mine moved up from a four-place single-engine airplane to a powerful light twin. In more than 800 hours of logged flight, my friend was never exposed to the concept of power and pitch management and the use of standard aircraft configurations to net desired performance.

For instance, in the particular airplane that my friend flies, I teach an "approach configuration" of 15 inches manifold pressure, 2500 propeller RPM, and approach flaps (about 15 degrees) to obtain a level-flight approach speed of 120 knots. From this point, extending the landing gear, letting the nose down to about 3 degrees below the horizon, and trimming off the pressures slows the airplane to around 100 knots while setting up a shallow descent that is desirable for the base leg and final approach prior to full-flap extension. The technique makes it very easy to set the airplane up precisely every time and therefore make minor corrections as necessary for glidepath and airspeed. My newly rated twin-engine pilot friend knew nothing of this and amazingly found that precise and smooth touchdowns were mastered after only a few trips around the traffic pattern.

Old habits die hard, however, and when my friend became tired by the end of the first training day, his mental awareness reverted to what had been the old standard operating procedure, which was to merely tug and push on the yoke, yank and haul on the throttles, and coerce the airplane to the pavement. The last landing was a wild affair, zigzagging back and forth across the final-approach course, carrying an airspeed that was 15 knots too fast, and generally turning into a bouncy, wobbly impact with the runway. My friend wondered out loud what could have been done to make that landing as smooth and precise as the eight or so others in the last three hours; I simply replied "You should have flown that approach the same way you had been all along."

In another example, let's say you're an instrument-rated pilot, flying along in the soup. Suddenly you experience an electrical fire. You promptly accomplish the appropriate checklist actions, cut off the overheat, and then review the emergency checklist to verify you haven't forgotten anything. You find that your number one navcom has bitten the dust, and you leave it turned off.

Now it's time to see about landing the airplane. You want to advise ATC of your problem and request vectors to the nearest ILS, but you haven't followed your standard operating procedure of tuning the active communications frequency in the number two radio after making contact on the number one, and now you can't remember what frequency you had been assigned. At this point it's a mad scramble to find the air route traffic control center frequency for the area in which you're flying after an actual in-flight emergency has already raised the stress level.

But it goes further. Prior to the fire, you had the airplane on autopilot tuned to follow the number one nav signal. When you shut down electrical power momentarily as part of the fire checklist, the autopilot disengaged; in your struggle to find the "missing" ATC frequency after the fire, you forgot to reengage the autopilot. With your head in the en route chart looking for a frequency, a bump in the air reminds you you're not on autopilot, and you hastily reengage "altitude hold" and "navigation" modes. The airplane settles down, but you're too busy to remember that the nav function has nothing to follow. Your plane drifts off course dangerously close to a mountaintop all because you didn't follow the standard operating procedure of backing up the comm frequency on the number two radio.

This was something of a peek into how these clues of loss of situational awareness can add up to an accident, by demanding so much of your attention that your situational awareness, your perception of the safety-related level of risk, goes so low as to cause an accident. If you find yourself deviating from standard operating procedures, ask yourself why you're doing so and expect that change to demand more of your time and consequently reduce your level of safety perception.

I think it was aviation editor Richard Collins who said that "the problem with most pilots is not that they have bad procedures, it's that they have no procedures at all." Develop a standard way of doing things to ensure that they are safely and efficiently done, and remember that doing things differently than you're used to is a sign that the risk level increases. Falling back to normal procedures will likely reduce risk and allow you to better sense the "big picture."

Violating minimums or limitations

A related situation that serves as a clue to the level of awareness in the cockpit is whether the pilot sticks to the rules of aircraft operation. Airplanes and pilots have limitations. Procedures have stated minimums, especially under instrument flight rules.

Airplanes are designed to fly in certain ways. (You probably wouldn't want to fly a highly unstable aerobatic airplane on instruments any more than you'd try to win an aerobatics competition in a Cherokee Six.) If an airplane is flown outside of prescribed limitations, obviously the level of risk has increased. How many times have you read of light airplanes crashing while attempting low-level aerobatics? When was the last time you saw an accident report citing flight into thunderstorms or known icing as a contributing factor?

Look at section 2, Limitations, in a GAMA-standard FAA-approved pilot's operating handbook and you find the parameters within which it's safe to fly the airplane. My A36 Bonanza handbook, for instance, starts with a table of safe airspeeds and the corresponding markings (where appropriate) on the airspeed indicator. Never-exceed speed (V_{NE}, the "red line"), maximum structural cruising speed (V_{NO} or V_C, top of the green arc), maneuvering speed (V_A, no marking as it is a variable), maximum flap extension/extended speeds (V_{FO}/V_{FE}, top of the white arc), and maximum gear operating/extended speed (V_{LO}/V_{LE}, marked by a white triangle) are all absolutes to be flown. Find yourself violating any of these airspeeds, and risk increases. If you have to violate limitations in order to fly, you're probably distracted enough that your level of situational awareness is reduced.

The FAA-approved manual goes on to list powerplant limitations (oil temperature and pressure, CHT limits, fuel flow, auxiliary fuel pump operation, approved fuels and oils, etc.) and corresponding markings on the engine instruments. Other instrument markings are enumerated. Instrument air pressure and minimum fuel quantity are also addressed. Weight, loading, and balance limits are listed, as are maneuvering limits, load factor limits, and whether the airplane is approved for day-VFR only, night, and/or IFR operations; the manual also describes the operational effects of "losing" various instruments and systems. There are even limitations concerning the positioning of passenger seats for takeoff and landing. ("Seat backs and tray tables in the full upright position.")

Every significant placard marking or aircraft limitation is listed in section 2 of an approved handbook. You need to be intimately familiar with these limitations to the extent that working within the rules is second nature. Is an aileron roll in a Malibu just to impress the crowds worth the added risk of working outside aircraft limits? Are you really in such a hurry to get airborne that not adding another quart of oil to the engine to bring it up to specs justifies the engine damage and off-airport landing or crash that might result?

Light icing was reported over your destination airport. Do you press on hoping that you won't encounter ice or hoping that your airplane can continue flying with an unpredictable change to its aerodynamic design, even if a dry and clear airfield is nearby? If you fail to maintain a healthy respect for what the airplane is and is not designed to do, you'll improve your ability to maintain situational awareness simply because you will not be preoccupied with the problems that might result from violating airplane limitations.

And what about your personal limitations? Are you fully qualified for IFR operations? If not rated *or* current, don't go near the clouds. Have you made the prescribed full-stop landings in that last 90 days to be legal carrying passengers at night? If you're not night current, the law says you can regain currency on your own, but you have no right to bring passengers along during your experimentations with nighttime illusions. Do you have a medical waiver, such as the need for corrective lenses? Such standards were created for a good reason; the FAA allows you the privilege, not the right, of exercising your pilot's license, only so long as you live up to your end of the bargain by sticking to the rules. If you can't find your glasses, for example, and they're required by your medical certificate, don't fly.

If you find yourself compelled to fly anyway, despite the fact that you'll violate your own limitations in the process, realize that you're about to commit yourself to an unacceptable level of risk, one from which it will be hard to extricate yourself after the flight has begun. Another old cliché: "Takeoffs are optional, landings are mandatory."

Previous chapters addressed the violation of flight-rule minimums. Suffice it to say that if you go "just a little bit lower" or "just a tiny bit farther" than the published procedure allows to try to find your intended destination, you have violated the rules and have artificially and unacceptably increased your level of risk. Execute a missed approach procedure immediately and think things through when the pressure of the approach has subsided. Decide whether the meeting you're trying to attend is worth dying for or the family gathering that waits below will be festive when word of your crash arrives. If you can't complete a flight as planned without busting minimums, go someplace else and rent a car or wait until conditions improve.

To repeat: When an airplane limitation, personal limitation, or published minimum has to be violated in order to fly as planned (expected), change the plan (and expectation), and do something that doesn't break the rules. If you suddenly find that your flight isn't going as predicted (the weather is worse than expected or headwinds have reduced your fuel-reserve margin), work out a way to avoid the risk, such as delaying a takeoff or diverting to an early alternate. If anyone ever cites your actions in a review of cockpit management, wouldn't you prefer to be an example of good decision making rather than the alternative?

No one flying the airplane

The "classic" case cited in crew resource management training is one of the incidents that led to the CRM concept in the first place: the crash of an Eastern Airlines Lockheed 1011 in the Florida Everglades that was brought on by a burned-out light bulb.

It was a clear and dark night over south Florida as the three-man crew of the wide-body jet made preparation for landing in Miami. Aboard the airplane was a fourth crew-qualified man, a passenger who was riding in the jumpseat of the airliner's cockpit. At the appropriate time, the captain called for gear extension; the first officer moved the landing gear switch to the "down" position and watched for three green indicators to prompt his callout that the gear was in fact down. Only two lights illuminated. The nosewheel landing gear light did not shine.

Wisely, the captain called ATC with a missed approach, asking for a vector over the Everglades to provide the time to troubleshoot the problem. Engaging the autopilot, the two crewmembers began the gear failure emergency procedure, watched closely by the other two crewmen in the cockpit. All cockpit efforts failed to verify that the nosewheel was down. Eventually, the flight engineer crawled down into the "hell hole," a narrow passageway through the nosewheel well, where he visually confirmed that the nosewheel was locked safely into position. He was on his way back to the cockpit to report his findings when the 350-passenger jet crashed, wings level, into the swamps.

NTSB findings revealed that the failed gear indication was the result of a simple burned-out light bulb in the nosewheel indicator. The crewmembers discovered this while their partner was in the "hell hole" and had begun to replace the bulb prior to impact. Unfortunately for all aboard, the simple process of changing a light bulb was so distracting to the three in the cockpit that they failed to notice when the autopilot disengaged and failed to detect the jet's gradual descent into the ground. Everyone assumed that "George" was flying the airplane.

This sort of accident is not limited to malfunctioning or disengaged autopilots. It occasionally crops up in accounts of training accidents or when two pilots are sharing flight duties, where both aboard think for whatever reason that the other pilot is flying the airplane.

I was flying right-seat in an A36 Bonanza while a colleague flew from the left. We were putting the airplane through a series of preplanned maneuvers and recording data to verify the performance of the Bonanza simulator we were employed to use. We had set up a cockpit voice recorder, but I was also logging data manually as fast as possible in case the tape recording failed.

We had the airplane set up slightly slower than maximum gear extension speed and about 3000 feet above central Kansas when the pilot lowered the wheels and let go of the control yoke. Our test was to plot the pitch, vertical speed, and airspeed oscillations to use in simulator programming. The nose started slowly downward with the pitch going lower and lower as the vertical speed and airspeed increased. I scrawled on my legal pad in the right seat while the pilot read performance into the tape recorder from the left. Suddenly a loud click signaled the end of our recording tape.

I reached down to begin tape replacement, only to find the pilot was doing the same thing. It was an almost comical moment when we looked at each other, then simultaneously sprung upright to see the brown fields coming rapidly at us. Of course the pilot recovered, pulling us smoothly out of the dive, but I learned an important lesson about division of cockpit duties that I've carried on into my preflight briefings to this day.

Whenever I'm to fly as instructor or "up front" with another pilot for any reason, I brief that I'm a stickler for making certain that somebody is on the controls or at least responsible for monitoring the autopilot all of the time. To that end, if I'm flying the airplane, for instance, and I want the other person to take over, I'll say "You have the controls," but won't actually relinquish responsibility until the other pilot clearly states "I have the controls." We both have to say it out loud before a change of command takes place. Similarly, if the other pilot wants me to fly, he or she will tell me I have the controls, but shouldn't assume I've taken over until I reply "I have the controls." In an emergency, I'll still take over using the same technique, although I might need to be a little more forceful about it.

A fine point of semantics: I recommend using "I have the controls" and not "I have the airplane." The latter is an almost instinctive way of saying that you have another airplane in sight to be pointed out as a traffic hazard. I don't want to confuse this terminology with a transfer of piloting responsibilities. I've found that this verbiage and technique is easily picked up by pilots who don't usually fly together. Since my "flight test" experience, I've never been in a situation when which pilot was on the controls was in doubt.

Accidents of this sort are relatively rare, but if you feel you've relinquished too much control to your autopilot, or if there's even the hint of a question about which of two pilots is flying the airplane, take control and settle things down. If you aren't keeping close tabs on "George" the autopilot, or if you're not certain exactly who is responsible for the controls, then it's obvious that you're not seeing the "big picture" and your level of risk has increased.

No one looking out the window

Similarly, when the attention of all pilots aboard is drawn inside the cockpit, such as in the Eastern Airlines accident, a vital part of the pilots' perception of safety is missing. It's no coincidence that the largest number of midair collisions involve at least one airplane with a pilot receiving instruction; the "student" pilot might be busy in the cockpit, dealing with a simulated emergency, or "under the hood" and flying on instruments; the instructor has to divide his or her attention between the inside world, where he or she is being paid to monitor and to teach, and the outside, where the instructor really earns his or her keep by acting as a safety observer. Is your head down looking at a chart or a checklist? Look up, and take in the outside world.

You should try to keep scans inside the cockpit to a minimum length, no more than a couple of seconds. This is where being familiar with the airplane, the charts, and the procedure to be flown beforehand works wonders. If you have to look around to find the carb heat handle or need to shuffle through reams of Jepp charts to find the approach plate you require, then you probably have not adequately prepared for the flight. Suffice it to say, the best information gatherers you have are your eyes; use them frequently to detect what's going on in the world around you.

Communications breakdowns

Communications failures come in three varieties: lack of communication within the cockpit, lack of communication from the airplane to the ground, and lack of communication from the ground to the airplane.

Crew resource management seminars spend a great deal of time discussing and role-playing cockpit communications scenarios. One of the findings in the development of the CRM concept was that crucial information is almost always available in the cockpit; in many cases, however, that information was not transmitted from one crewmember to another, or if an attempt to relay the data was made, it was dismissed or misunderstood.

For communication to be effective, four elements have to be working together:

- The sender who is delivering the information must detect the need for communication.
- That information must be put into a code or a language for transmission.
- The message must travel through a medium that might enhance or distort the message.
- The receiver must receive the information in the manner in which the sender intended.

For instance, a commuter turboprop with a crew of two begins to stray below the glideslope on a tricky ILS in turbulent and icy conditions. The captain is on the controls (the "pilot flying," or PF in CRM parlance), while the first officer (the "pilot not flying," or PNF) is charged with monitoring the approach and scanning outside for the runway environment.

Perhaps the PF is so wrapped up in trying to make the ride smooth for his passengers that he doesn't notice the trend away from glideslope. It's the PNF's responsibility to point out this transgression, to correct it before it becomes critical, and even to wrest control from her captain if the PF does not make an appropriate correction. The first officer sees the trend (detects the need for change) and taps the PF's glideslope indicator, stating clearly "glideslope low, fly up," or some standard operations phraseology (puts that information into code). The PF is pulled out of his trance by his first officer's action, which was clearly visible and audible (the medium), and correctly interprets the message to execute a small pitch and power adjustment to safely conclude the flight.

But what if the PNF is so distracted that she too fails to detect the need to communicate a transgression from the glideslope? Maybe the captain has asked the PNF to keep an eye on the ice buildup on the wings and to activate deicing equipment every few minutes in the turbulent air. Such duties, although essential, might distract the first officer from her primary job at this crucial point in the flight, which is to act as safety observer and emergency backup to the captain if the flight does not progress as planned. The need for communication might not be detected before it is too late.

Let's say that the first officer is new to the commuter airline and is flying with a high-time captain from the chief pilot's office. Low paid and wet behind the ears, our eager PNF is intimidated by the years of experience symbolized by her captain's presence and is hesitant to point out the PF's failure to maintain glideslope, perhaps even fearing for her job. When the turboprop descends below glideslope, the PNF notices but fails to communicate the message; the PF, still distracted by the weather, flies ever lower, until the airplane impacts treetops and cartwheels onto the ground.

Perhaps the turbulence is intense, and the dark cockpit is noisy with the sound of nearby propellers at high RPM. The PNF properly detects the need for change, and reaches over to tap the HSI on her captain's instrument panel. As the airplane bounces, the first officer's arm waves up and down across the captain's instrument panel, and the hand does not clearly identify the glideslope indicator; engine and propeller noises that are coupled with icy rain hitting the windshield obscure her voice when she calls "Glideslope low, fly up" to the PF. The environment, or the medium in which the message is delivered, distorts or overrides the message; crucial information never makes it to the captain.

Maybe the PF is truly caught up in other concerns: trying to smooth out the ride for his charges, worried about the financial state of the carrier and the security of his job, or anxious about a problem at home. Maybe he is a new hire from a failed airline elsewhere and, despite the required transitional training, is not yet fully up to speed with all the procedures and phraseology of his new employer. Perhaps he is a high-time U.S. Air Force fighter pilot who was forced out of the service by a military downsizing, and prefers to do things on his own, without what he considers the "nagging" of a copilot. For whatever reason, he might nod or grunt or even verbalize a response to the PNF's warning, but fails to respond or even chooses to ignore the dire warnings of his right-seat counterpart.

The PNF might think her part has been played out when the PF nods to the glideslope statement, but the aircraft continues to drift dangerously below glidepath. If the first officer doesn't detect that a change has been made, it's up to her to be more forceful, or even to assume command if the situation becomes critical.

What good does this discussion of crew-communication techniques do for the pilot of a single-pilot airplane? It's even more crucial for single-pilot operators to anticipate the effects of barriers to good communication because *there will be no one along for the ride to objectively point out when a safety transgression is being made.* Your job is to try to remove those barriers before they become roadblocks and prevent the flow of safety-related data.

We've already discussed certain things that you can do to eliminate the distractions that might prevent you from detecting the need for "communicating" safety-related information to yourself. Strict adherence to the disciplines of the altitude-critical area and the "sterile cockpit" will help keep you focused on your true duties during the most crucial phases of flight. Using the *altitude, distance, missed approach* (ADM) method of extracting precise approach information from an approach plate and posting it in the cockpit can prevent you from an overload of data if you need to double-check something inside the final approach fix.

Be smooth but be quick about making corrections if you notice the need for change. If you're one dot below glideslope and descending at the normal rate, the airplane will only get farther below the glideslope as you get closer to decision height. Make small corrections before the need for a big modification arises. Not only will this establish a trend toward a safer state and make things more comfortable for your passengers, it will also help you to maintain a higher level of situational awareness by tending not to preoccupy yourself with excessive corrections.

Keep the environment conducive to good communication. Have you ever gone from using a headset, boom mike, and push-to-talk switch back to an overhead speaker and a hand-held microphone? The added workload alone is a big distraction, but the change in the cockpit environment is enough to make it hard for you to think clearly. The first time I flew a Baron without a headset, it seemed so loud that I almost aborted the takeoff for fear something was wrong. I almost always wore custom-molded ear plugs to protect my hearing in the Cessna 120 that I owned. One time I forgot them when I went to the airport, and I actually did stop short on my takeoff roll to give the engine another runup. In these sorts of situations, my internal "communication" was clouded by the unusual noise and unfamiliar sensations of flight. My risk level was definitely higher than normal, but I took steps to compensate for the scrambled communications.

And how do you keep yourself from "failing to communicate" safety information to yourself? This is where good health and a clear head, familiarity and currency in the airplane and procedure to be flown, and knowledge of those personality traits that tend to dominate and impair your judgment come in. If you capitalize on your strength and compensate for your weaknesses, you should be best able to "see the big picture" and take in and properly evaluate the information available that will make your flight a safe one.

External communications. We've looked at the effects of good and bad communication within the cockpit. What about the other two varieties of communications failure: air-to-ground and ground-to-air?

Recall the crash of an Avianca Boeing 707 several miles short of New York's John F. Kennedy Airport. This accident serves as a classic CRM case, illustrating the negative effects of bad air-to-ground and ground-to-air communications. The heavily laden Boeing was on a nonstop flight from Latin America to the New York airport. Weather was poor along the Northeast seaboard, and airplanes were being "stacked up" in holding patterns, taking their turn at the approach. The Avianca was no exception; in fact, it was ordered into an en route hold well south of its destination airport where it burned off crucial fuel for something like 45 minutes before being accepted for vectors into the megalopolis.

The crew, as noted by the cockpit voice recorder, was already getting nervous about the jetliner's fuel state even at this point but said nothing to air traffic control; they were routed into the queue and eventually onto the final approach course into JFK. Arriving at the missed approach point and still unable to see the runway, the captain ordered a missed approach, pouring volumes of fuel through the first-generation jetliner engines as they climbed back into the murk.

Now critically low on fuel, the crew radioed that they would have to get on the ground quickly. ATC acknowledged their call and asked if they wished to declare an emergency, which would allow the controllers to divert other traffic and put the 707 first in line to retry the approach. The Colombian crew, either because of the language barrier, fear of the supposed implications of declaring an emergency, or some brand of machismo that would not allow them to ask for help, declined the emergency call. The Avianca jet resumed its place in line, vectored well away from the airport for another turn at the approach.

The rest, as they say, is history. Some few miles short of the airport, on the final approach course inbound, one engine cut off, then another, and soon the fuel-less jet made contact with the earth and subsequently the front page of most of the world's newspapers.

How could this tragedy have been avoided? The NTSB findings found fault not only with the crew, who failed to employ the tool that would have placed them first in line, declaring an emergency, but also with the controllers, who had been told that the Avianca's crew was concerned about their fuel state, and failed to assertively present the option of declaring an emergency, the vehicle that could have allowed ATC to prevent the crash.

If you need something, ask somebody! ATC and other off-airplane agencies often have the resources to help you get out of trouble, but they can't make the decision for you, and you're on your own unless you initiate communication. Are you lost? Ask for a position check. Getting conflicting signals from the nav radios? Ask for a ground-speed check. Afraid the gear isn't down? Ask the tower to look.

Using standard phraseology helps convey true meanings as well. One result of the Avianca crash was an emphasis on standard terminology for fuel-related situations. A "minimum-fuel advisory," for instance, warns controllers that although an emergency is not yet imminent, any undue delays might be critical. Call a "minimum-fuel advisory" when you calculate that the flight will start to consume the legal fuel minimums if placed in a hold or in a long line for the approach. ATC won't immediately give you priority, but will be ready to reroute you to another destination if traffic begins to stack up. A "low-fuel emergency" is exactly what the phrase implies: an emergency situation where if you don't go to the head of the line for the nearest suitable airport, you'll run out of gas. ATC will give you priority over all traffic, as in any declared emergency. Be prepared to account for any imprudent pre-flight and in-flight decision making with regard to fuel, but don't hesitate to declare the emergency and get the plane safely on the ground. The *Airman's Information Manual* includes a *Pilot/Controller Glossary* that details the proper phraseology to maintain good communications.

If you feel that communications are breaking down because you don't know where you are or you don't understand what the instruments are showing or you can't seem to understand ATC's routing of the flight, then take the required steps that are necessary to resolve the communications question before moving on.

Ambiguity

Ambiguity is the result of poor cockpit communications, whether between you and the airplane or between you and persons on the other end of the communications link. When you have ambiguities or you are unclear about your situation relative to others or what the instruments are indicating, you've obviously lost situational awareness, and your level of risk has increased manyfold.

I was flying a Beech Baron one evening when the ADF needle showed the outer marker compass locator for Wichita's Mid-Continent Airport to be about thirty degrees off to my left while all other indicators (HSI on the localizer frequency and loran) detected that the locator should have been off to my right. I had properly tuned and identified the NDB signal. I was still tuned to the Morse-code sequence, barely within the range of hearing and was still receiving a strong signal. My conclusion: A malfunctioning bearing needle had become stuck in position when the NDB was off to the left and had not changed indication while I was being vectored for the approach. I resolved the ambiguity by deciding that the ADF was unreliable; I informed ATC and continued the approach without referring to the ADF.

In another case, I was flying a Bellanca Super Viking VFR above a scattered cumulus deck on a sunny winter's day when I noticed that I was consistently turning to get back on heading. Concerned that I should be having so much trouble holding heading in such smooth and clear conditions, I soon found the source of my trouble. A weak vacuum pump was indicated on the instrument air-pressure gauge, which effectively degraded the attitude indicator (my primary means of determining wings-level to maintain course) and the heading indicator itself, which was slowly precessing to the right. I covered the offending instruments with adhesive-backed office notepaper to remove them from my scan and completed the short VFR trip using outside references and the magnetic compass alone.

Early on in my flying career with a newly minted private certificate in my wallet, I ventured westward in my Cessna 120. With nothing but the magnetic compass for guidance, I headed cross-country from Higginsville, Missouri, to Newton, Kansas. When I crossed the Kansas border, familiar section lines disappeared in the vast expanse of grasslands known as the Flint Hills. Without a handy heading reference outside of the airplane, I found that I kept turning to the left, instinctively banking into the sun for some base psychological reason I as yet don't understand. I had to force myself to keep the wings level, even in pristine conditions, to avoid turning south of course. Eventually I found a railroad track headed the right way and followed it uneventfully to the intended destination.

All of these examples had ambiguities, or conflicting information. It would have been easy for me to become quite distracted, perhaps following the wrong signal and ending up far off course lost and unsafe. Instead, I searched around for the source of the informational conflict and used multiple pieces of information to put me back on course. I resolved the ambiguity and eliminated it as a possible accident cause.

Regardless of the cause, if you find an ambiguity in your flying, or a question arises that you can't resolve, take steps to get more information. Only then will you reduce your level of risk.

Unresolved discrepancies

If you feel you are receiving contradictory information in the cockpit and you do nothing about the contradiction, you're operating with an unresolved discrepancy. Recall the Baron's ADF needle pointing to the left when all other sources indicated the outer marker was to the right. Not doing anything to verify the true location of the outer marker locator might have led to enough of a distraction to cause an accident. I might have remained so confused that I might have "locked in" on the navigational problem, letting the altitude stray or missing an ATC handoff to another communications frequency.

Some pilots don't even tune the ADF to the locator frequency figuring that ATC will always vector them to the final-approach course. I checked out in a high-performance single-engine airplane that was owned by a practicing CFII himself who told me the plane didn't have an ADF because "nobody really uses them anymore, anyway." Undoubtedly, many more pilots tune the device out of some sense of obligation but never identify it audibly or use it in their orientation scan to plot their way around the approach course.

I prefer to use every bit of information I have available to verify the location of the marker and my glideslope intercept. Case in point: A pilot descended into terrain eight miles short of an airport by following the ILS glideslope all the way into the trees. I've seen cases of false glideslope intercepts (due to some of the inherent transmission characteristics of glideslope antennas), but I would have to assume that there was some way of verifying the glideslope intercept on this approach. If there had been a marker or ADF compass locator for the pilot of this airplane to see and/or hear, its absence on this particular approach might have been enough of a discrepancy for the pilot to climb clear of the terminal altitude-critical area and rethink the approach.

Not all discrepancies might be related to instrument procedures. What if your airplane isn't meeting performance targets, such as fuel flow or initial climb rate on takeoff? What if it takes an inordinate amount of throttle reduction to get the desired manifold pressure for a known altitude? What if oil temperature is running higher than normal or doesn't vary with the corresponding oil pressure? All of these things are discrepancies. Will they alone cause an accident? Probably not. But left unchecked, seemingly minor items can add up to catastrophe.

Preoccupation or distraction

The *Flight Training Handbook* and its offshoots refer to preoccupation and distraction as "fixation." Any time that your attention is drawn to one object, indication, or situation to the point that it draws you away from the monitoring of other information, you've lost a part of the "big picture" and are potentially setting yourself up for a loss. Think about how easily the Eastern L-1011 crew could have avoided becoming a textbook case if only the captain had delegated troubleshooting of the gear problem to his subordinates and had not allowed himself to become preoccupied with the landing-gear indication.

In another accident, an errant fuel-flow indication after takeoff prompted the pilot to request a return to the departure airport. Digital and analog fuel-flow devices (which receive information from the same mechanical sensor) showed wild fluctuations. There were no corresponding surges or reductions in engine power, and the engine continued to run smoothly. Of course a precautionary landing was in order, but the pilot became distracted by the jumpy indicators and was preoccupied with a possible engine failure. Apparently the lack of attention caused the pilot to prematurely flare upon landing, and the airplane was substantially damaged after stalling roughly 30 feet above the runway. No one was hurt.[2]

Your job as pilot-in-command is to occasionally step back and ask yourself, "Am I doing everything I can to assure a safe flight?" If you can't remember the last time you checked the engine readings or aligned the heading indicator or identified the Morse-code signal of the primary navaid, then it's time to do so. If you are busy looking up a radio frequency or plotting your way around special-use airspace, look up inside the cockpit and outside the airplane and take in the "big picture" before again sticking your nose in a map.

A former instructor colleague taught the "one potato, two potato" method. Don't look at any one thing longer than the time it takes to say "one potato, two potato." He was trying to emphasize that virtually any cockpit chore, normal or emergency, has the potential to become a distraction. If you feel that you might have spent too much time working on one thing, you probably have. Take a fresh look around to heighten your level of situational awareness.

"Bad feeling"

Have you ever had a feeling that things weren't going the way you had hoped? Have you ever wished that you had never left the ground in the first place? If you have a "bad feeling" about a flight, chances are you can easily become distracted away from the disciplines that are keeping you safe in the air. I had the opportunity to deliver a Baron for a friend who had just purchased but not flown the airplane. My schedule mandated an hour-long night flight from northern Kansas to Wichita where a dual-control yoke would be installed for my friend's checkout training.

Conditions were forecast to be 25,000-feet broken with 25 miles visibility, but the flight up with a friend in a Piper Archer included about 20 minutes of actual IFR time in an overcast layer that spread about 50 miles north of Wichita. The wind was out of the south, which was increasing the amount of moisture available for condensation, and the sun was already down, meaning temperatures were dropping as well. Cloudiness in the Wichita area would undoubtedly increase.

It took some effort to crank up the Baron, but once started, its engines responded well. Takeoff was uneventful as was leveling off in the dark night sky. I found that the communications radios were not illuminated at all, meaning that I had to keep one of my flashlights on the copilot's seat to see the frequencies I had selected. I was beginning to have a "bad feeling" about this flight.

I air-filed an IFR clearance with flight service, then checked in with Kansas City Center for the trip to Wichita. Given vectors direct to the airport, I tuned the number-one navigation receiver to the localizer in use at Mid-Continent: nothing. I was within 30 miles and still unable to receive the localizer although I was almost directly in line with the runway, so I tried the number-two receiver, which I had already set for a cross-bearing that helps identify the outer marker for Runway 19R. I got the localizer okay on number two, but still had nothing on the primary nav receiver or the HSI. My "bad feeling" was beginning to become justified.

Soon I was switched over to the localizer/back course for Runway 19L, which removed my "no-way-to-receive-the-glideslope" problem, but made me fly a true reverse-sensing approach (without the HSI, which can remove this troublesome feature of a back-course signal), using the number-two nav receiver to an uneventful breakout a couple hundred feet above minimums.

The point? I really should have declined to deliver the airplane after dark, especially in instrument conditions, as the first time I ever flew it. I had a "bad feeling" about that arrangement before I ever got into the airplane. That sense of foreboding might have distracted me to the point of an accident if I had not realized that it existed. As it was, I knew that my situational awareness was at risk and constantly "kicked myself" to remain focused on the task at hand, which was safely landing an unfamiliar airplane in partial-panel conditions. I also set a new personal limitation to never fly at night or in instrument conditions in an airplane that I've never flown before.

Look again at the list of 11 indicators of your level of situational awareness. Detecting that any single indicator or clue to a loss of situational awareness exists does not mean than an accident is imminent or that only some divine grace has kept you from an untimely contact with the earth. Instead, if you sense that any of these indicators describe the way you're flying at the time, you'll have discovered the opportunity to regain your lost level of situational awareness by reflecting back on the "big picture."

We can demonstrate that virtually all accidents are not the result of a single cause, which was the bent of investigations for so long. Instead, when an accident does occur, it's because several of these clues to a loss of situational awareness were allowed to continue unchecked. In most cases, a majority of the clues to loss of situational awareness were evident by the time an accident took place; incidents became linked like a chain, additive in their nature, until finally events exceeded the capabilities of the pilot or the airplane. If the pilot had detected even one link in this "judgment chain," perhaps the accident would have been avoided.

THE JUDGMENT CHAIN

If, as the name implies, an accident is the result of a chain of events, or judgments, then it should be possible to prevent the accident by "breaking" one of the links of that chain. In fact, recognizing that one or more links even exists might be enough to allow you to reverse the trend toward a mishap.

Let's look at a couple of accident studies to identify links in the judgment chain and how the pilot or pilots involved might have broken the chain and avoided a crash. Let's do another review of the L-1011 accident in the Everglades in terms of the clues to a loss of situational awareness and the judgment chain.

- Failure to meet targets. The airplane was doing everything its crew was asking of it, except confirming that the nosewheel was down and locked. The autopilot flew the plane fine until it was accidentally disengaged. Failure to meet targets was arguably not a player in this example.

- Use of an undocumented procedure. I'd say that this definitely was a factor in this accident. I don't know what emergency procedure Eastern had adopted for a failed-gear indication at the time of this crash, but I'm reasonably certain that it did not involve all of the gyrations the crew seems to have gone through to try to remedy the situation, especially when it was later determined to have been caused by a burned-out light bulb. Use of an undocumented procedure was a factor in this accident. If the crew had recognized that the checklist existed and should be followed, then the light bulb probably would have been replaced safely.

- Departure from standard operating procedure. Similarly, SOPs dictate that when abnormal conditions exist, one or more crewmembers should be detailed to deal with the problem while at least one other should be left in charge of the actual flying of the airplane. Not following this procedure became a major player as events unfolded.

- Violating minimums or limitations. Yes, the L-1011 eventually violated minimum altitudes, so the case could be made that this was a factor. But because the violation was not intentional, I tend to say it wasn't a player.

- No one flying the airplane. Need I say more? Obviously, the crew was so caught up in dealing with the gear indicator that no one retained responsibility for the flying, and it was a costly oversight.

- No one looking out the window. It was a dark night over the Everglades with little in the way of visual clues for the crew. It might not have been possible to see the surface at all, even if someone were looking outside (apparently no one was); therefore, I'll say that this was not a factor in the accident.

- Communications breakdown. Yes poor communications was a factor on two counts. First, the captain should have clearly defined crew responsibilities during the gear investigation so that there would be no question as to who was flying the airplane. Second, the airplane was under positive ATC control at the time of the crash; the controllers had a responsibility to assertively warn the crew when radar indicated that the jumbo jet was sliding below a safe altitude. A communications breakdown was most certainly evident in this crash.

- Ambiguity. Yes, the airplane gave every indication except for a green light of having a proper gear extension. A visual check in the "hell hole" confirmed that the nosewheel was locked into place. Misleading and contradictory signals were confusing the crew, and they gave themselves too little an altitude margin to figure things out.

- Unresolved discrepancies. I could go either way on this count but tend to say no because the crew was trying to resolve the discrepancies, albeit using an undocumented procedure.

- Preoccupation or distraction. Not paying attention was a major player.

- "Bad feeling." There is no evidence that any of the crewmembers felt their procedure was unwise or unlikely to fix the problem, so I'll say that a bad feeling was not a factor in this accident.

Even not considering those links in the judgment chain that could be ruled either way, a solid majority (6 of 11) of the factors were in evidence at the time of the crash:

- Use of an undocumented procedure
- Departure from standard operating procedures
- No one flying the airplane
- Communications breakdown
- Ambiguity
- Preoccupation or distraction

If a single crewmember had detected any one of these factors, he might have spoken up and remedied the situation before it was too late. If the flight engineer had said simply "You know, no one is flying the airplane," or if the captain had radioed ATC and said "Please keep an eye on my altitude and track while we work out this problem," then the judgment chain could have been broken, and the accident might never have occurred.

What happened?

A second example is a more common accident that is so "everyday" in its occurrence that it might almost be brushed aside as an "aw shucks" sort of blunder. After takeoff in VFR conditions, a Beech Bonanza suffered a gear-up landing. Although the airplane was substantially damaged, the solo pilot was unhurt. What happened?

According to the NTSB conclusions, the pilot reported that the cylinder head temperatures were "falling back out of the green" shortly after takeoff. The pilot reversed direction and landed at his departure airport but forgot to extend the landing gear. Later investigation revealed a stuck exhaust valve on the number 3 cylinder.[3] What factors might have helped this Bonanza pilot limit damage to his airplane?

- Failure to meet targets. Bonanzas are very slick airplanes aerodynamically. It's hard to slow a Bonanza down for landing without use of the drag-producing wheels. The pitch attitude (visually or on the gauges) required to maintain a normal final approach speed gear-up is quite a bit higher than that if the gear is properly extended. The pilot in this case was probably either on speed and way off normal attitude, or on attitude and quite a bit faster that normal for a landing in the Bonanza. In either case, if the pilot had recognized that pitch and performance targets were not being met, he might have gone around or extended the landing gear in time to limit his losses to the overheated engine.

- Undocumented procedure. Unless you want to argue that landing without extending the gear is in itself an undocumented procedure, I'd say that this was not a factor in the accident.

- Departure from standard operating procedures. There is a point in a normal VFR approach and landing when it is appropriate to extend the landing gear. Many pilots do this at many different times during the approach, but the point is that it should be done at the same time, every time, just so that in times of increased tension such as this the pilot won't forget to lower the wheels. Similarly, there should be some ingrained response to double-check the gear extension on short final (a modified "GUMPS" check, for instance), and, if the pilot had employed this SOP, perhaps the accident report would have never materialized.

- Violating minimums or limitations. These violations were not really a player in this mishap.

- No one flying the airplane. It could be argued that the pilot was really just along for the ride in the final moments of this flight because he didn't appear to be actively managing the approach and landing. Let's cautiously say "yes" to this factor.

- No one looking out the window. Scanning outside the airplane was not a factor.

- Communications breakdown. I'd say "yes" because the pilot needs to actively "communicate" with an airplane. When trying to manage power, pitch, and airspeed for the landing, this pilot apparently was not receiving the Bonanza's messages.

- Ambiguity. The report doesn't mention any actual loss of power in the Bonanza, just an indicated cylinder head temperature problem. That the gauge indicated a problem and the pilot recognized this problem existed prior to getting far from the airport is testimony to his superior scan technique. I'd say that any ambiguity was caught and processed by the pilot in this case, so I won't call it a factor in this accident.

- Unresolved discrepancies. Again, there is the pitch versus airspeed question, about which the pilot apparently did nothing to resolve prior to impact. This was definitely a player in the accident.

- Preoccupation or distraction. Not paying attention is probably the most obvious link in this airplane's accident chain. The pilot was so fixated on the CHT indication that he failed to direct and monitor the remainder of his flight.
- "Bad feeling." I would surely have a bad feeling if the engine in an airplane were acting up during takeoff. I'm sufficiently convinced that the pilot's decision to immediately return to his departure airport is indication that he had a bad feeling in this situation. That knowledge alone, admitting to himself that he was nervous, might have been enough to remind the pilot to check his procedures very carefully and allowed him to avoid the gear-up landing.

Again, we have a majority (six or seven if we include "no one flying the airplane") of the clues to loss of situational awareness evident in the moments leading up to the crash. If the pilot had noticed even one of these clues in time to take action, he might easily have avoided this "mental lapse" sort of mishap.

What's your job as the pilot in command of a single-pilot airplane? Be familiar with the clues to a loss of situational awareness (clues to an increase in risk), and constantly ask yourself in flight if you see evidence of any of these clues creeping up on you. If you do, cautiously take action immediately to get yourself back on track. Use a checklist if you find yourself freewheeling, or go around and figure things out before reentering an altitude critical area.

Monitor your level of situational awareness and the varying level of risk that it implies. Watch for some of the clues to a loss of situational awareness that themselves become links in a judgment chain. Remember that accidents are rarely the result of a single catastrophic event but instead are usually the result of a chain of errors that eventually becomes stronger than your airplane, your training, or your experience can withstand.

12
Teaching cockpit management

ADHERING TO THE PRINCIPLES OF COCKPIT RESOURCE MANAGEMENT HOLDS the promise of greatly increased safety in flight. Pilots who know how to apply airline-style CRM to their own brand of flying will likely be more confident and more competent in the skies.

If you're a certified flight instructor for primary or advanced certificates and ratings, you need to introduce your students to the tactics of cockpit resource management. But how can you integrate the safety-enhancing principles of CRM into even the earliest of flying lessons?

KNOW YOUR EXAMINERS

Talk to the examiners in your area. Ask them exactly how they evaluate "Area of Operations II, Task B (Cockpit Management)" and those references to CRM, decision making, and dealing with distractions found in the practical test standards. Part of your job as instructor is to prepare your students for their checkrides, so it can't hurt to know how they are likely to be judged.

These meetings can be a two-way exchange. Many flight examiners have been in the business for a long time. Despite the wealth of their knowledge and experience, they might not have fully "spooled up" to the sort of life-saving techniques taught under the banner of CRM. Discuss some of the techniques you've learned and the way you like to teach them. Checkrides can be learning experiences as well as evaluations for applicants, and if the examiner learns to reinforce your teachings with the same procedures you taught your students, cockpit management will gain an even greater validity in their eyes.

INCORPORATE CRM TECHNIQUES
IN THE TRAINING SYLLABUS

Be an example to your students. There is a lot of "do as I say, not as I do" in flight instruction. Some of the most demanding and meticulous instructors I've known revert to a devil-may-care flying style when away from the duties of instruction. If you're to impress a level of professionalism onto your charges, then you're going to have to demonstrate that this is exactly how you fly an airplane when on your own. If you're seen rushing through a preflight or lunging into night or instrument flight still folding charts on the way to the airplane, you'll destroy a student's confidence in you and break down his or her CRM discipline.

Introduce your students to cockpit resource management gradually. If you try to lump everything you know about CRM into the first flying lesson, you'll completely overload your student at a time when he or she is already deluged with information. You can start talking about cockpit management on the very first lesson toward a private or recreational certificate. I like to introduce three topics during the first lesson: transfer of airplane control, the altitude-critical area, and the "sterile cockpit" rule.

For instance, I'll spend time with the customer discussing the training route toward a pilot certificate and demonstrate a thorough preflight inspection. Now it's time for the flight briefing. I'll briefly run through the syllabus highlights for the flight without spending too much time explaining things on the first lesson. I end the briefing with what I call "safety notes." I want to impress upon the student the need for safety rules without sounding like airplanes are crashing left and right, so I proceed cautiously. I'll say something like this:

"I'm going to be 'talking you through' most of the flight maneuvers, letting you work the controls while I tell you what to do. Don't worry. I'm always there to step in if you need me and to take the controls to demonstrate things or provide you a moment to take a break.

"Obviously, we need to make it clear who's actually flying the airplane at all times. If you're flying the airplane and want me to take the controls, tell me 'You have the controls' and I'll take over; however, don't assume that I'm the one flying until I echo back 'I have the controls.' We want a positive transfer of authority.

"If I'm the one flying and I want you to practice something, I'll transfer authority in the same way. I'll say 'You have the controls,' but won't assume you're flying until you repeat 'I have the controls' back to me.

"Unless I tell you otherwise, keep flying through a maneuver. I'll take over in the manner prescribed if I need to step in in the interest of safety."

From there I'll go to the concept of the altitude-critical area.

"Close to the ground and when we're nearing our level-off altitudes on the way up and back down, there's a range of airspace known as the 'altitude-critical area.' Consider yourself to be inside an ACA anytime you're within 1000 feet of leveling off during a climb or descent and when within 1000 feet of the ground, especially near an airport. The function of the ACA is merely to remind us that we need to concentrate on the task at hand, which is safely flying the airplane, and not to let extraneous details distract us from making a safe takeoff, leveling off, or landing.

"I'll be showing you some ACA techniques that keep us from flying through our desired altitude once we get in the airplane; however, the most important is the 'sterile cockpit rule.' This rule was modeled after airline regulations and simply states that when flying in an altitude-critical area we should not engage in conversation not directly related to that phase of flight and that we need to defer extraneous tasks that can wait a few minutes longer."

What has this briefing provided? You've introduced techniques designed to avoid altitude busts and controlled-flight-into-terrain accidents. The student will assume everybody learns about altitude-critical areas and the "sterile cockpit rule." With you as an example, the student will likely carry these techniques throughout his or her flying career.

"Takeoff targets" and the sticky-note quick-reference checklist are introduced on the second lesson. I used this on the first lesson with minimal explanation to prevent overloading the new pilot-in-training but promising to cover its use on the next flight. Ready for the second lesson: I review transfer of aircraft control, the ACA, and the "sterile cockpit rule" in my "safety notes," then I move on to explaining what indications to expect on takeoff. To drive the point home, I brief that I'll be simulating a takeoff problem, a target not met, during this lesson.

When I line up to go, I'll apply power, check power development, and simulate a problem. I'll simply retard the throttle, being careful to maintain directional control, and exit the runway to check things out. After resolution of the problem (by changing airplane configuration as necessary, or after "maintenance"), we'll taxi back to the runway and take off.

During the third lesson, I like to introduce the beginnings of judgment and the go/no-go decision. "What are my preflight safety check items?" I'll ask the student pilot and then guide the discussion toward evaluating the pilot, the airplane, the environment, and the situation. We'll briefly discuss the "airworthiness" of the pilot and the weather, as well as the airplane, and combine that information with an introduction to risk factors and the goals of the flight to make a go/no-go decision.

From this flight on, the student will make his or her own go/no-go decision for each training flight, guided and double-checked by me until evaluating each airworthiness element and the risks and goals involved become a natural element of his or her everyday flight planning.

You can see how easy it will be to divide cockpit resource management tasks and techniques into small teaching units and to incorporate them into the traditional flight-training syllabus. Be careful not to overload your student. You should maintain positive control of the airplane at all times and present "safety notes" in a positive fashion, not a "do this, or die" sort of threat. The end of this chapter includes recommended lesson plans for the teaching of cockpit resource management fundamentals, as well as guidance for teaching CRM principles as part of presenting the practical test standards for the Private Pilot certificate and the instrument rating. It also contains recommendations for including CRM safety training as part of biennial flight reviews and instrument competency checks.

Additionally, demonstrate and adhere to all your CRM techniques in every flight from the first lesson onward, telling your student that you'll cover the procedures in subsequent flights. If you do this, you'll be demonstrating that you think CRM is important for every flight, even local training missions. By example, you'll condition your student to incorporate the techniques of cockpit resource management long after the last time you fly with him or her.

RAINY DAYS

When I was learning to fly and again during my commercial and instrument training, I'd call out to the airport if the weather was bad and ask my instructor whether we were going to fly. I was always told to come on out and fly when conditions were favorable or rescheduled with little explanation when conditions were unfavorable. My instructor failed to take advantage of a fantastic training tool, the "bad day" when weather or other conditions made flying unfavorable.

Instead of making the decision for me, as was universally the case, my instructor could have taught me much more if he had asked me to decide whether we could fly and to support my decision with firm facts. That would have forced me to get more familiar with the flight service station's briefing process and the hazards that weather presents to airplanes in flight. With practice, I could have become much more capable of making a safe go/no-go decision when finally turned loose with my advanced certificates and ratings.

A bad day for flying is a wonderful opportunity to catch up on a little ground school. You and your student have already budgeted this time together, so use it wisely. You as instructor might pull out some magazines and review recent accidents. Analyze each mishap in terms of goal-setting and the possible chain of events that led up to the accident. What could have been done differently with safety in mind? Discuss making good decisions and role-play a few scenarios. For instance, assume you detect an engine exhaust leak in flight. What indications will alert you to the problem? What are the likely outcomes of an exhaust leak? This will lead to a review of aeromedical factors and carbon monoxide poisoning as well as the engine fire and emergency landing checklists. If you're flying a turbocharged and/or pressurized airplane, you'll eventually touch on partial power failures, precautionary shutdowns, depressurizations, and emergency descents, all possible results of a simple exhaust-gas leak. A "rainy day" is an excellent time for this sort of review.

HAZARDOUS ATTITUDES

Sometime very early in your association with your student, have him or her complete the "Self-Assessment of Hazardous Attitudes" (Advisory Circular AC 60-22, also included in Chapter 4 of this book). Caution the student to answer honestly, but not to take too much time on any single question. The inventory is most telling when the student logs his or her first "gut" reaction to each question posed. Tell your student that you'll "score" the assessment together after a training flight or on a rainy day.

After your student has taken the inventory, but before you actually tally results, provide an overview of the five hazardous attitudes, how they can affect pilot judgment, and the "antidotes" for those attitudes as outlined in the advisory circular. Then "grade" your student's assessment. You'll probably find one dominant personality trait that can disrupt sound judgment in your student; challenge him or her to come up with a few scenarios where that dominant trait could cause trouble. Discuss solutions to those problems and how recognizing the dominant attitude can help the pilot avoid the hazard. Remember how I discussed my flight over darkest Kansas without electricity in my Cessna 120? If I had been aware of my dominant attitude, invulnerability, I might have had the foresight to avoid making that takeoff. This is the sort of thing your student needs to know about himself or herself.

You might ask the student to retake the inventory just before you sign off for the first solo cross-country and again just before the checkride. Challenge applicants for higher certificates and ratings to test themselves at various points in their training as well. This can alert pilots to the fact that attitudes can change (and should change for the better, if you're doing your job), thereby allowing some other trait to become dominant. Self-assessment needs to be done on a periodic basis. It won't hurt you to quiz yourself once a year.

OTHER TECHNIQUES

This book has been filled with suggestions for improving the safety of single-pilot flight in light airplanes. Become familiar with the techniques we've discussed, and add the insights that your experience provides. Then make a concerted effort to present the skills you've amassed to your students, with a nonthreatening building-block approach. Especially with your primary students, make it look as though everybody practices the philosophy of cockpit resource management on every flight.

Use your in-flight checklists, point out performance targets, and "what if?" your way through actual and simulated decision points during briefings and in flight. Look at how stress and other motivators affect your judgment. Take the time to point out how your airplane is predictable when given changes in power, pitch, or configuration and how knowledge of those changes can dramatically reduce cockpit workload.

In short, turn this book and your experiences into a living and learning experience for your students. You should serve as an example for them to follow in their everyday flying when you've completed your job and they're on their own. Preparing your students to fly as good risk managers and decision makers will have a tremendously positive impact on their flying careers; the discipline you instill in yourself to serve as their mentor will likely assure you a long and safe flying career as well.

CRM lesson plans

Just as with any other piloting technique, you'll find teaching the principles of Cockpit Resource Management easier if you have a plan for presenting each topic. What follows is a set of recommended, FAA-format lesson plans for presenting the precepts of CRM. After the lesson plans you'll find suggestions for presenting selected topics as part of teaching the Practical Test Standards for the Private Pilot certificate and the Instrument rating. Use these as a guide for developing your own syllabus for teaching these and other certificates and ratings.

Instructors, feel free to modify these as you see fit to meet the needs of your students. Students, ask your instructors and other pilots for the benefit of their experience by reviewing the lesson plans with them.

The Principles

The principles of Cockpit Resource Management presented in this book can be listed as 18 topics for discussion and study:

1. **Setting goals of the flight:** determining priorities by establishing goals of the flight, and evaluating decisions based on their impact on achieving those goals.

2. **Decision making:** making informed decisions in normal, abnormal, and emergency situations.

3. **Factors affecting decision making:** external factors that aid or impair your ability to make informed decisions.

4. **Pilot attitudes:** how personality traits can influence the decisions you make.

5. **Performance targets:** predicting anticipated aircraft performance for each maneuver or phase of flight, monitoring actual performance, and comparing actual to expected to aid in pilot decision making.

6. **Departure alternate:** preparing beforehand for alternatives should abnormalities or emergencies arise during or shortly after takeoff.

7. **Cockpit set-up:** alignment of materials or accomplishment of tasks in the cockpit as a means of reducing workload.

8. **Altitude critical areas:** techniques for eliminating "altitude busts" and controlled flight into terrain-type accidents.

9. **Checklist use:** ensuring proper completion of normal, abnormal, and emergency tasks by using checklists.

10. **Autopilot use:** use of automation to reduce workload while not becoming dependent on its use.

11. **Engine monitoring:** enhancing safety by eliminating, detecting, or correcting engine abnormalities.

12. **Weather monitoring:** comparing actual to forecast weather conditions as an aid in continually reevaluating your go/no-go decision.

13. **Altitude-distance-missed:** simplifying the information you need from the Final Approach Fix inbound through and including the missed approach procedure.

14. **Evaluating risk:** making the go/no-go decision by evaluating the total risk picture.

15. **Transfer of aircraft control:** ensuring there's no doubt as to who is responsible for flying the airplane.

16. **Airworthiness—the aircraft and the pilot:** evaluating the legal and safety status of the pilot and the machine.

17. **Sources of information:** where to find help in reducing workload and making decisions.

18. **Situational awareness and the judgment chain:** awareness of the chain of decisions that often leads to an accident; avoiding distractions, and gathering as much information as possible for informed decision making.

Lesson 1: Setting goals of the flight

OBJECTIVE	To teach the pilot to determine priorities by establishing goals of the flight, and evaluating decisions based on their impact on achieving those goals.
ELEMENTS	• Listing goals or desired outcomes of a flight
	• Prioritizing those goals
	• Evaluating in-flight decisions on the basis of their impact on achieving those goals in the order of priority
SCHEDULE	• Listing goals of the flight :05
	• Prioritizing goals :05
	• Discussing impact of decisions :10
EQUIPMENT	• CRM book, Chapter 2
	• Writing tool, writing surface
INSTRUCTOR ACTION	• Review Chapter 2 prior to lesson.
	• Ask student to identify and prioritize goals for a typical pleasure and/or business flight.
	• Discuss with student how scheduling pressures, weather, and aircraft maintenance issues might force a decision.
	• Coach student in evaluating how possible outcomes of decisions might impact achieving flight goals.
	• Discuss with student when decisions might mean sacrificing lesser goals in order to achieve the goal of safety.

STUDENT ACTION	• Review Chapter 2 prior to lesson. • Actively participate in discussion. • Define what a "typical" flight is for the student personally; list and prioritize goals for those typical flights. • Suggest scenarios when inflight goal evaluation might be necessary.
COMPLETION STANDARD	Student will be able to define and prioritize goals for personal and business flights, and explain how inflight decisions can be evaluated in terms of their impact on attaining flight goals.

Lesson 2: Decision making

OBJECTIVE	To teach the pilot to make informed safety-related decisions, in normal, abnormal, and emergency situations.
ELEMENTS	• Using the "DECIDE" model
SCHEDULE	• Defining the "DECIDE" model :10 • Tracing the steps of decision making :10 • Discussing "DIE" in emergencies :10
EQUIPMENT	• CRM book, Chapter 3 • Writing tool, writing surface • Aircraft checklists
INSTRUCTOR ACTION	• Review Chapter 3 prior to lesson. • Define elements of decision making. • Provide examples for normal, abnormal, and emergency situations. • Show how aircraft emergency procedures relate to the "DECIDE" model.
STUDENT ACTION	• Review Chapter 3 prior to lesson. • Actively participate in discussion. • Using examples, discuss decision making in normal, abnormal, and emergency situations from onset of the need to make a decision to safe arrival on the ground. • Suggest scenarios when preflight and inflight decision making is necessary.
COMPLETION STANDARD	Student will be able to determine when a decision needs to be made; demonstrate gathering information and making a decision in normal, abnormal, and emergency situations; and discuss how those decisions will likely affect the remainder of a flight in real-world conditions.

Lesson 3: Factors affecting decision making

OBJECTIVE	To teach the pilot to recognize factors that enhance or inhibit information gathering and decision making.

ELEMENTS	• The "DECIDE" model for decision making
	• Factors that increase information and aid in making decisions
	• Factors that detract from information gathering and decision making
SCHEDULE	• Review the "DECIDE" model :05
	• Factors that aid decision making :10
	• Factors that hinder decision making :10
EQUIPMENT	• CRM book, Chapter 4
	• Writing tool, writing surface
INSTRUCTOR ACTION	• Review Chapter 4 prior to lesson.
	• Ask student to review decision-making process for normal, abnormal, and emergency procedures.
	• Discuss factors that aid or inhibit information gathering and decision making.
	• Discuss how awareness of those factors can affect safety.
STUDENT ACTION	• Review Chapter 4 prior to lesson.
	• Actively participate in discussion.
	• Suggest scenarios when preflight and inflight decision making might be affected by outside factors.
COMPLETION STANDARD	Student will be able to list factors that affect decision making and discuss how those factors can be exploited or overcome to safely conduct a flight.

Lesson 4: Pilot attitudes

OBJECTIVE	To teach the pilot to recognize personality traits that enhance or inhibit information gathering and decision making.
ELEMENTS	• The "DECIDE" model for decision making
	• Pilot attitudes, and how they affect safety
SCHEDULE	• Review the "DECIDE" model :05
	• Attitudes that enhance safety :05
	• Attitudes that hinder decision making :05
	• Review the student's Attitude Inventory :15
EQUIPMENT	• CRM book, Chapter 4
	• Student's completed Attitude Inventory
	• Writing tool, writing surface
INSTRUCTOR ACTION	• Review Chapter 4 prior to lesson.
	• Ask student to review decision-making process for normal, abnormal, and emergency procedures.
	• Discuss attitudes that aid or inhibit information gathering and decision making.
	• Discuss how awareness of those attitudes can affect safety.
	• Review student's completed Attitude Inventory.

STUDENT ACTION	• Review Chapter 4 and complete Attitude Inventory prior to lesson.
	• Actively participate in discussion.
	• Suggest scenarios when preflight and inflight decision making might be affected by pilot attitude.
COMPLETION STANDARD	Student will be able to list attitudes that affect decision making and discuss how those factors can be exploited or overcome to safely conduct a flight.

Lesson 5: Performance targets

OBJECTIVE	To teach the pilot to predict aircraft performance in all phases of flight, to actively compare predicted performance to that actually attained, and to use that comparison to make decisions regarding the safety of flight.
ELEMENTS	• Aircraft performance information
	• Techniques for improving aircraft performance
SCHEDULE	• Calculating aircraft performance 1:00
	• Monitoring aircraft performance :15
	• Techniques for optimizing performance :15
EQUIPMENT	• CRM book, Chapters 5, 6, and 7
	• Pilot's Operating Handbook performance charts
	• Writing tool, writing surface
INSTRUCTOR ACTION	• Review Chapters 5, 6, and 7 prior to lesson.
	• Demonstrate and review method of calculating aircraft performance.
	• Discuss factors that limit aircraft performance.
	• Present methods of optimizing aircraft performances.
STUDENT ACTION	• Review Chapters 5, 6, and 7 prior to lesson.
	• Actively participate in discussion.
	• Suggest scenarios when aircraft performance is critical, and when early determination of a problem can prevent an accident.
COMPLETION STANDARD	The student will be able to predict airplane performance in all phases of flight and under all conditions, will be able to monitor actual performance in flight and compare that to the prediction, and will be able to take action to achieve maximum aircraft performance should the airplane not at first perform to expectations.

Lesson 6: Departure alternate

| OBJECTIVE | To teach the pilot to plan for a quick landing at the departure airport, if suitable, another nearby airport, or at a preselected off-airport location when faced with an abnormality or emergency shortly after takeoff. |

ELEMENTS	• Air navigation charts and approach plates • Weather information • Dealing with inflight emergencies
SCHEDULE	• Situations mandating a departure alternate :15 • Criteria for returning to departure airport :05 • Criteria for landing at another location :05 • Cockpit set-up for the departure alternate :05
EQUIPMENT	• CRM book, Chapters 5 and 7 • Air navigation charts and approach plates • Writing tool, writing surface
INSTRUCTOR ACTION	• Review Chapters 5 and 7 prior to lesson. • Ask student to review decision-making process for emergencies encountered shortly after takeoff. • Discuss preflight selection of a departure alternate. • Discuss cockpit organization for the departure alternate.
STUDENT ACTION	• Review Chapters 5 and 7 prior to the lesson. • Actively participate in discussion. • Using air navigation charts, designate a departure alternate for various airports, given simulated aircraft and weather conditions. • Explain cockpit organization for the departure alternate.
COMPLETION STANDARD	The student will be able to determine the safest airport for landing if faced with an abnormal or emergency condition shortly after take-off, and will organize the cockpit to reduce workload if faced with deviating to a departure alternate.

Lesson 7: Cockpit set-up

OBJECTIVE	To teach the pilot to organize the cockpit to minimize pilot workload.
ELEMENTS	• Arranging air navigation charts and other materials • Standardized use of radio equipment
SCHEDULE	• Cockpit organization :05 • Radio discipline :05
EQUIPMENT	• CRM book, Chapters 5 and 6 • Writing tool, writing surface
INSTRUCTOR ACTION	• Review Chapters 5 and 6 prior to lesson. • Discuss possible methods of cockpit organization. • Discuss set-up and use of radio equipment.
STUDENT ACTION	• Review Chapters 5 and 6 prior to the lesson. • Actively participate in discussion. • Suggest scenarios when preplanning can reduce pilot workload.

| COMPLETION STANDARD | Student will organize the cockpit and make use of radio and other equipment to minimize workload. |

Lesson 8: Altitude critical areas

| OBJECTIVE | To teach the pilot to avoid "altitude busts" and Controlled Flight Into Terrain accidents. |

ELEMENTS	• Altitude Critical Areas
	• Sterile cockpit rule
	• Techniques for reducing workload

SCHEDULE	• Define Altitude Critical Areas :10
	• The Sterile Cockpit Rule :05
	• Techniques for reducing workload in Altitude Critical Areas :15

| EQUIPMENT | • CRM book, Chapters 6 and 9 |
| | • Writing tool, writing surface |

INSTRUCTOR ACTION	• Review Chapters 6 and 9 prior to lesson.
	• Define "altitude busts" and "controlled flight into terrain," and discuss the accident record related to each.
	• Define Altitude Critical Areas.
	• Discuss methods of reducing cockpit workload.

STUDENT ACTION	• Review Chapters 6 and 9 prior to lesson.
	• Actively participate in discussion.
	• Define actions that can safely be deferred until after transitioning out of Altitude Critical Areas.

| COMPLETION STANDARD | The student will be able to recognize the hazards of "altitude busts" and controlled flight into terrain, will be able to define Altitude Critical Areas, and will be able to reduce workload while flying in Altitude Critical Areas. |

Lesson 9: Use of checklists

| OBJECTIVE | To teach the pilot to use approved aircraft checklists to enhance flight safety. |

| ELEMENTS | • Aircraft checklists |

| SCHEDULE | • Review normal, abnormal, and emergency procedures checklists 1:00 |

EQUIPMENT	• CRM book, Chapter 6
	• Pilot's Operating Handbook or other approved checklists
	• Writing tool, writing surface

| INSTRUCTOR ACTION | • Review Chapter 6 prior to lesson. |
| | • Discuss how normal procedures checklists can be used to back up memory, to avoid missed items. |

- Discuss use of checklists for abnormal and emergency procedures.
- Discuss need to study checklists to remain current.

STUDENT
ACTION
- Review Chapter 6 prior to lesson.
- Actively participate in discussion.
- Suggest situations where the pilot may miss critical normal, abnormal, and emergency procedure steps if not backed up by use of approved checklists.

COMPLETION
STANDARD
The student will use approved aircraft checklists in all phases of flight, as an aid in accomplishing critical safety in normal, abnormal, or emergency procedures.

Lesson 10: Use of the autopilot

OBJECTIVE
To teach the pilot to use the autopilot as a safety and workload-reduction device, and to recognize the mechanical and pilot-interface limitations of autopilots.

ELEMENTS
- Autopilot use
- Autopilot failure modes
- The autopilot-related accident record

SCHEDULE
- Autopilot use   :05
- Autopilot operation and failure modes   :20
- The autopilot-related accident record   :05

EQUIPMENT
- CRM book, Chapter 6
- Pilot's Operating Handbook autopilot supplement
- Writing tool, writing surface

INSTRUCTOR
ACTION
- Review Chapter 6 prior to lesson.
- Review autopilot normal, abnormal, and emergency checklists.
- Review autopilot failure modes.
- Discuss how pilot mistakes can lead to autopilot-related accidents.

STUDENT
ACTION
- Review Chapter 6 prior to lesson.
- Actively participate in discussion.
- Discuss use and abuse of autopilot systems.

COMPLETION
STANDARD
The student will be able to engage and operate the autopilot in all modes and in all phase of flight. The student will use the autopilot as a workload- and fatigue-reducing aid, but will recognize the potential for accidents related to autopilot use, improper pilot control of the autopilot, and overreliance on the autopilot to fly the airplane.

Lesson 11: Engine monitoring

OBJECTIVE
To teach the pilot to continually monitor the aircraft engine(s), to ensure safe operation of the airplane.

ELEMENTS	• Engine monitoring instruments
	• Engine management techniques
SCHEDULE	• Engine instrumentation :30
	• Engine management 1:30
EQUIPMENT	• CRM book, Chapter 6
	• Engine monitoring instruments
	• *Aircraft Pilot's Operating Handbook* and supplements
	• Writing tool, writing surface
INSTRUCTOR ACTION	• Review Chapter 6 prior to lesson.
	• Discuss engine monitoring systems.
	• Discuss engine management techniques.
STUDENT ACTION	• Review Chapter 6 and POH/Supplements prior to lesson.
	• Actively participate in discussion.
	• Suggest normal, abnormal, and emergency engine indications, and actions to be taken upon noting those indications.
COMPLETION STANDARD	The student will understand and apply approved techniques for proper engine management. The student will monitor engine function and take action to correct problems/divert for a landing should any unusual indications be noted.

Lesson 12: Weather monitoring

OBJECTIVE	To teach the pilot techniques for comparing forecast to actual weather, to constantly reevaluate the go/no-go decision.
ELEMENTS	• Obtaining weather information
	• The "DECIDE" model
SCHEDULE	• Review the "DECIDE" model :05
	• Preflight weather briefings :30
	• Inflight weather briefings :30
	• Avoiding aviation weather hazards 1:00
EQUIPMENT	• CRM book, Chapter 6
	• Other weather texts at discretion of instructor
	• Telephone and/or computer for FSS/DUATs briefing
	• Writing tool, writing surface
INSTRUCTOR ACTION	• Review Chapter 6 and texts prior to lesson.
	• Ask student to review decision-making process for normal, abnormal, and emergency procedures.
	• Discuss preflight and inflight weather decision making.
	• Describe aviation weather hazards and their avoidance.
STUDENT ACTION	• Review Chapter 6 and texts prior to lesson.
	• Actively participate in discussion.

- Obtain a preflight weather briefing for use in discussion.
- List methods of obtaining and reporting weather hazards en route.

COMPLETION STANDARD
The student will be able to obtain accurate preflight and inflight weather briefings, and use that information in making and evaluating a go/no-go decision. The student will be able to recognize meteorological hazards to safe flight.

Lesson 13: Altitude-distance-missed

OBJECTIVE
To teach the pilot techniques for increasing precision and decreasing workload during instrument approach and missed approach procedures

ELEMENTS
- Reviewing instrument approach procedure plates

SCHEDULE
- Review instrument approach plates   :15
- Selecting items critical for the approach   :10
- Organizing information in the cockpit   :05

EQUIPMENT
- CRM book, Chapter 7
- Instrument Approach Procedure plates
- Writing tool, writing surface

INSTRUCTOR ACTION
- Review Chapter 7 and approach plates prior to lesson.
- Discuss what items are critical from the Final Approach Fix inbound, through and including the Missed Approach procedure.
- Discuss organizing this information in the cockpit.

STUDENT ACTION
- Review Chapter 7 and approach plates prior to lesson.
- Actively participate in discussion.

COMPLETION STANDARD
The student will be able to determine which information is most critical for use in the descent phase of and instrument approach, as well as that required to initiate the missed approach procedure. The student will organize this information in the cockpit to reduce workload.

Lesson 14: Evaluating risk

OBJECTIVE
To teach the pilot techniques for evaluating the total level of risk associated with a flight or a maneuver, for use in making a go/no-go decision.

ELEMENTS
- Identifying high-risk situations
- Methods of reducing total risk

SCHEDULE
- Review the "DECIDE" model   :05
- Determining risk level   :10
- Identifying high-risk situations   :10
- Techniques for reducing risk   :10

EQUIPMENT	• CRM book, Chapters 8 and 9
	• Writing tool, writing surface
INSTRUCTOR ACTION	• Review Chapters 8 and 9 prior to lesson.
	• Ask student to review decision-making process for normal, abnormal, and emergency procedures.
	• Discuss determining level of risk for a flight.
	• Identify high-risk flight operations.
	• Discuss methods of reducing total risk.
STUDENT ACTION	• Review Chapters 8 and 9 prior to lesson.
	• Actively participate in discussion.
COMPLETION STANDARD	The student will be able to identify high-risk operations, and determine the total risk level for a flight for use in making a go/no-go decision. The student will command techniques for reducing the total level of risk.

Lesson 15: Transfer of aircraft control

OBJECTIVE	To teach the pilot techniques for ensuring there's never any doubt as to who is responsible for aircraft control.
ELEMENTS	• Technique for transferring aircraft control
SCHEDULE	• Technique for transferring aircraft control :05
EQUIPMENT	• CRM book, Chapter 11
	• Writing tool, writing surface
INSTRUCTOR ACTION	• Review Chapter 11 prior to lesson.
	• Present technique for transferring aircraft control.
STUDENT ACTION	• Review Chapter 11 prior to lesson.
	• Actively participate in discussion.
COMPLETION STANDARD	The student will employ a positive transfer of aircraft control in all cases where another person is in a position to manipulate aircraft controls.

Lesson 16: Airworthiness—the aircraft and the pilot

OBJECTIVE	To teach the pilot techniques for determining personal and aircraft fitness for flight.
ELEMENTS	• Preflight aircraft inspection
	• The "IMSAFE" model
SCHEDULE	• Review aircraft inspection procedures :15
	• Discuss the "IMSAFE" model :15
	• Evaluating airworthiness while in flight :10

EQUIPMENT	• CRM book, Chapters 4, 9, and 10
	• Pilot's Operating Handbook inspection checklists
	• Aircraft limitations and/or equipment list
	• Writing tool, writing surface

INSTRUCTOR ACTION	• Review Chapters 4, 9, and 10 prior to lesson.
	• Ask student to review procedures for inspecting airplane for airworthiness prior to flight, for accomplishing minor airworthiness items (adding engine oil, etc.), and making a maintenance go/no-go decision.
	• Discuss the "IMSAFE" model for personal airworthiness.
	• Review aircraft limitations and/or required equipment list.

STUDENT ACTION	• Review Chapters 4, 9, and 10 prior to lesson.
	• Actively participate in discussion.
	• List commonly used medications, etc., that affect airworthiness
	• List method of making a go/no-go decision when faced with inoperative equipment either before or during flight.

COMPLETION STANDARD	The student will be able to evaluate pilot fitness for flight, as well as that of the airplane during preflight and while en route.

Lesson 17: Sources of information

OBJECTIVE	To teach the pilot to obtain decision-making information from all available sources.

ELEMENTS	• The safety equation

SCHEDULE	• Review sources of information available for pilots to use in decision making :15

EQUIPMENT	• CRM book, Chapter 10
	• *Pilot's Operating Handbook* inspection checklists
	• Aircraft limitations and/or equipment list
	• Writing tool, writing surface

INSTRUCTOR ACTION	• Review Chapter 10 prior to lesson.
	• Ask student to list sources of information available in flight.
	• Discuss possible roles of nonflying passengers in the cockpit.
	• Review radio and checklist procedures.

STUDENT ACTION	• Review Chapter 10 prior to lesson.
	• Actively participate in discussion.
	• List and detail aviation experience level of typical or anticipated passengers.

COMPLETION STANDARD	The student will be able to use all available sources of information when making decisions in flight.

Lesson 18: Situation awareness and the judgment chain

OBJECTIVE To teach the pilot techniques that most accidents are the result of a chain of decision making, and how the pilot can avoid accidents by actively monitoring the decision-making process.

ELEMENTS
- The "DECIDE" model
- Aircraft accident case studies

SCHEDULE
- Define the Judgment Chain   :05
- Detecting a loss of situational awareness   :10
- Reacquiring situational awareness to make good decisions   :15
- Case studies   :30

EQUIPMENT
- CRM book, Chapter 11
- Aircraft accident case histories
- Writing tool, writing surface

INSTRUCTOR ACTION
- Review Chapter 11 prior to lesson.
- Discuss how most accidents are result of a chain of decisions.
- Discuss clues to loss of situational awareness, and method for reestablishing awareness.
- Use case studies of aircraft accidents to detect what clues to a loss of situational awareness likely existed, and how the pilot might have reestablished control.

STUDENT ACTION
- Review Chapters 11 prior to lesson.
- Actively participate in discussion.
- Discuss ways to retain a high degree of situational awareness.

COMPLETION STANDARD The student will be able to list clues to a loss of situational awareness and a method of reestablishing control. The student will be able to analyze accident records from a judgment chain/loss of situational awareness standpoint and suggest ways the pilot might have avoided the accident.

Presenting CRM training with the practical test standards

Whether presenting items from the FAA Practical Test Standards for the first time or reviewing them as part of a checkride preparation, Instrument Proficiency Check, or a Flight Review, you can help make your students safer by including a discussion and in-flight practice of the elements of Cockpit Resource Management. What follows is a description of the Practical Test Standards of the Private Pilot certificate and Instrument ratings, with a list of those of the 18 topics which most directly pertain to each task. Be careful not to overwhelm a student with information; instead, pick one or two of the CRM topics to discuss with each task presentation. Among other things, this will allow you to present your students with fresh (at least to them) material each time you get together.

Private Pilot Certificate practical test standards (May 1, 1995, as amended 4/28/97)

Area of Operation	Task	CRM Topics
I. Preflight Preparation	A. Certificates and documents	16
	B. Weather information	12
	C. Cross-country planning	1, 2, 3, 6, 14, 17
	D. Airspace	12, 17, 18
	E. Performance and limitations	5, 9, 11
	F. Systems	7, 9, 11, 15, 16
	G. Minimum Equipment List	2, 7, 9, 14, 16, 18
	H. Aeromedical factors	3, 4, 14, 16
II. Preflight procedures	A. Preflight inspection	1, 2, 3, 4, 14, 16
	B. Cockpit management	7, 9, 15, 18
	C. Engine starting	9, 11
	D. Taxiing	9, 18
	E. Before takeoff check	5, 6, 9, 11, 12, 14, 16, 18
III. Airport operations	A. Radio communications	7, 17
	B. Traffic patterns	5, 6, 8, 9, 14, 18
	C. Airport markings	17
IV. Takeoff landings	A. Normal takeoff	5, 6, 7, 8, 9, 11, 12, 14, 15, 18
	B. Normal, crosswind landing	2, 5, 7, 8, 9, 14, 16, 18
	C. Soft-field takeoff	2, 3, 5, 6, 7, 8, 9, 11, 12, 14, 18
	D. Soft-field landing	2, 3, 5, 7, 8, 9, 14, 16, 18
	E. Short-field takeoff	2, 3, 5, 6, 7, 8, 9, 11, 12, 14, 18
	F. Short-field landing	2, 3, 5, 7, 8, 9, 14, 16, 18
	G. Forward slip to landing	2, 3, 5, 7, 8, 9, 14, 16, 18
	H. Go-around	2, 3, 5, 6, 7, 8, 9, 11, 12, 14, 18
V. Maneuver	A. Steep turns	5, 14, 18
VI. Ground reference	A. Rectangular course	14, 18
	B. S-turns	14, 18
	C. Turns around a point	14, 18
VII. Navigation	A. Pilotage and D.R.	1, 2, 3, 5, 7, 9, 10, 11, 12, 14, 18
	B. Navigation systems	7, 9, 10, 11, 12, 14, 16, 17, 18
	C. Diversion	1, 2, 3, 4, 7, 9, 10, 11, 12, 14, 16, 17, 18
	D. Lost procedures	2, 3, 4, 7, 9, 10, 14, 17, 18
VIII. Slow flight/stalls	A. Slow flight	5, 9, 11, 14, 18
	B. Power-off stalls	5, 9, 11, 14, 18
	C. Power-on stalls	5, 9, 11, 14, 18
	D. Spin awareness	5, 9, 11, 14, 18
IX. Instruments	A. Straight and level flight	3, 5, 9, 10, 11, 12, 17, 18
	B. Airspeed climbs	3, 5, 8, 9, 10, 11, 12, 17, 18
	C. Airspeed descents	3, 5, 8, 9, 10, 11, 12, 17, 18
	D. Turns to headings	3, 5, 9, 10, 11, 12, 17, 18
	E. Unusual attitudes	3, 5, 9, 10, 11, 17, 18
	F. Radio communications	2, 3, 4, 7, 9, 10, 17, 18
X. Emergencies	A. Emergency descent	2, 3, 5, 8, 9, 14, 18

Area of Operation	Task	CRM Topics
X. Emergencies (*cont.*)	B. Emergency landing	2, 3, 5, 7, 8, 9, 14, 16, 18
	C. Malfunctions	2, 3, 5, 7, 9, 10, 11, 14, 16, 18
	D. Equipment	7, 9, 14, 18
XI. Night Operations	A. Night preparations	1, 2, 3, 4, 5, 6, 7, 8, 9, 11, 12, 14, 16, 17, 18
	B. Night flight	1, 2, 3, 4, 5, 6, 7, 8, 9, 11, 12, 14, 16, 17, 18
XII. Postflight	A. After landing	2, 9, 14, 17, 18
	B. Securing	2, 9

Instrument Pilot Rating Practical Test Standards (Oct. 1, 1994)

Area of Operation	Task	CRM Topics
I. Preflight preparation	A. Weather information	1, 2, 3, 4, 5, 6, 7, 9, 12, 14, 16, 17, 18
	B. Cross-country planning	1, 2, 3, 5, 7, 9, 10, 12, 14, 17, 18
II. Preflight procedures	A. Aircraft systems	5, 7, 9, 11, 14, 16
	B. Instruments	5, 7, 9, 10, 14, 16
	C. Cockpit check	2, 3, 4, 9, 14, 15, 16, 18
III. ATC procedures	A. Clearances	7, 9, 14, 17, 18
	B. Compliance	6, 7, 8, 9, 10, 17, 20
	C. Holding	1, 2, 3, 4, 5, 7, 8, 9, 10, 11, 12, 14, 17, 20
IV. Instrument flight	A. Straight and level flight	3, 5, 9, 10, 11, 12, 17, 18
	B. Change of airspeed	5, 18
	C. Airspeed climbs	5, 8, 18
	D. Rate climbs	5, 8, 18
	E. Timed turns	5, 8, 17, 20
	F. Steep turns	5, 18
	G. Unusual attitudes	3, 5, 9, 10, 11, 17, 18
V. Navigation aids	A. VOR and DME arcs	5, 7, 8, 10, 17, 18
	B. NDB	5, 7, 8, 10, 17, 18
VI. Approach procedures	A. VOR approach	5, 7, 8, 9, 10, 13, 14, 17, 18
	B. NDB approach	5, 7, 8, 9, 10, 13, 14, 17, 18
	C. ILS approach	5, 7, 8, 9, 10, 13, 14, 17, 18
	D. Missed approach	2, 3, 4, 5, 7, 8, 9, 10, 11, 12, 13, 14, 17, 18
	E. Circling approach	1, 2, 3, 4, 5, 7, 8, 9, 10, 13, 14, 17, 18
	F. Landing from approach	4, 5, 9, 14, 18
VII. Emergencies	A. Lost communications	1, 2, 3, 4, 6, 7, 9, 10, 14, 16, 17, 18
	B. Engine failure (ME only)	1, 2, 3, 4, 5, 6, 7, 8, 9, 10, 11, 16, 18
	C. Single-engine approach (ME)	2, 3, 4, 5, 8, 9, 10, 11, 13, 14, 18
	D. Partial panel flight	2, 3, 4, 5, 7, 8, 9, 10, 13, 14, 16, 17, 18
VIII. Postflight	A. Checking instruments	7, 9, 14, 16

Afterword

There's nothing really new about crew or cockpit resource management. Generally, CRM is the compilation of the best techniques and procedures for dealing with the stresses and distractions of an airplane cockpit, identified with a few "buzzwords" that make those philosophies a little easier to remember.

The airlines and especially corporate aviation have made great strides in improving flying safety. Large training organizations, especially those who make their profits from teaching the airline and corporate flight crews, do an excellent job of promoting and teaching CRM to their customers. What's missing for the most part is a vehicle to get these life-saving principles to the largest segment of aviation, the owners and pilots of privately flown light airplanes.

I hope that this book will open your eyes to the power that you hold as pilot in command to safely command your craft and more actively determine the safe outcome of your flights. Remember the FAA's definition of "acceptable performance" from the practical test standards: "The pilot is the obvious master of the airplane and the successful outcome of the maneuver is never seriously in doubt."

References

Chapter 1

1. *General Aviation Accident Analysis Book, 1982–1988*. AOPA Air Safety Foundation, Frederick, MD. 1991.
2. *FAA Private Pilot Practical Test Standards*, 1994.
3. FlightSafety International Cockpit Resource Management seminar, Wichita, KS. September 1992.
4. AOPA Air Safety Foundation, 1991.

Chapter 2

1. Peter Garrison, "Aftermath: Hidden Pressure." *FLYING* Vol. 115 No. 5 (May 1988), pp. 20–23. Reprinted by permission of author.
2. Peter Garrison, "Aftermath: Late For Work." *FLYING* Vol. 115 No. 9 (September 1988), pp. 24–26. Reprinted by permission of author.

Chapter 3

1. FAA Advisory Circular AC 60-22, 12/13/91.
2. "Safety Information: Piper Malibu/Mirage." AOPA Air Safety Foundation, Frederick, MD. 1994.

Chapter 4

1. "Safety Information/Safety Review: Cessna 182." AOPA Air Safety Foundation, Frederick, MD. 1993.
2. "Safety Review: Beech Bonanza/Debonair." AOPA Air Safety Foundation, Frederick, MD. 1994.

References

3. Advisory Circular AC 60-22, 12/13/91.

4. "Safety Information: Piper Malibu/Mirage." AOPA Air Safety Foundation, Frederick, MD. 1994.

Chapter 5

1. *General Aviation Accident Analysis Book, 1982–1988.* AOPA Air Safety Foundation, Frederick, MD. 1991.

2. Thomas P. Turner, "Takeoff Targets." *Private Pilot*, October 1994. pp. 36–41.

3. Unpublished account of takeoff incident reprinted by permission of author/instructor who remains anonymous.

Chapter 6

1. FlightSafety International CRM seminar, Wichita, KS. September 1992.

2. Robert Sumwalt, "Altitude Awareness." *Professional Pilot*, September 1990. p. 84.

3. Sumwalt, 1990.

4. Sumwalt, 1990.

5. Sumwalt, 1990.

6. Sumwalt, 1990.

7. Sumwalt, 1990.

Chapter 7

1. *General Aviation Accident Analysis Book, 1982–1988.* AOPA Air Safety Foundation, Frederick, MD. 1991.

2. *General Aviation Accident Analysis Book, 1982–1988.* AOPA Air Safety Foundation, Frederick, MD. 1991.

Chapter 8

1. R. Jerry Falkner, "Never Again: Engine Out, Forest Below." AOPA *Pilot*, December 1993. Reprinted by permission of author.

2. Advisory Circular AC 60-22, 12/13/91.

3. Advisory Circular AC 60-22, 12/13/91.

Chapter 9

1. FlightSafety International CRM seminar, Wichita, KS. September 1992.

2. FAA information related by FSDO officer, at Flight Instructor Refresher Clinic, Wichita, KS. March 1993.

Chapter 11

1. FlightSafety International CRM seminar, Wichita, KS. September 1992.

2. "Safety Information: Piper Malibu/Mirage." AOPA Air Safety Foundation, Frederick, MD. 1994.

3. "Safety Review: Beech Bonanza/Debonair." AOPA Air Safety Foundation, Frederick, MD. 1994.

Index

About the author

Thomas P. Turner's diverse background includes a stint as Lead Instructor of Flight-Safety International's Beech Bonanza school, tenure as Chief Pilot for an aftermarket engine modification firm, aviation sales, and duty as an officer in the U.S. Air Force. Turner heads Mastery Flight Training, an aviation safety consulting firm. He's a Contributing Editor to *Private Pilot* magazine and the journal of the World Beechcraft Society; he's frequently published in the *American Bonanza Society* and over 30 other magazines, and is a regular speaker at the annual Oshkosh and other aviation conventions.